ALLSTON-BRIGHTON

MASSACHUSETTS

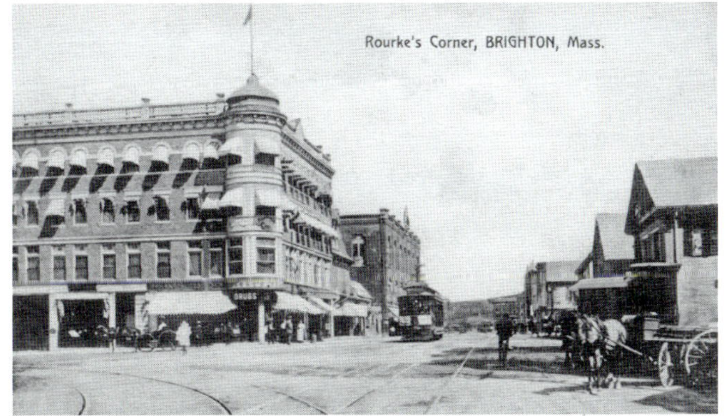

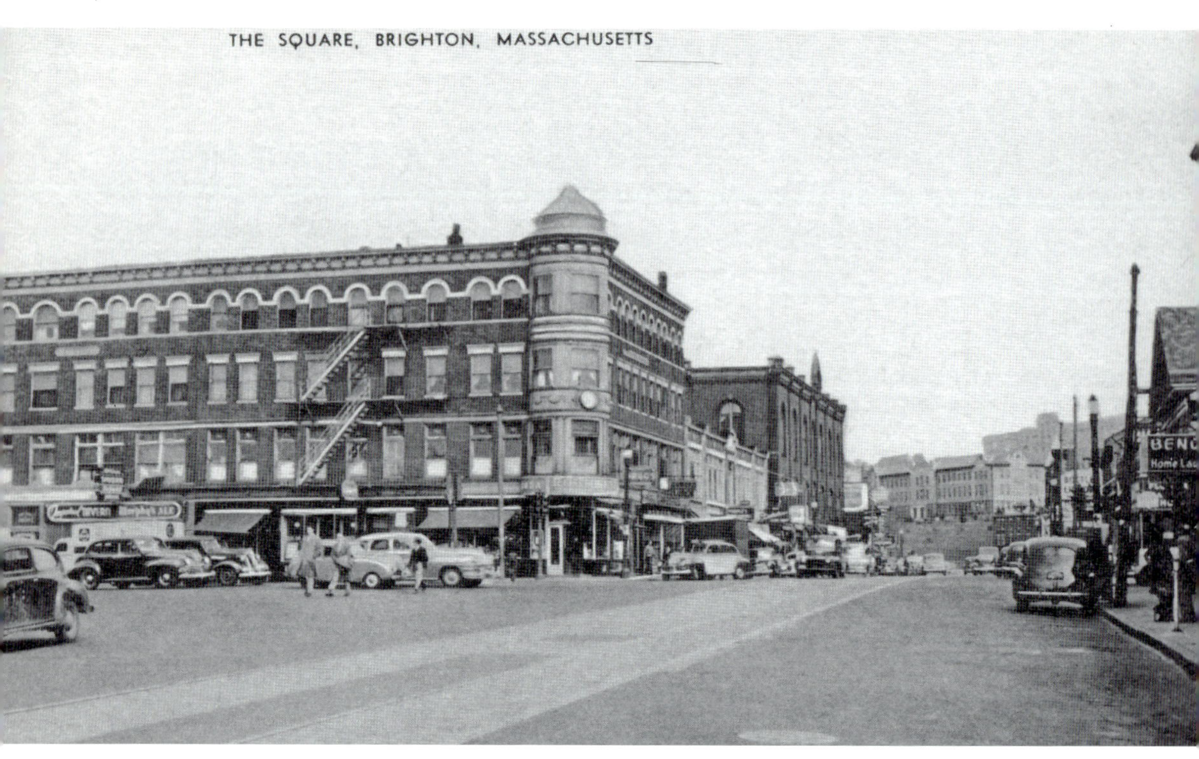

Brighton Center, 1950
In this c. 1950 view of Brighton Center, St. Elizabeth's Hospital is visible in the distance. (Boston Public Library.)

Page 1: Brighton Center
This is a c. 1905 view of Brighton Center looking east. (Brighton-Allston Historical Society archives.)

LEGENDARY LOCALS

OF

ALLSTON-BRIGHTON

MASSACHUSETTS

LINDA MISHKIN
FOREWORD BY WILLIAM MARCHIONE

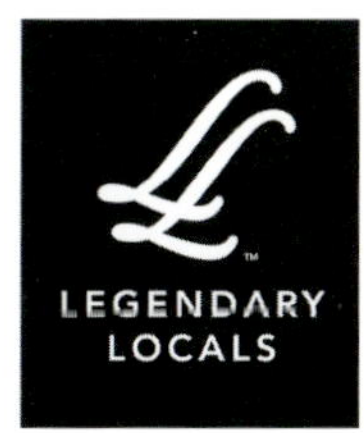

ISBN 978-1-4671-0051-9

Legendary Locals is an imprint of Arcadia Publishing
Charleston, South Carolina

Printed in the United States of America

Library of Congress Control Number: 2012944873

For all general information, please contact Arcadia Publishing:
Telephone 843-853-2070
Fax 843-853-0044
E-mail sales@arcadiapublishing.com
For customer service and orders:
Toll-Free 1-888-313-2665

Visit us on the Internet at www.arcadiapublishing.com

On the Cover: From left to right:
(TOP ROW) Robert Webber, owner of Model Hardware (Photograph by Linda Mishkin, page 27); Sam Cornish, poet laureate of Boston (Photograph by Linda Mishkin, page 76); Joseph Breck, horticulturist (Brighton-Allston Historical Society archives, page 29); Elli Crocker, muralist (Photograph by Liane Brandon, page 107); Sal Barone, owner of Mr. Music (Photograph by Linda Mishkin, page 40).
(MIDDLE ROW) Mary Jane Kinglsey Merwin, historian (BAHS archives, page 68); Valter Vitorino, owner of Café Brazil (Photograph by Linda Mishkin, page 20); William Wirt Warren, US congressman and Massachusetts state senator (BAHS archives, page 123); Kevin Honan, Massachusetts state representative (Photograph by Linda Mishkin, page 120); Sara Willis Eldredge "Fanny Fern," writer (BAHS archives, page 82).
(BOTTOM ROW) Harold Connolly, Olympic gold medal winner (Photograph by Linda Mishkin, page 112); Liane Brandon, documentary filmmaker (Photograph by Boyd Estus, page 113); William Marchione, historian (Marchione family, page 71); Elizabeth Rowell Thompson, philanthropist (BAHS archives, page 53); Richard Salvucci, artist (Photograph by Marjorie Hilton, page 110).

CONTENTS

ACKNOWLEDGMENTS

This book truly represents a group activity. It was great working with so many people on this project. I want to give special thanks to Bill Marchione. His books provided material for many of the historical narratives and his ongoing research and writing added many more. Bill has been an instructive and supportive mentor to me through all phases of this project. Thank you, Liane Brandon for improving many of the images and getting them to Arcadia. Thanks also for taking some of the photographs. Your talent as a professional photographer is much appreciated. I want to thank Margie Hilton for working with me on several aspects of this project. Margie researched and wrote some of the narratives and was enormously helpful in selecting and organizing images. Margie also worked very hard and effectively on getting the necessary releases for numerous images. I want to acknowledge the contribution of Margaret R. Sullivan, records manager and archivist, Boston Police Department. Thank you, Peg Collins, president of the Brighton-Allston Historical Society, for your suggestions, edits, and for tracking down some of the images. I want to thank many of the members of the board of the Brighton-Allston Historical Society for suggestions of whom to include in this book. I want to thank the Women's Heritage Committee; their booklet, *Women of Vision*, provided material for some of the narratives in this book. Thank you to Charlie Vassilades, Nancy O'Hara, and John Broderick for jumping in at the last minute to supply images necessary to complete this project. And thank you John Broderick for coming up with the photographs at the last minute that are included in the introductory section of the book. Thank you Sharon Cayley for your support and calming words. Thank you Erin Vosgien for working so patiently with me throughout this process and providing timely responses to my numerous questions. I also want to thank my husband, Paul, for his patience and support.

FOREWORD

The present volume approaches the history of Allston-Brighton from a somewhat different and much more personal perspective than earlier works; the focus here is on the *people* who helped to shape the fascinating and incredibly diverse community that is Allston-Brighton today.

In every decade of this community's long and rich history, from the 17th century to the present, Allston-Brighton has produced a panoply of interesting personalities. This volume seeks to systematically document the careers of some 122 of these interesting individuals.

This work makes no claim to comprehensiveness. There are so many interesting Allston-Brighton stories out there that we could easily fill several volumes of this kind.

Allston-Brighton is most fortunate in having Dr. Linda Mishkin heading up this Brighton-Allston Historical Society publication project. Linda, as readers of the *Allston-Brighton Tab* will remember, has long been involved in conducting oral interviews of Allston-Brighton's business leaders and sharing the details of their careers with the reading public. I can personally attest to her great talent and competence as both historian and writer. Back in 2008, prior to my retirement and relocation in Georgia, I had the distinct privilege of co-editing the *Women of Vision* guide to the Brighton-Allston Women's Heritage Trail with Linda. She is a superb writer and a highly talented editor.

This Legendary Locals book represents another contribution by the Brighton-Allston Historical Society and Heritage Museum to the community's expanding knowledge and appreciation of its fascinating history. What the BAHS has demonstrated over and over again since it was founded almost 50 years ago is that there are endless new facts to be uncovered about the fascinating community of Allston-Brighton.

I'm very proud to have played a role over the years in helping to build up this dynamic local historical society, arguably the most active in the city of Boston, an organization that has—through its myriad programs, publications, and exhibits—unearthed endless interesting stories about the historically rich community of Allston-Brighton. The present volume bears additional testimony to the richness of Allston-Brighton's history and to the commitment of its local historical society to sharing its story with the reading public.

—Dr. William P. Marchione
Smyrna, Georgia

INTRODUCTION

Historian J.P.C. Winship, in Volume I of his book, *Historical Brighton, An Illustrated History of Brighton And Its Citizens*, notes that the growth of Brighton (still part of Cambridge at the time) was slow in the beginning. By 1689, the area had only about 30 families. They were drawn by land grants that were presented to any person willing to settle there. Religion played a large role in the lives of early settlers, and farming was the principal occupation. Historian William Marchione notes in Images of America: *Allston-Brighton* that the area had natural advantages, including fertile soil and healthy, elevated, and well-drained farmsteads.

Modern-day Allston-Brighton has approximately 75,000 residents. Farmers markets and produce stores have replaced the sprawling farms of earlier generations. Nearby universities, hospitals, and corporations draw students and people of various professions to the area. A large number of families with children and even a good number of multigenerational families reside in many of the neighborhoods. Because the focus of this book is on individuals and their accomplishments, the history told here is as vibrant as the people who made it. It is hoped that this collection will inspire further research.

These brief narratives provide only a glimpse of the many legendary locals of Allston-Brighton. To quote from the preface of Winshop's book, due to the practical conditions of space and time, "a number of very worthy people are not given the prominence that they deserve." This book still highlights some remarkable people.

Whether it's colonist Rev. John Eliot preaching in the 1600s, Mary Jane Kinglsy Merwin's reminiscences of the 1800s, Charles J. Artesani's longtime service as state representative in the 1900s, or Jim Gentile finding the perfect home for one of his small animals last week, the images and stories presented here show a tremendous versatility of talent and interests. Sam Cornish, Boston's poet laureate, lives in the neighborhood and gives public readings. Benjamin Faneuil Jr. accepted a shipment of tea from England and had to flee for his safety. Ava Chan directs the food pantry at the Congregational Church and is starting her own textile business. William C. Strong gave up a career in law to grow grapes. Harold Connolly won an Olympic gold medal in spite of a physical disability. Lazaro Ponce left Cuba alone in a small boat, was stranded, and later rescued. A park was named for Theresa Hynes, who is currently working on the Brighton Common project, including a time capsule.

With its treasured parks, close neighborhood feel, access to public transportation, libraries, abundant social services, art exhibits, ethnic and cultural diversity, and bustling retail centers, Allston-Brighton draws people (whether for a short time or a lifetime) into the fabric of this thriving urban community.

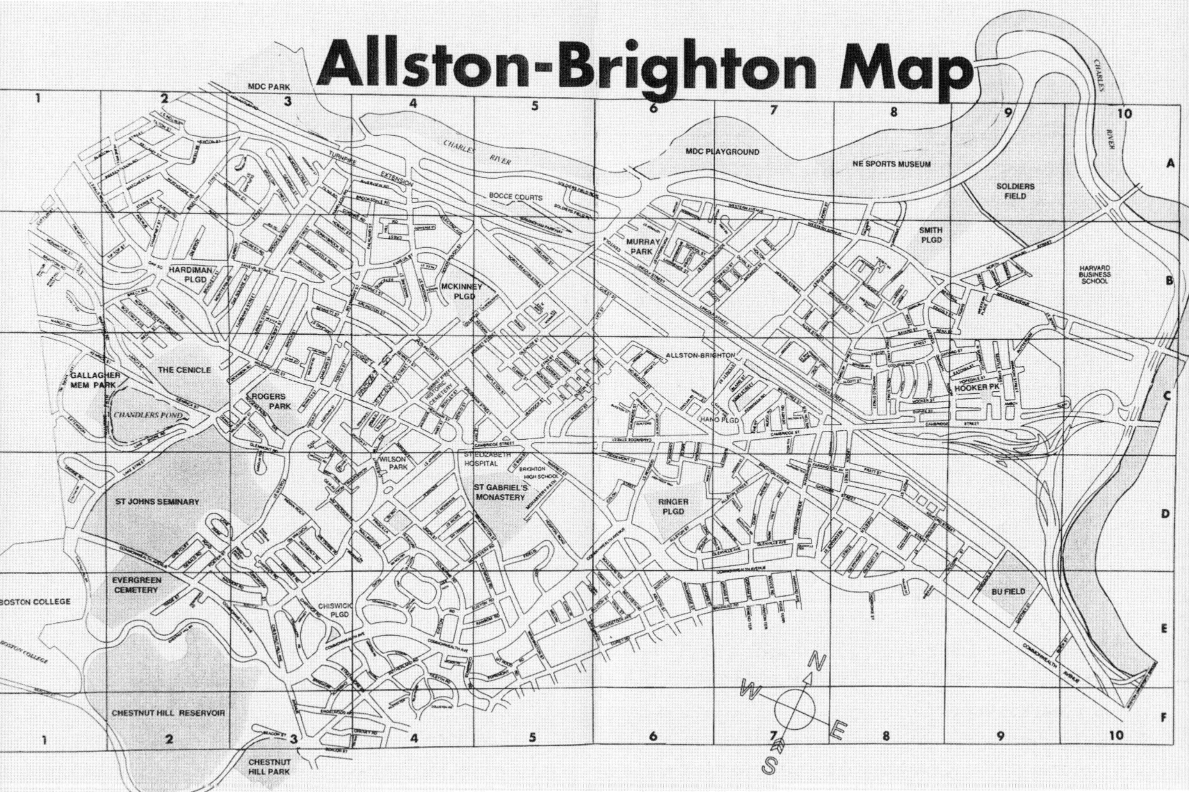

Map
Pictured here is a modern-day street map of Allston-Brighton. (Prime Realty Group.)

CHAPTER ONE

Laying the Historic Foundation

Some of the narratives in this history begin before there was an Allston-Brighton and predate the Revolutionary War. Among these stories are those of the earliest settlers, whose actions built what later became Allston-Brighton. These stories give life to the foundation of this thriving community. Included here are themes of religious conversion, political loyalty, and industry building. Early settlers were key players in early American history, including such events as the Boston Tea Party and the Revolutionary War.

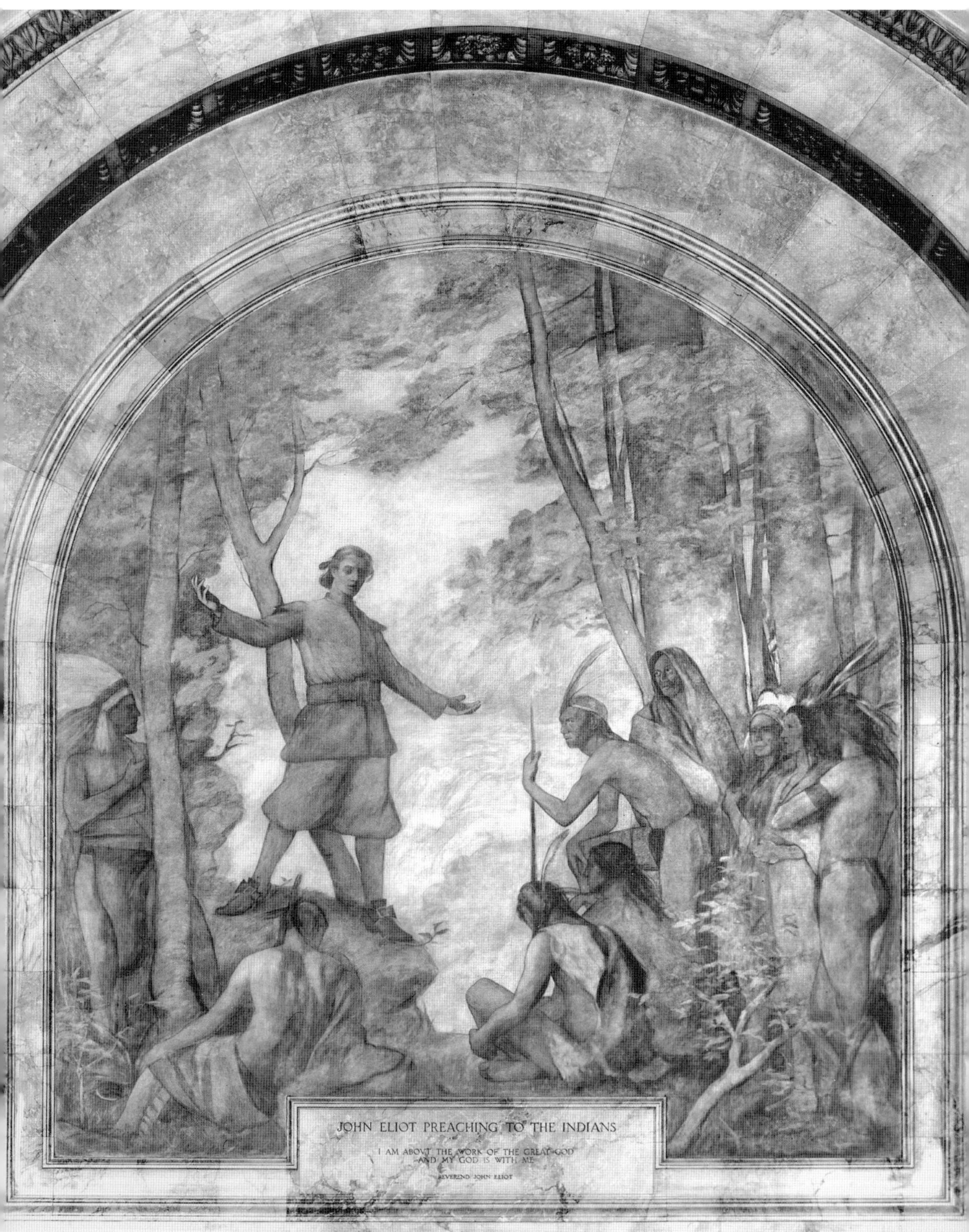
JOHN ELIOT PREACHING TO THE INDIANS
I AM ABOVT THE WORK OF THE GREAT GOD
AND MY GOD IS WITH ME
REVEREND JOHN ELIOT

John Eliot

Religious conversion of the native population to Christianity was a priority of the English government in chartering the Bay Colony in 1628. Colonist Rev. John Eliot eagerly accepted the challenge. After a humiliating, unsuccessful attempt with a native leader elsewhere, Eliot set his sights on Waban, a native leader whose extended family had settled on what is now the Brighton-Newton boundary area. This time, Eliot's proselytizing met with a more receptive audience in Waban and his followers. Eliot was enormously aided in his effort because he had command of the native language, Algonquian. He even devised an Algonquian grammar, giving the language written form. He painstakingly translated the Old and New Testaments into this newly devised written language so that the natives would be able to read the Bible. Being able to read and interpret the Bible was a basic tenet of the Puritan faith. The conversion of these natives led to the creation of a Praying Indian town on land granted by the general court and supervised by the Puritan Church. Eliot suggested the town be named *Nonantum*, the Algonquian word for "Rejoicing." Present-day Nonantum Road in Brighton sits in the area that once belonged to this early community. Nonantum was the first of many such communities. Over his career, Eliot converted some 1,100 Massachusetts natives to Christianity and developed 14 Praying Indian communities. King Philip's War (1675–1676), the most severe Indian conflict in the history of Massachusetts, led to the abandonment of most of these communities. (BAHS archives.)

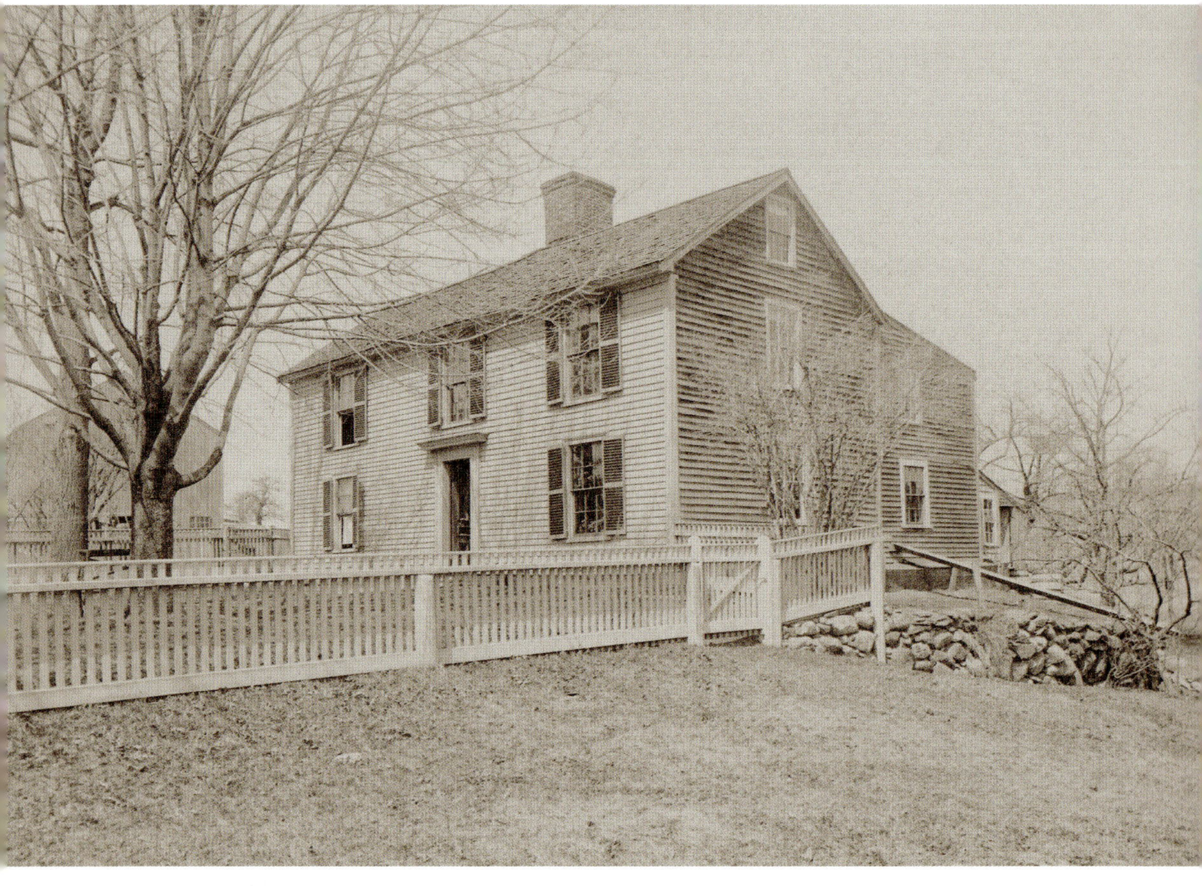

Founders of Little Cambridge
In 1647, Richard and Susannah Champney moved to a 149-acre tract of land in what was then called Little Cambridge. That same year, Richard Dana and his new bride, Anne, moved nearby on a 58-acre lot. Nathanial Sparhawk and his new wife moved to the area in 1649. These three families became known as the founders of Little Cambridge. Generations of these families dominated the political structure of Little Cambridge through much of the 18th century. (BAHS archives.)

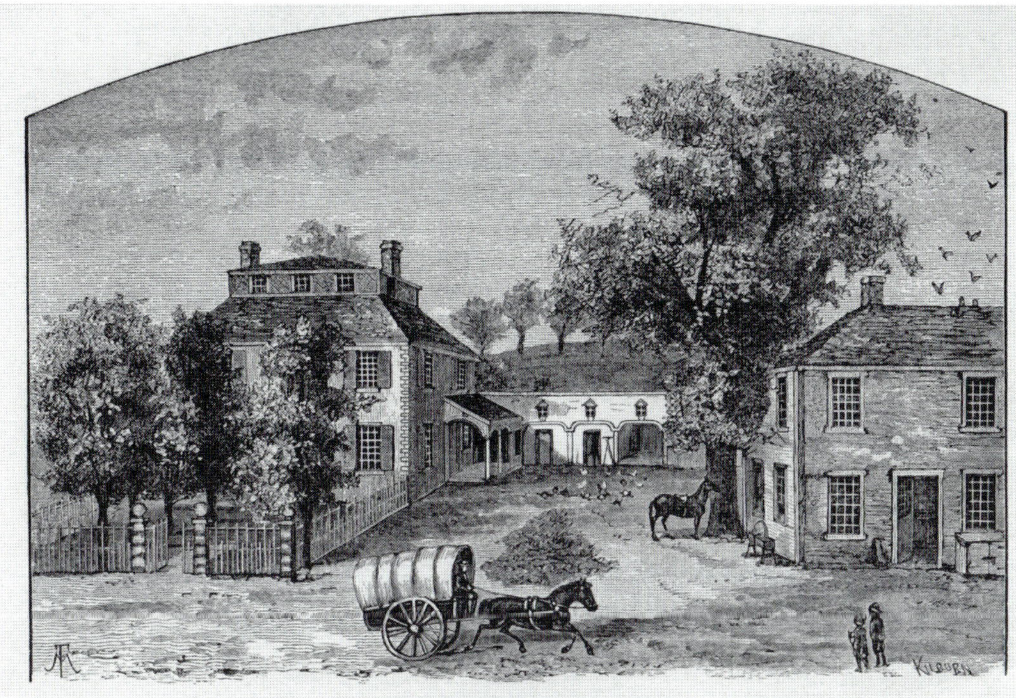

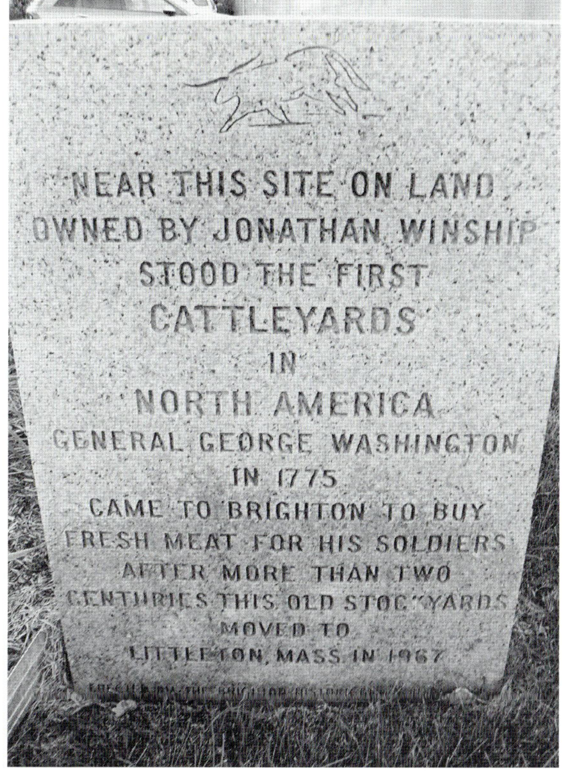

Jonathan Winship I and Jonathan Winship II

Jonathan Winship I and Jonathan Winship II, father and son, responded to Gen. George Washington's plea for meat to feed his troops. At the time, Allston-Brighton was part of Cambridge, headquarters for the Continental army. The Winships contracted with the government and arranged for Middlesex farmers to send cattle. The Winships purchased the livestock and processed the meat for the army, contributing significantly to the Patriot cause. This started what became Brighton-Allston's lucrative cattle market. By 1790, the elder Winship had died, but Jonathan Winship II had become the largest meatpacker in Massachusetts. Others joined the trade. In 1807, Brighton became a separate town from Cambridge. By 1818, Brighton was headquarters of the fairgrounds and exhibition hall of the Massachusetts Society for Promoting Agriculture and site of the annual Brighton Fair and Cattle Show. (Above, BAHS archives; left, Linda Mishkin.)

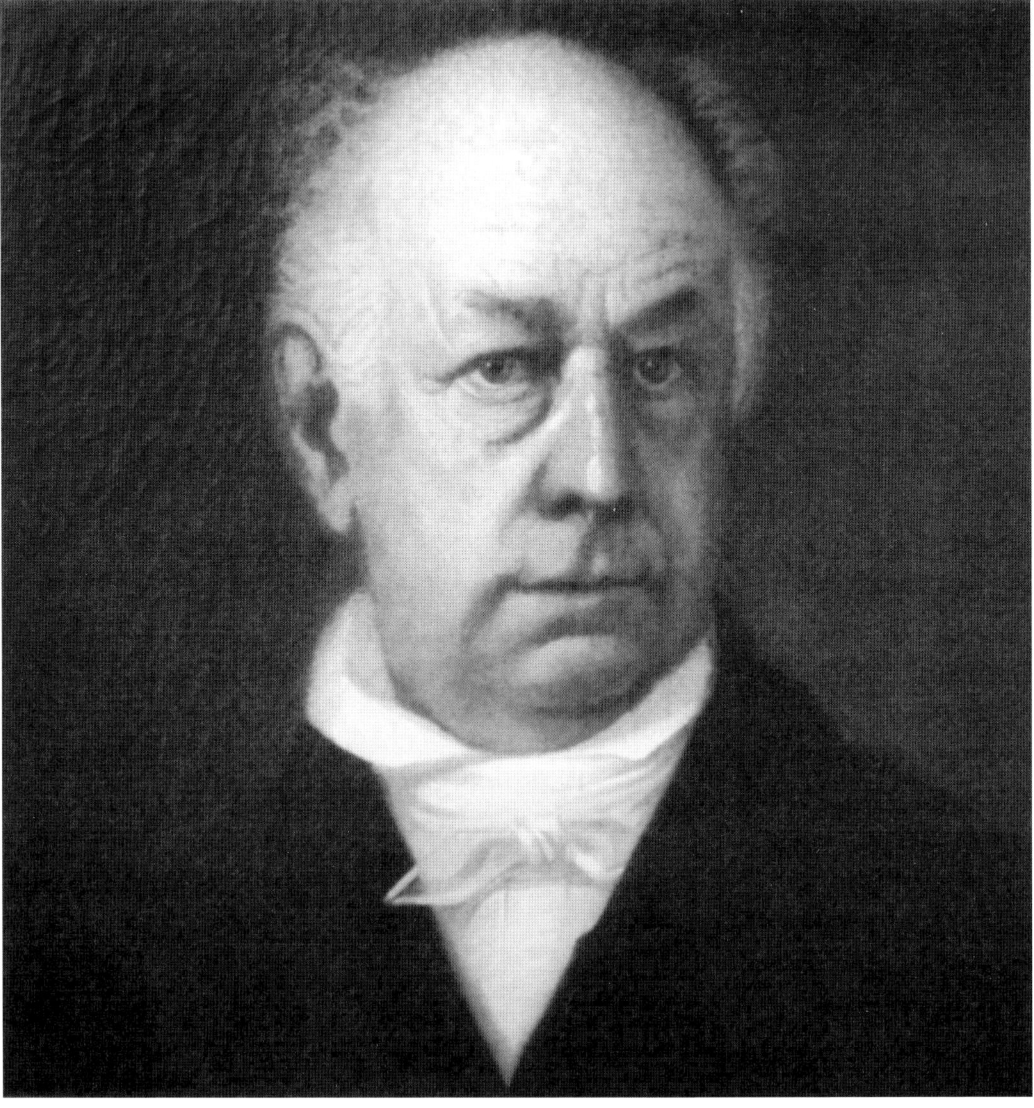

Jonathan Winship III (1780–1847)
Born in 1780 in Brighton (then still Little Cambridge), Jonathan Winship III, son and grandson of the team that founded the Brighton Cattle Market during the American Revolution, distinguished himself in the Pacific trade from 1801 to 1815 while working for the firm of Homer and Winship, headed by his brother Abiel. His Pacific adventures, carried out in collaboration with his brothers, included trading along the west coast of the present United States between California and the Pacific Northwest, the Hawaiian Islands, Alaska, and Canton, China, in activities that included provisioning the Russian Colony in Alaska, attempting to colonize the Columbia River Valley, engaging in highly lucrative seal and otter hunting expeditions, securing a monopoly on the sandalwood trade from King Kamehameha of Hawaii, and spending time in China during the War of 1812. It was in China that Jonathan, during a period of forced leisure, acquired the skills in horticulture that led to a partnership with his youngest brother, Francis. Together, in 1820, they founded Winships' Gardens, Brighton's pioneer horticultural enterprise. Later, Capt. Jonathan Winship also played a key role in founding the Massachusetts Horticultural Society, serving as that organization's vice president from 1835 until his death in 1847. (BAHS archives.)

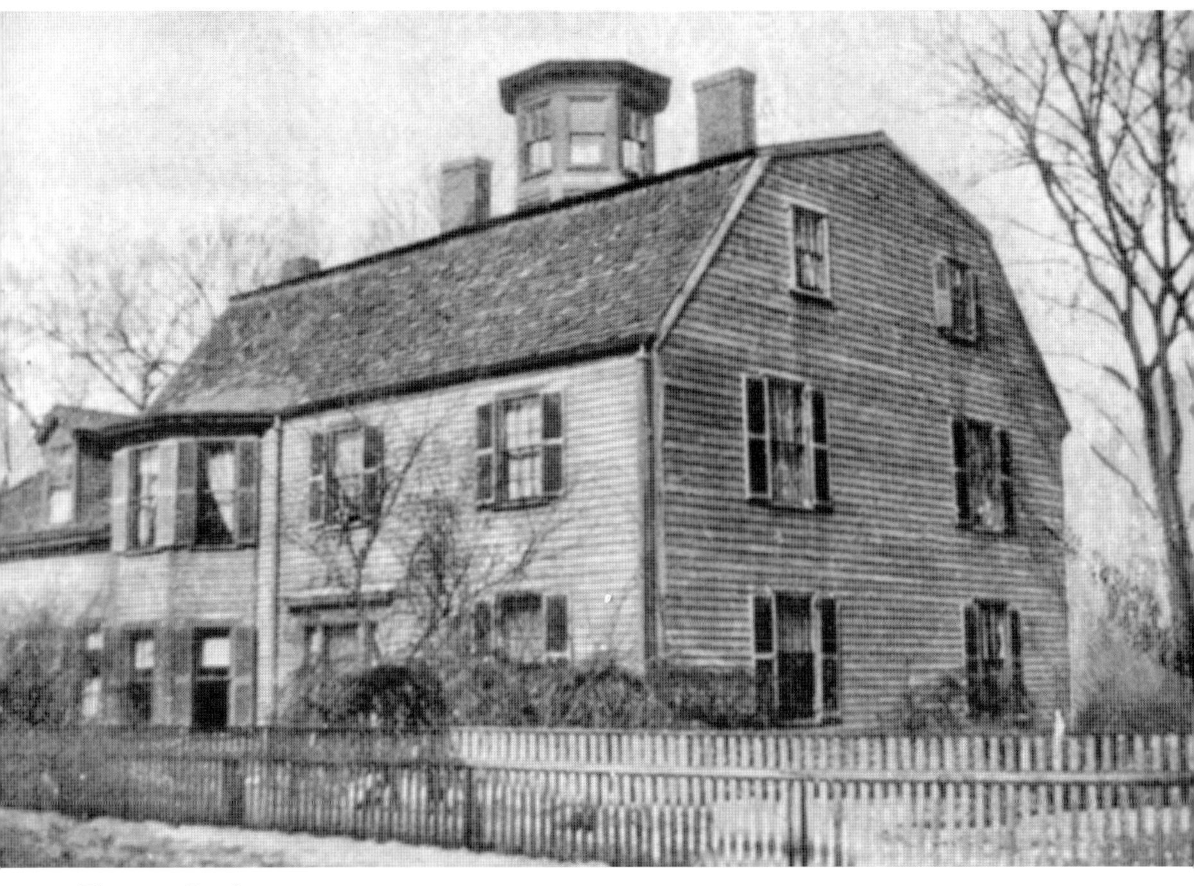

Thomas Gardner

Thomas Gardner, who married Joanna Sparhawk in 1755, was a strong voice for Little Cambridge in Cambridge town government. He was elected representative to the general court in 1769 and remained there until the king dissolved the court in 1774, following the Boston Tea Party. Gardner was a fervent revolutionary at the forefront of those urging resistance. In 1775, he was commissioned colonel of a regiment he had organized largely at his own expense. He was severely wounded at the Battle of Bunker Hill and died in Brighton at the home of his sister. Gardner was the second-highest ranking officer mortally wounded at Bunker Hill. General Washington attended his funeral services. A Massachusetts town, Gardner, was named in his honor. (BAHS archives.)

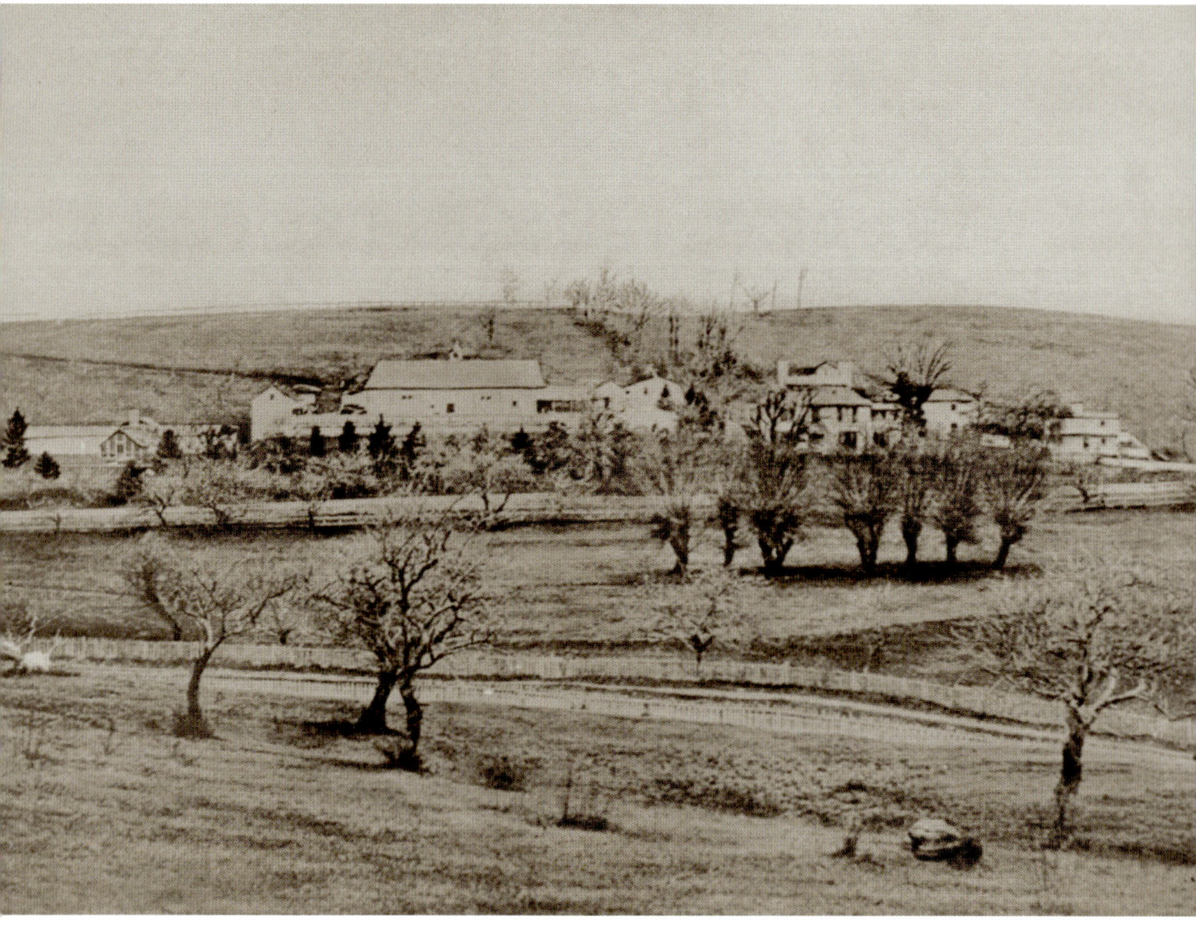

The Faneuil Family

The Faneuil family was prominent in Brighton's early commercial history when it was still part of Cambridge. Benjamin Faneuil was brother and heir to the benefactor, Peter Faneuil, for whom Boston's Faneuil Hall is named. After a successful career in the family mercantile business, in 1760, Benjamin retired to a 70-acre estate in Little Cambridge, turning the family business over to his sons. For many years, while living on this side of the Atlantic, the Faneuils had maintained strong business and property ties with England. Their loyalty became apparent in 1773 when Benjamin Faneuil Jr. decided to accept a shipment of British tea. This action provoked public anger. Fearing for their safety, Benjamin Jr. and his brother fled to England. When the quick departure of the two brothers became publicly known, an angry mob marched on Faneuil Hall and destroyed a portrait of Peter Faneuil that had hung there. At this time, the aged and blind Benjamin, still residing in Little Cambridge, was under the care of his daughter, Mary Faneuil Bethune. Perhaps fearing that her father's property would be seized by the revolutionary authorities, Mary hosted General Washington and some officers at her father's estate for dinner. Accompanying Washington was Gen. Arthur Lee, a deserter from the British Army. At the close of the dinner, elderly Benjamin entered the room. He praised General Washington for his patriotism to the colonies and then castigated Lee for his disloyalty to the throne. Later that evening, General Washington asked for an explanation from Mary. She replied that her father, being blind and out of the world for 20 years, still stated the ideas on which he was educated. The evening ended peacefully. The property remained in the family until 1811, when Bethune's heirs sold it. (BAHS archives.)

CHAPTER TWO

Business and Trade

This chapter focuses on past and present business people of Allston-Brighton. Many overcame the challenges associated with starting a new business or adapting a business to changing times. In many cases, family and networking provided support and resources to overcome obstacles. It is the internal enthusiasm and fortitude of each individual that is portrayed in these brief stories. Local businesses bring more than goods and services to an area. They also help solidify a community by providing places for people to meet and greet, thereby maintaining the human scale of urban life. The variety of stores nestled in present day Allston Village, Packards Corner, Brighton Center, and Oak Square encourage pedestrian traffic and are all accessible by public transportation.

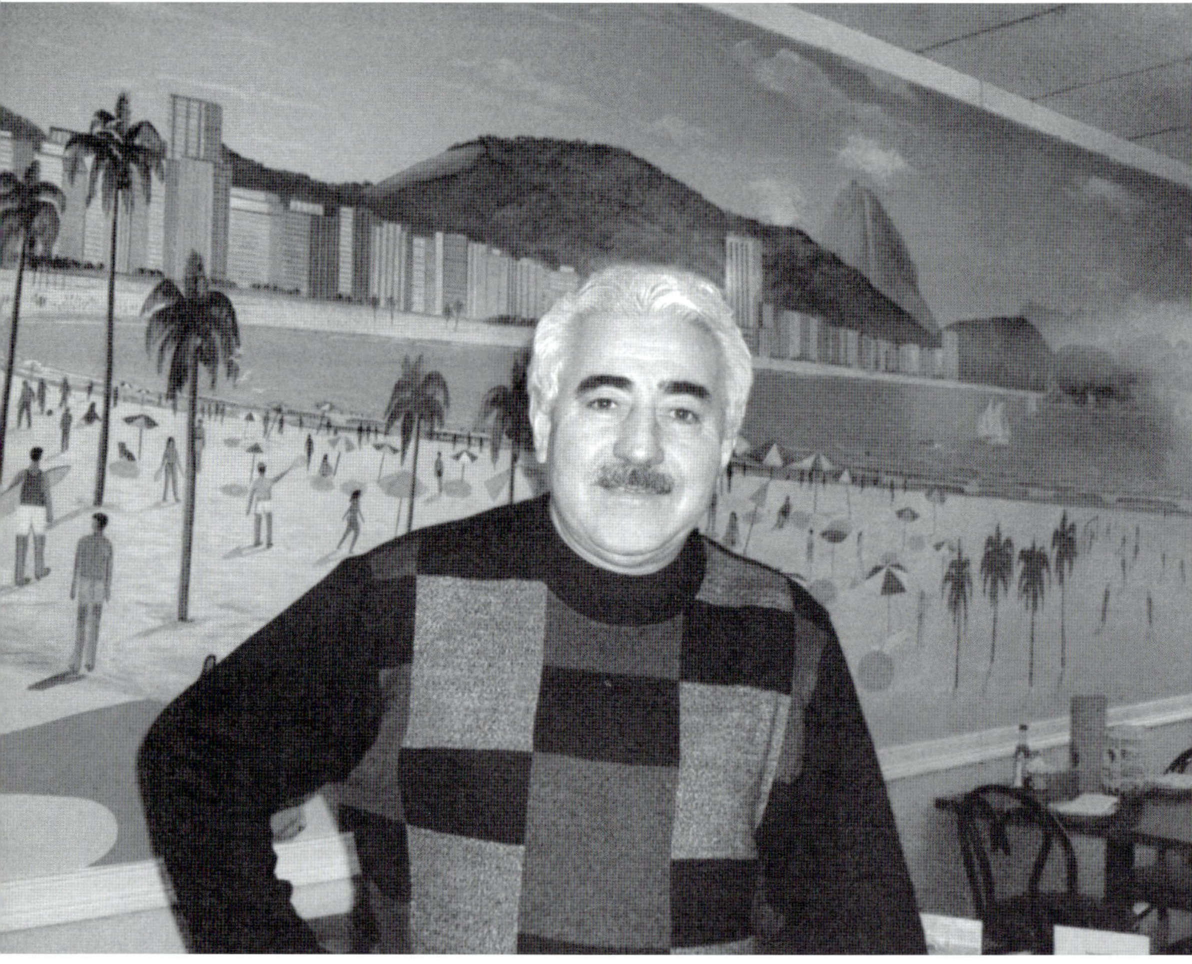

Valter Vitorino

Valter Vitorino, along with business partner Gilmar Pinto, opened Allston restaurant Café Brazil in 1986. His partner subsequently left, leaving Vitorino sole owner. He was 19 years old when, in 1969, he came to the United States from Conselheiro-Pena, Brazil. He expected to stay only one year. He first went to New York City but could not find work. Friends urged him to try Boston. He found Boston a good place to work, with people who were friendly and welcoming. He worked in several restaurants, including a job as headwaiter at Anthony's Pier 4 where he met many famous people, Frank Sinatra among them. The dream to run his own business remained. (Photograph by Linda Mishkin.)

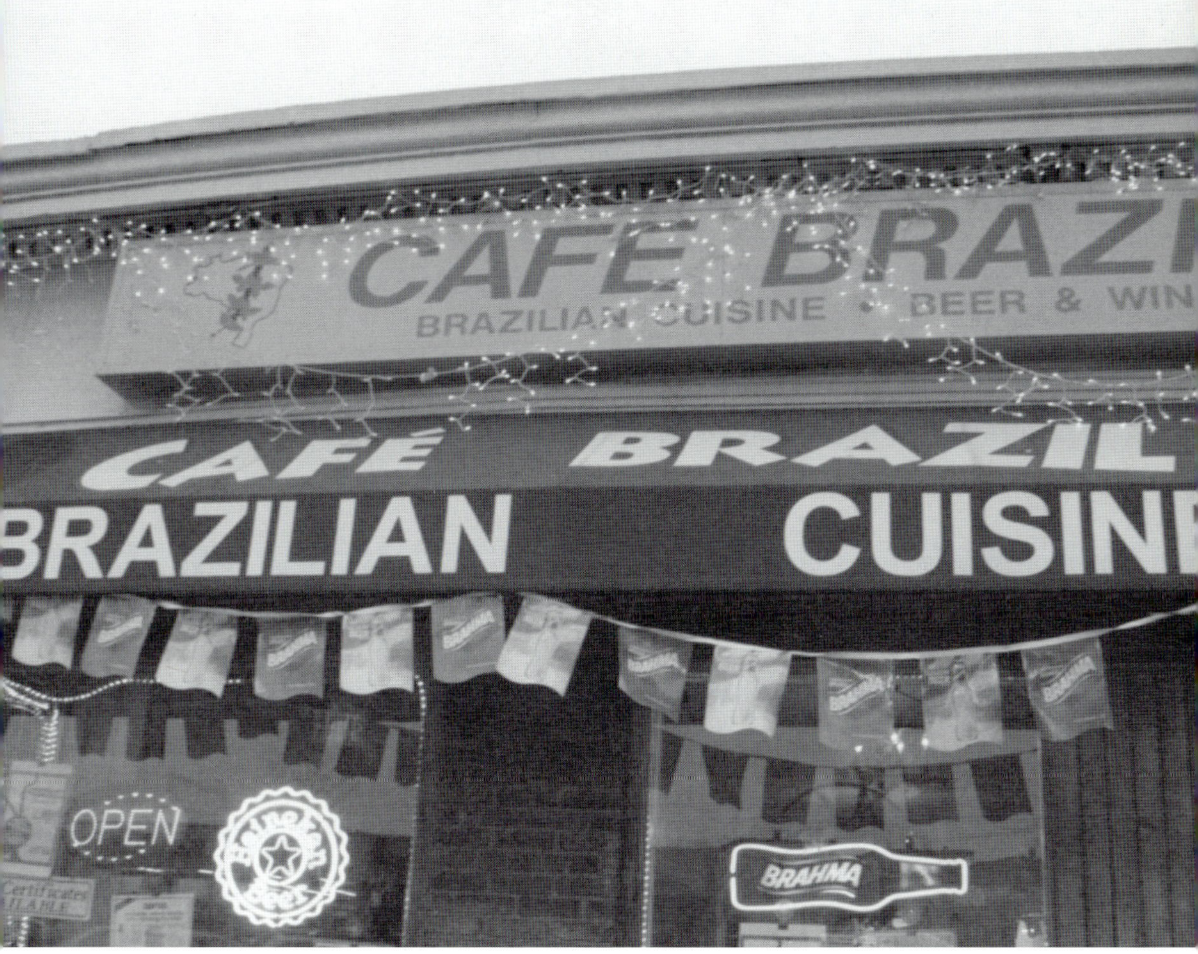

Café Brazil

Vitorino was drawn to Allston because of its growing Brazilian community and because of Boston's public transportation system, which he credits with enabling people to get around easily, even without cars. He describes the cuisine as "home style." He enjoys hearing from customers that it reminds them of family meals back in Brazil. His loyal customer base, which spans generations, includes many Brazilians but also represents the cultural diversity of the city and surrounding towns. Children who began coming to his restaurant with their parents now come as adults and bring their own children. (Photograph by Linda Mishkin.)

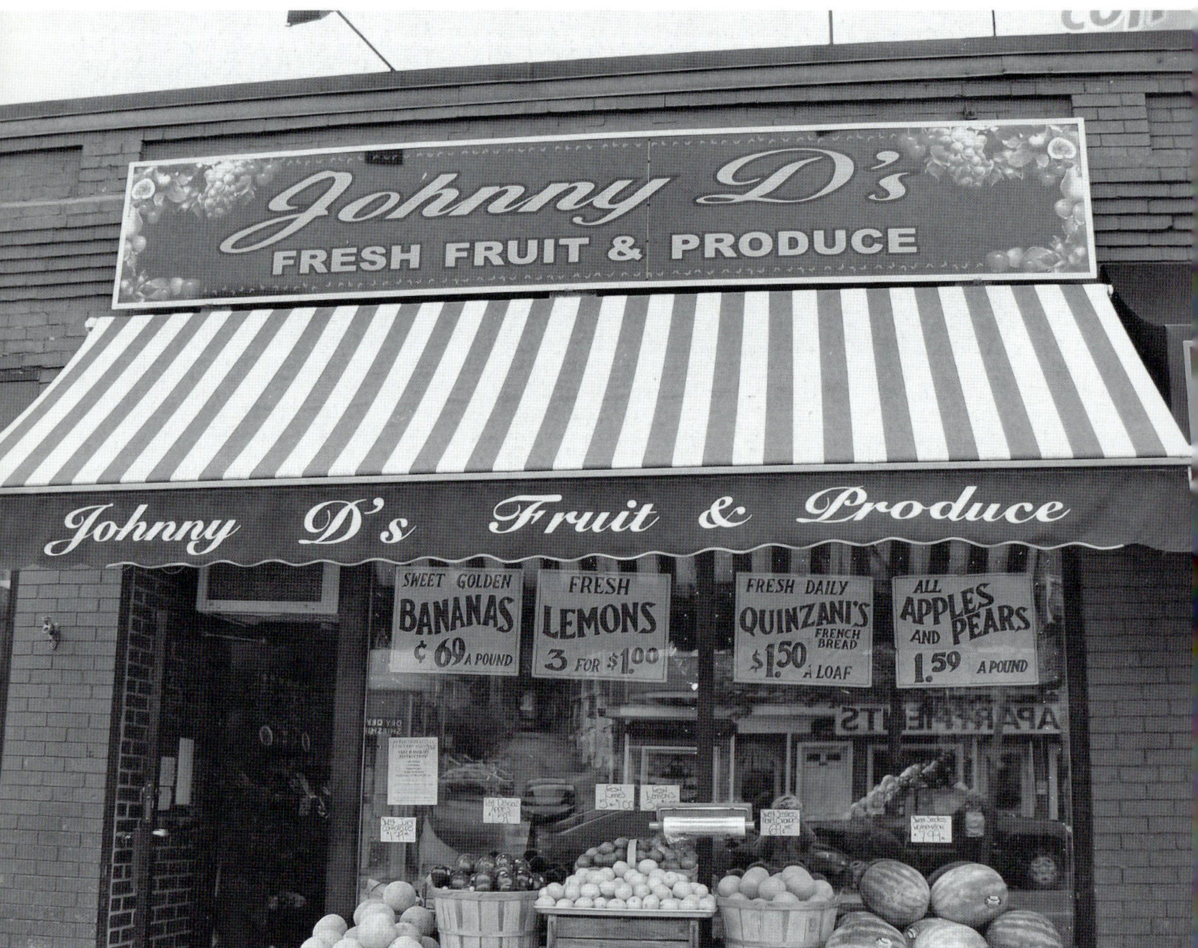

Johnny D's Fruit & Produce

John DePietro is owner of Brighton Center landmark Johnny D's Fruit and Produce. Taking a job out of high school at a produce section of a food store, DePietro fell in love with the business. As his knowledge grew and conversations with customers increased, his shyness disappeared. He later became the store's produce manager. He expanded his knowledge while working at Wilson Farms in Lexington, where he learned the farming side of the industry. He enjoyed his job, but knew that eventually he would open his own business. (Photograph by Linda Mishkin.)

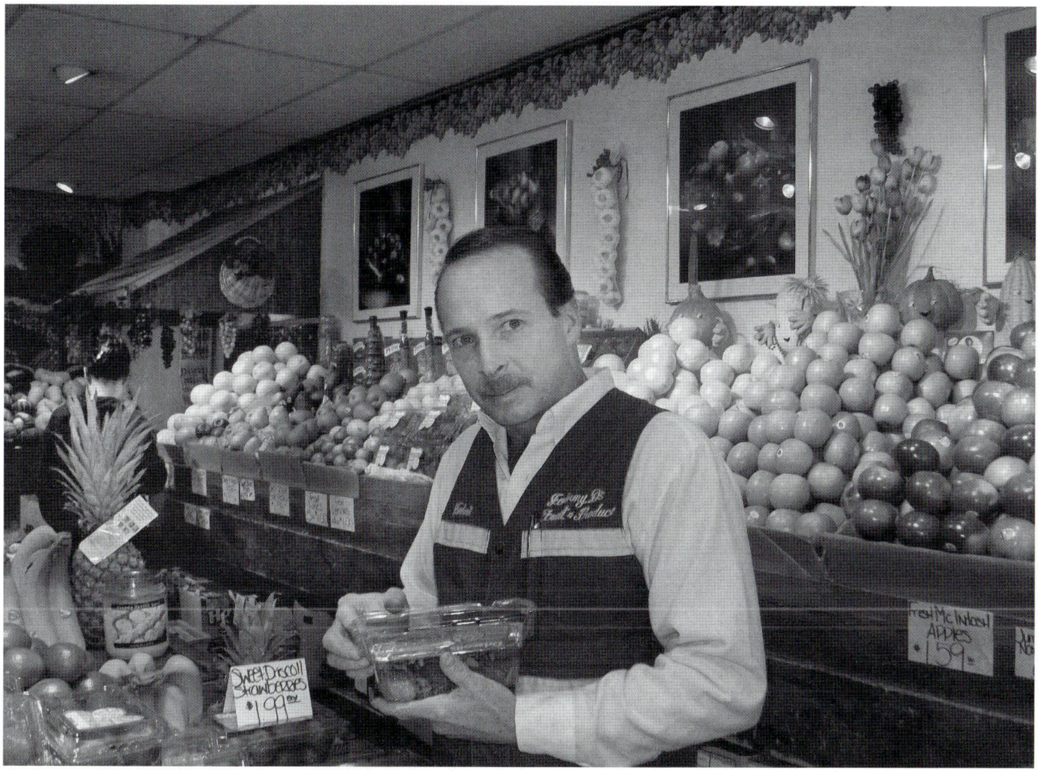

John DePietro
DePietro started with a fruit stand on a corner of Denis Minihane's lot, which he tended from April 15 until Thanksgiving. Then in 1992, he opened his store. He considers himself to be fortunate in doing what he loves in a community where he wants to stay. No matter what the season, Johnny D's is a comfortable and colorful place that encourages people to ask questions, swap recipes, and chat with neighbors while in pursuit of the perfectly ripe tomato or tangerine. (Photograph by Linda Mishkin.)

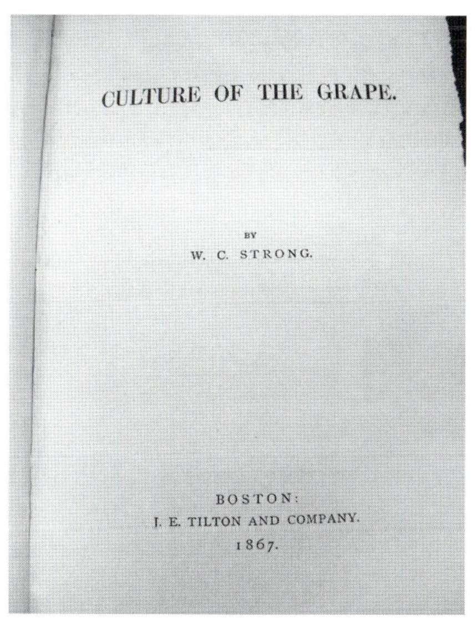

CULTURE OF THE GRAPE.

BY
W. C. STRONG.

BOSTON:
J. E. TILTON AND COMPANY.
1867.

William C. Strong
William C. Strong was a law clerk in the Boston law firm of Senator Daniel Webster at the time that Horace Gray owned his Brighton grapery. In his capacity as clerk, Strong was frequently sent by Webster to Gray's estate on business matters. According to historian Winship, Strong was so charmed with the estate and especially the graperies that in 1848, when the estate was sold at auction, he became the purchaser. The estate covered more than 100 acres. The magnitude of owning the graperies was such that he gave up the profession of law and devoted himself full time to his horticultural interests. (BAHS archives.)

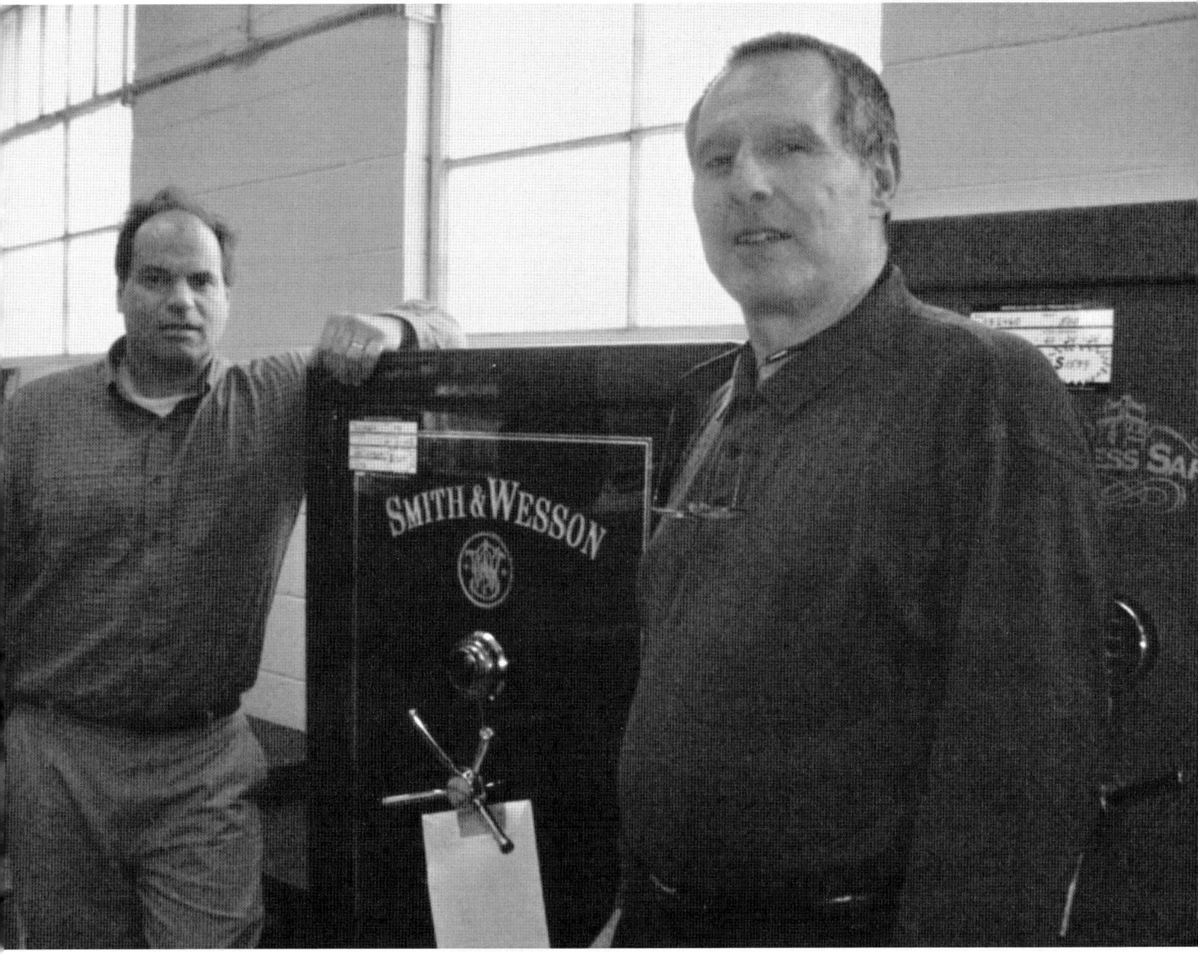

David Stoia and Joe Bartholomew

David Stoia (left) is owner of Boston Lock and Safe Company; Joe Bartholomew (right) is vice president. In 1975, soon after the Massachusetts Turnpike extension was built, Stoia and Bartholomew relocated the company to Brighton from its previous site in Boston. The Brighton location provided better space and access for huge truckloads of deliveries. Boston Lock and Safe dates back to Colonial times. Over its long history, the company has had different names, including Boston Lock, Boston Lock and Clock, and Boston Lock and Key. It is America's oldest lock company. In 1776, James and Thomas Winship opened a combination locksmith and blacksmith shop. In 1790, the company focused exclusively on the manufacture and distribution of locking devices and hardware. About 1900, Vangel Stoia, a priest in Albania, immigrated to the United States. To support his 14 children, Vangel needed to supplement his meager clergyman's salary. He got a job cutting keys for the company, then still owned by the Winship family. (Photograph by Linda Mishkin.)

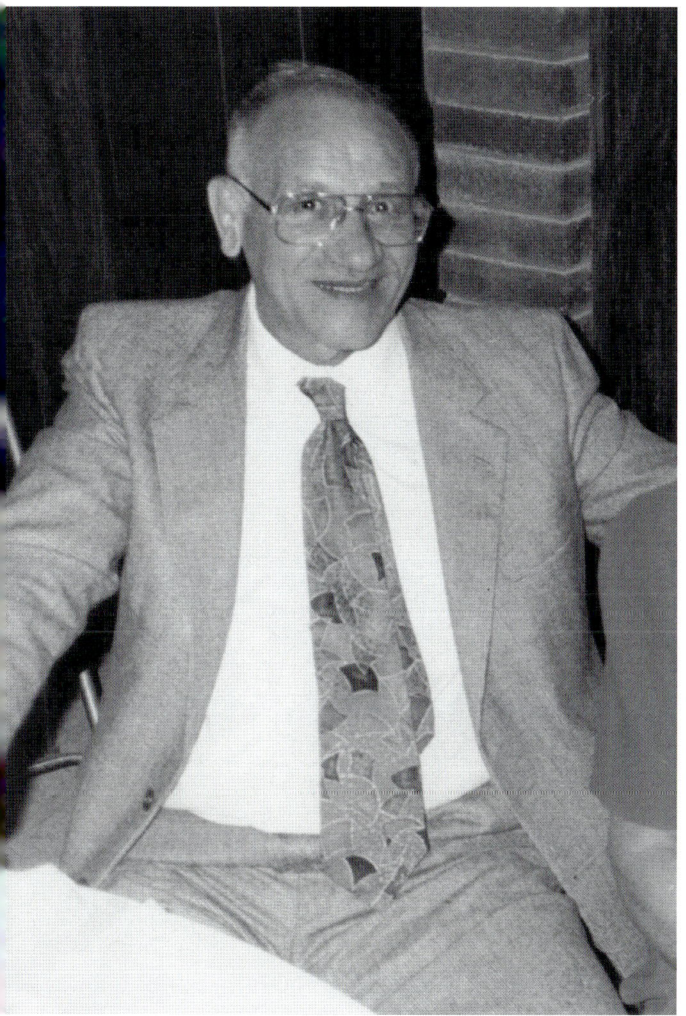

Harry Stoia
Vangel succeeded in making the company one of the biggest key-making businesses in the world. In time, he became owner. He was succeeded by his son James and grandson Harry. When Harry Stoia, David's father, became owner in the early 1940s, he still had to sell hardware items along with locksmithing to make a living. But Harry was a practical visionary. By the late 1940s, he saw the potential new demand for keying systems for the sprouting phenomenon of food and other chain stores. Under Harry's ownership, the company became federally registered, spurring its future growth. In the last 60 to 70 years, the lock and safe business has grown exponentially with sophisticated alarm and security systems. Since 9/11, the industry has become even more specialized with audit control and closed circuit television. David Stoia and Joe Bartholomew have created a niche in the burgeoning industry that includes safes, alarms, access control, and specialty hardware. Together, they continue the company's long tradition of being in the forefront of change. (The Stoia family.)

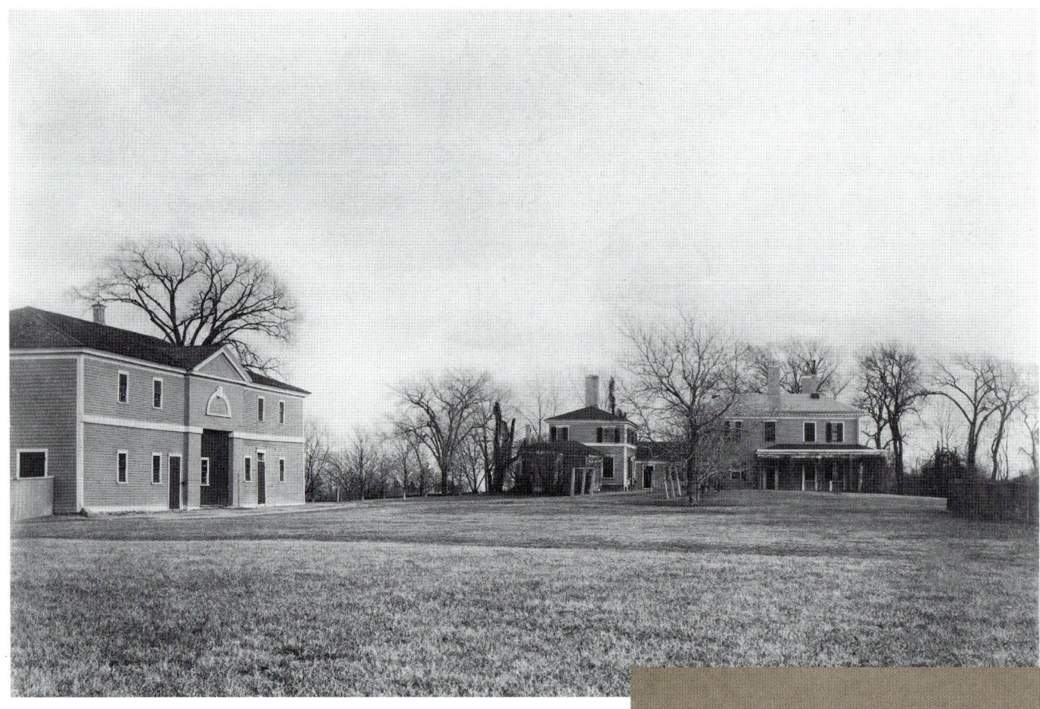

David Nevins Sr. (1809–1881)
Born in Salem, New Hampshire, David Nevins Sr. became a wealthy New England textile manufacturer. He owned several mills in Lawrence, Salem, and Methuen, Massachusetts, including the Pemberton Mill in Lawrence. The latter was the scene of a January 1860 building collapse and fire that killed as many as 145 workers, mostly Irish and Scottish immigrants. After the disaster, Nevins bought out his partner and rebuilt the mill, which still stands. Nevins resided for many years on an estate in Brighton called Bellvue, a property that today comprises the grounds of St. Elizabeth's Hospital and the former St. Gabriel's Monastery. The hill on which Bellvue Estate stood is commonly referred to as Nevins Hill. (BAHS archives.)

Joseph L.L.F. Warren
In 1820, Joseph L.L.F. Warren established Brighton's second horticultural firm, which he named Nonantum Vale Gardens. The nursery attracted many visitors, including Ralph Waldo Emerson, Daniel Webster, and Henry Wadsworth Longfellow. Warren won many prizes, including an 1838 award from the Boston Horticultural society for raising the first tomatoes in Massachusetts. (BAHS archives.)

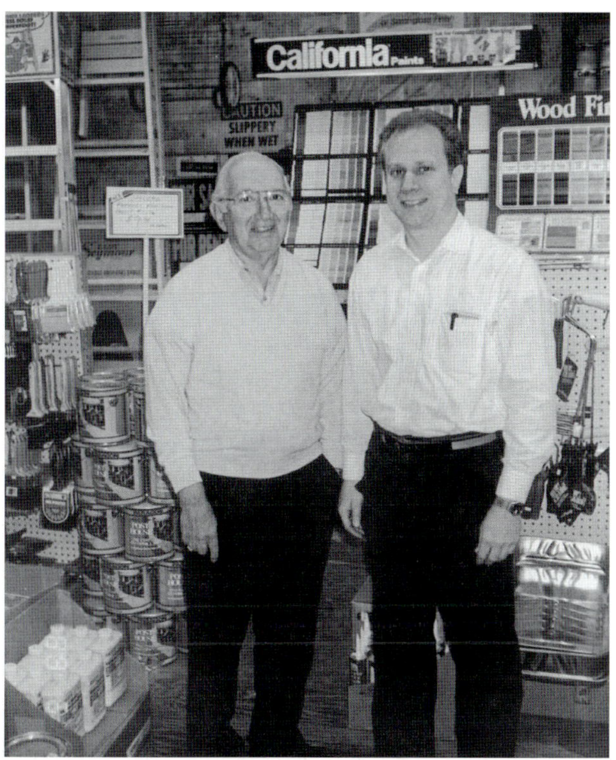

Robert Webber

Robert Webber (below) is current owner of Model Hardware. His father, Ike (left, with young Robert), bought the Allston store in 1959. Ike had been working in the store for its previous owner, Abraham Rome, since 1938. Over the years, and in response to economic fluctuations and competition from big box stores, several small local hardware stores went out of business. Model Hardware prevailed. Webber credits the store's durability to managing change effectively and sticking to the principles his father taught him: to provide great personal service, attend to details, train the staff to be well-informed, and treat customers well. Webber takes great pride in following these principles, which have benefited both the business and its customers for decades. (Left, Webber family; below, Linda Mishkin.)

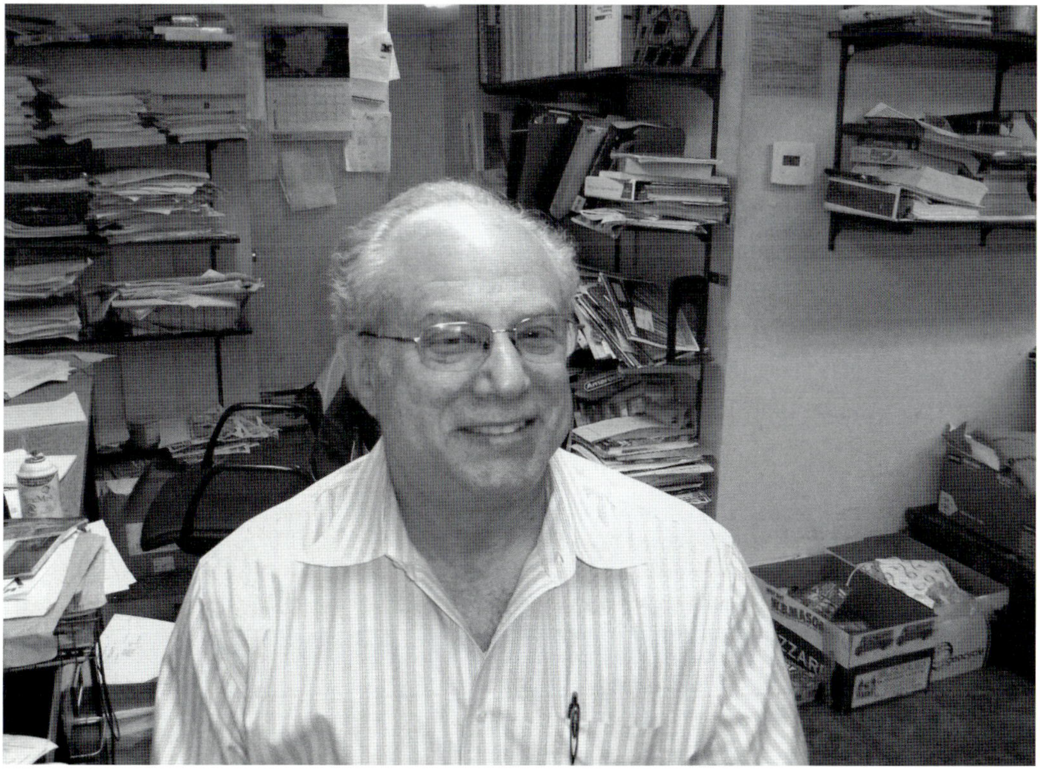

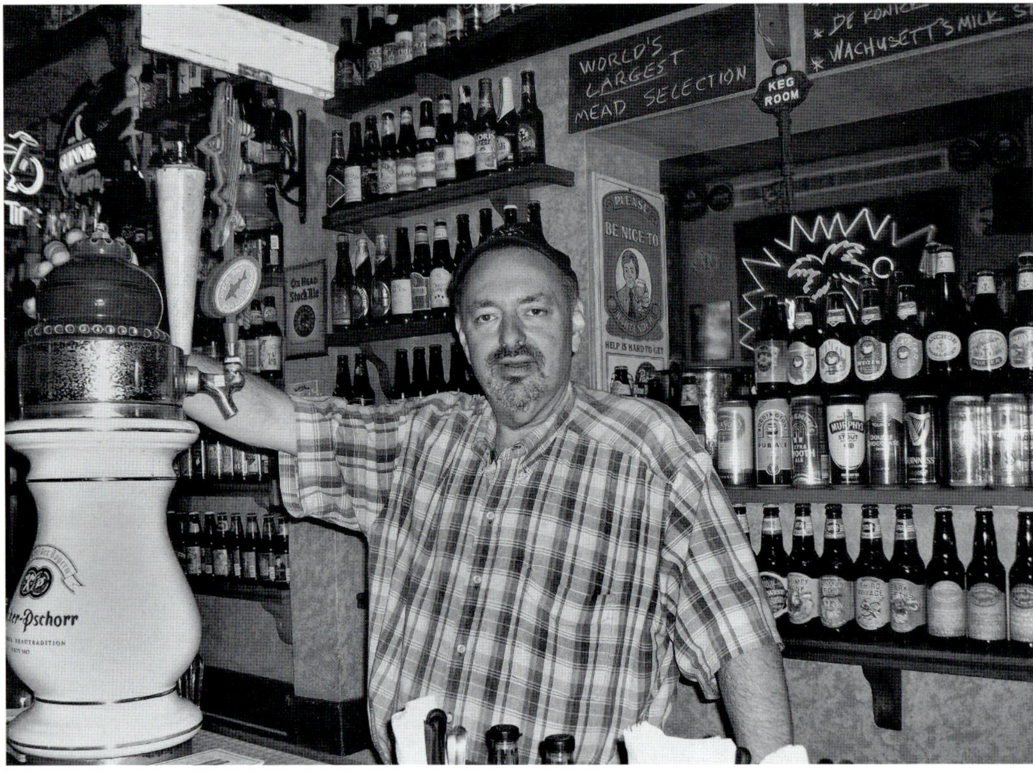

Marc Kadish

Marc Kadish is owner of Sunset Grill and Tap and Big City, both in Allston, and Sunset Cantina in Brookline. Throughout his life, Kadish has always loved food. As a kid, he had a great time hanging out in the kitchen of a Boston restaurant where his father worked. That early experience influenced Marc's later decision to pursue a career in food service. He worked as a chef while studying hotel and restaurant management on Cape Cod and interned at Disney World, where he attended the chef's apprentice program. He later worked as an executive chef on a cruise ship. By 1986, he decided to return to Boston. He was attracted to Allston because of the high foot traffic and reasonable rents. The area also had lots of successful restaurants and bars. He quickly found a restaurant for sale and has been there ever since. He describes his restaurant's décor as "real junk." Over the years, Kadish has accumulated what he believes to be one of the largest breweriana collections in the United States, including such items as cocktail trays that date back to the 1930s, coasters from all over the world, and beer steins. He also collects license plates, which are displayed on the walls of the restaurants. He credits his staff for supplying great ideas that have helped the businesses flourish. Many of his 60 employees have been with him for over 20 years. For more than 20 years, the restaurant's beer selection has won Best in Boston awards. The food menus include ribs, steak tips, burgers, pastas, and what he claims to be the best nachos in town. The *Improper Bostonian* magazine has said as much several years in a row. Kadish is invested in Allston and has served as president of the board of Allston Village Main Streets since 1996. Over the years, he has seen the streets in the Allston business district become safer and storefronts become more attractive. With a concerted effort on behalf of local merchants and Allston Village Main Streets, the City of Boston has installed outdoor seating areas, planted trees and gardens, and repaved sidewalks. Now, he says, Allston offers even more reason to live here, eat here, and shop here because, "We have a little bit of everything." (Photograph by Linda Mishkin.)

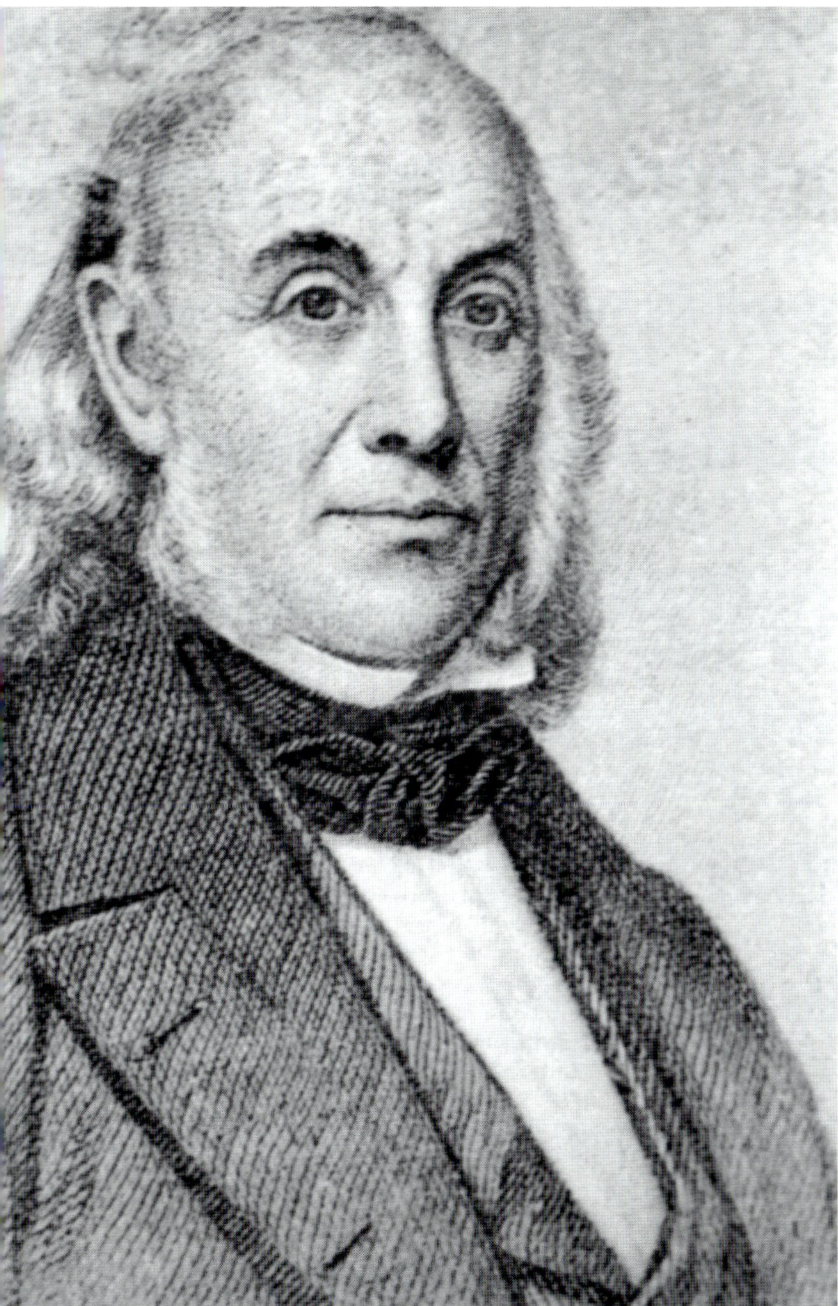

Joseph Breck
As editor of the *New England Farmer*, Joseph Breck was already a leading horticulturist when he moved to Brighton and established the town's third major horticultural business. He first specialized in growing vegetables and flower seeds and then added shrubs and other flowering plants. In 1851, he discontinued his nursery and sold most of the stock to his son-in-law William C. Strong for use at the grapery he had acquired from Horace Gray. Then, in 1854, he opened a second nursery in Brighton. Breck served as president of the Massachusetts Horticultural Society from 1859 to 1862. Today there is still a Breck flower catalog. (BAHS archives.)

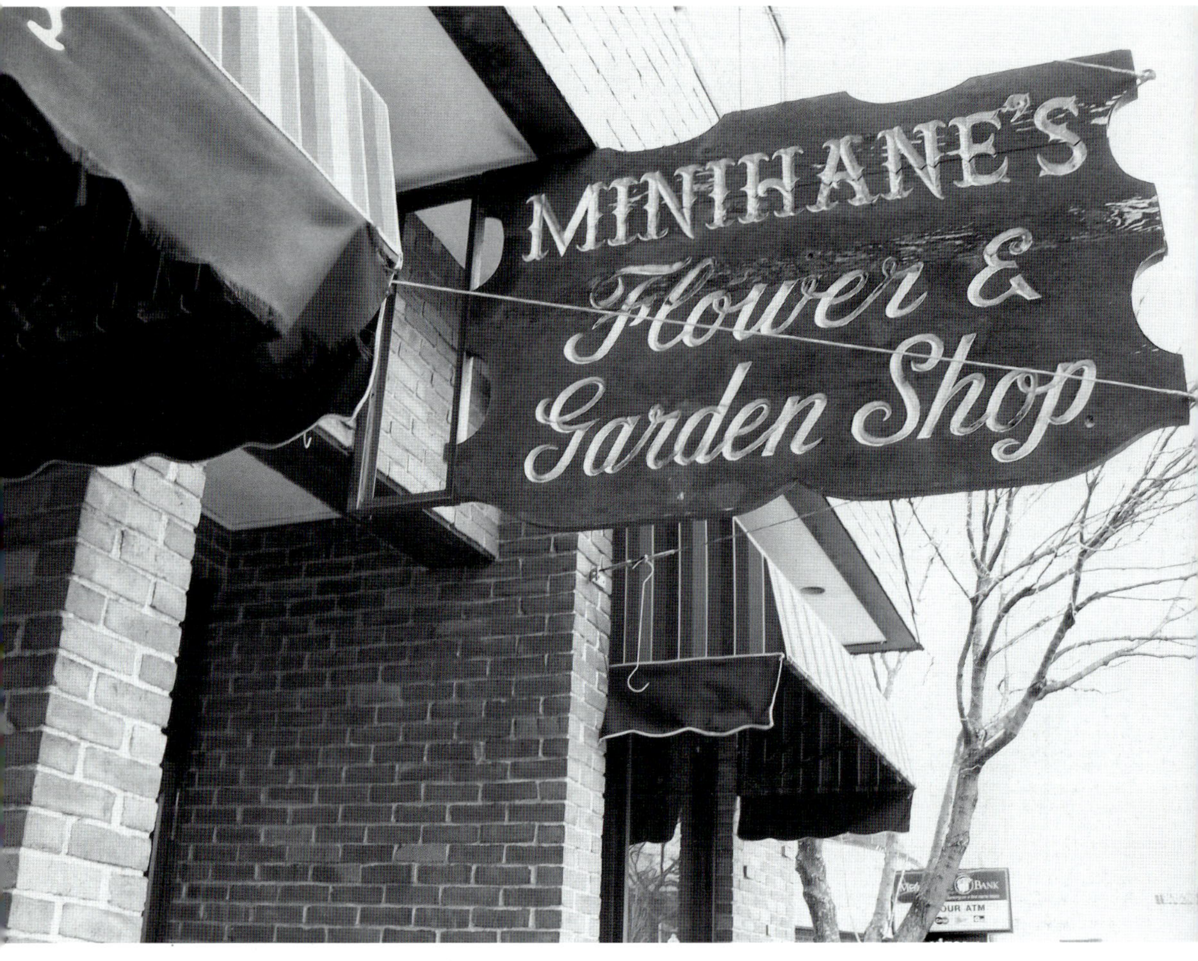

Minihane's Flower & Garden Shop

Denis Minihane worked at a greenhouse called Arlington Conservatory when he was young. It was located in Brighton Center. He cleaned, ran errands, watered the plants, and eventually learned how to take orders over the phone and operate the cash register. He also learned how to make flower arrangements. During the years he worked and learned the flower business, he promised himself to one day own a shop of his own. He made good on that promise. After college and a few years in the Marine Corps, he married and started a family. In 1965, he opened his flower shop in Brighton Center. (Photograph by Linda Mishkin.)

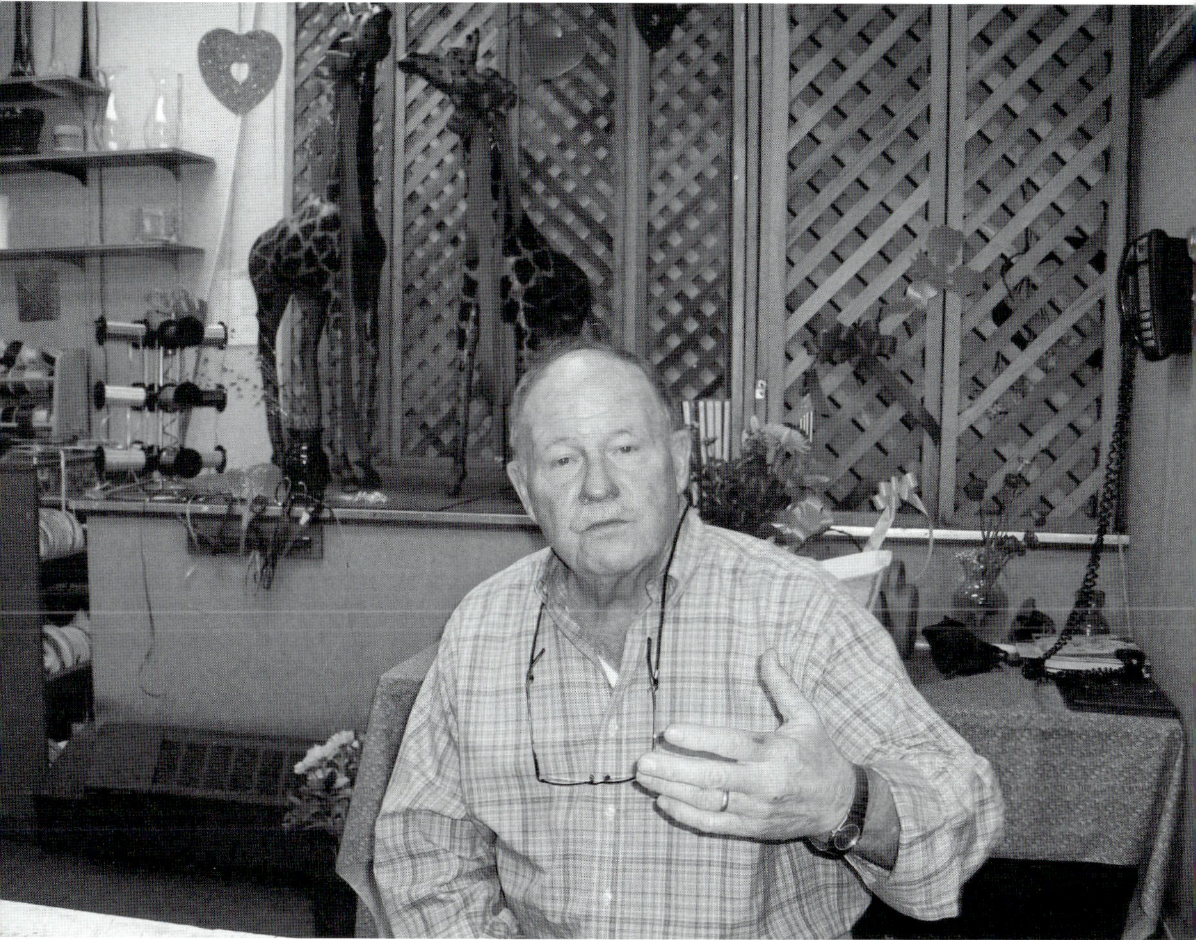

Denis Minihane

At first, the new business did not bring in enough income for him to raise his growing family. So, he took a second job selling power equipment, including snowblowers and chain saws. Gradually, he was able to focus full time on his beloved flower business. It flourished. Over time, the inventory expanded to include greeting cards and beautiful gift shop items. The business became a very popular spot for shoppers and browsers alike. Minihane's Flower & Garden Shop was an integral part of Brighton Center for over four decades. It closed in 2011. (Photograph by Linda Mishkin.)

Cindy Nguyen

Cindy Nguyen is the owner of Chez Bella Salon in Allston. She came alone to the United States from Viet Nam when she was 15 years old, leaving behind her parents and eight siblings. She spoke no English. She lived with a family who also had emigrated from Viet Nam. She was able to attend a Catholic high school because of the church's sponsorship. After school, she worked at the church. Cindy attended college for two years and during the summers attended beauty school. It was there that she found her real passion for the beauty business. (Photograph by Linda Mishkin.)

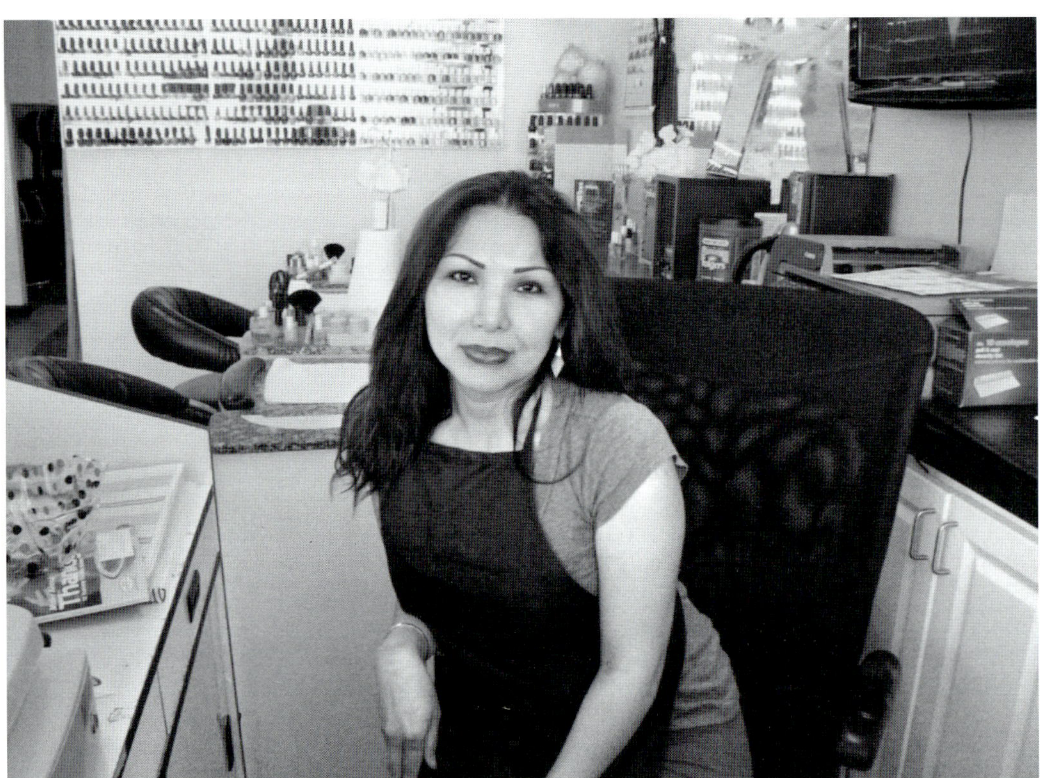

Chez Bella Salon (opposite)

Now after nearly 25 years, she still loves it. She also loves Allston and plans to stay here forever. From the beginning, she felt welcomed by the community. Looking back, she remembers leaving all she had ever known in Viet Nam. But now, she feels that Allston is her home. Two of her siblings have subsequently moved to the United States and live in Dorchester. Family get-togethers require them to come to Allston because Cindy works seven days a week. In spite of her busy schedule, Cindy and her husband are involved with the Allston-Brighton community through the West End House. They help support the girls' basketball team. (Photograph by Linda Mishkin.)

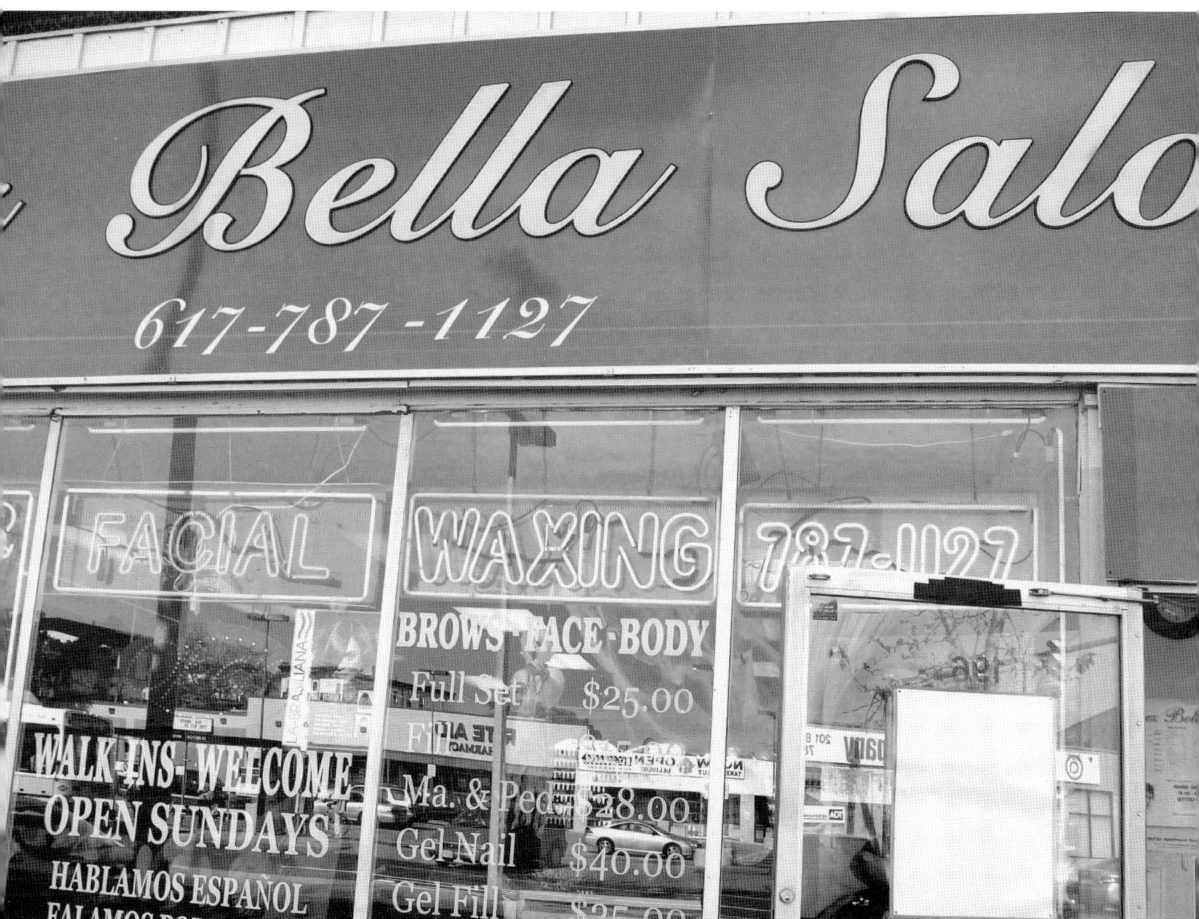
Bella Salo
617-787-1127
FACIAL
WAXING
BROWS-FACE-BODY
Full Set $25.00
Ma. & Ped. $28.00
Gel-Nail $40.00
Gel Fill $25.00
WALK-INS- WELCOME
OPEN SUNDAYS
HABLAMOS ESPAÑOL
FALAMOS PORTUGUÉS

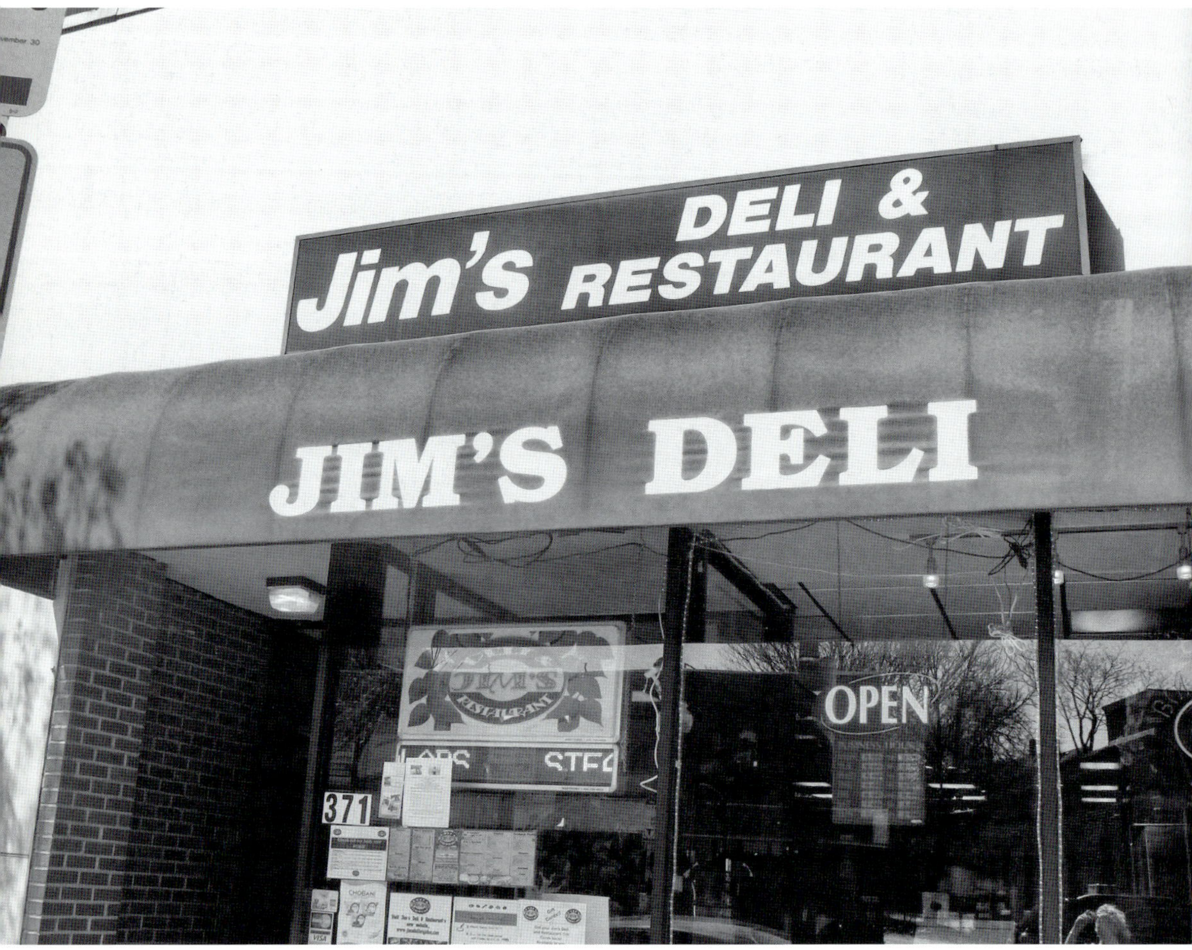

Jim's Deli

Brothers Jim and Nick Tziavas are the current owners of Jim's Deli in Brighton Center. It is a family-owned, second-generation business. Their parents came to the United States from Greece with a dream of owning their own restaurant. They opened their first restaurant in Brookline in 1985 and in 1990 opened another in Brighton Center, where they still continue to work. (Photograph by Linda Mishkin.)

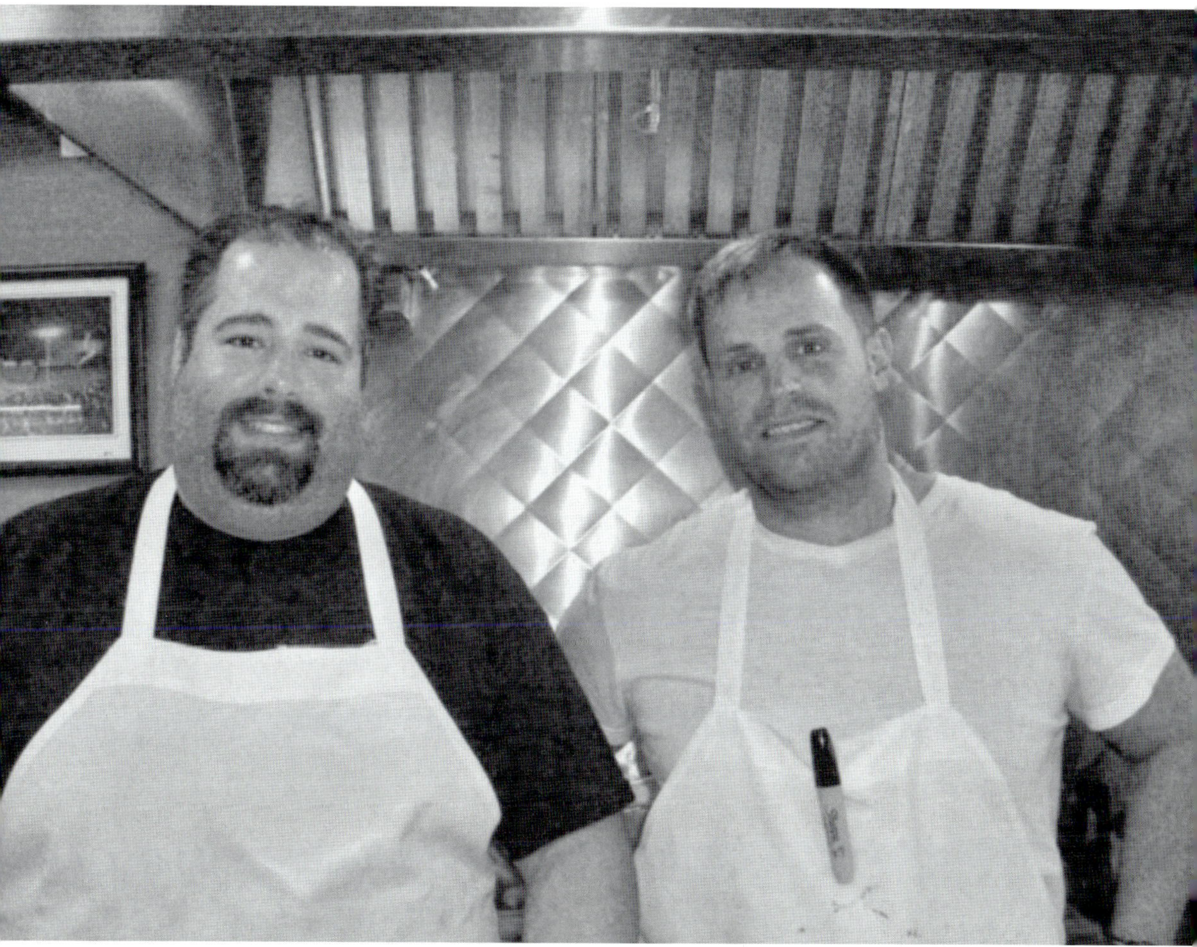

Jim and Nick Tziavas
Breakfast service begins at 6 a.m., which requires Jim and Nick to arrive at 4 a.m. to get things ready. The menu is large, as are the portions. Recipes include many family secrets. Several items have been featured on the television show *Phantom Gourmet*. (Photograph by Linda Mishkin.)

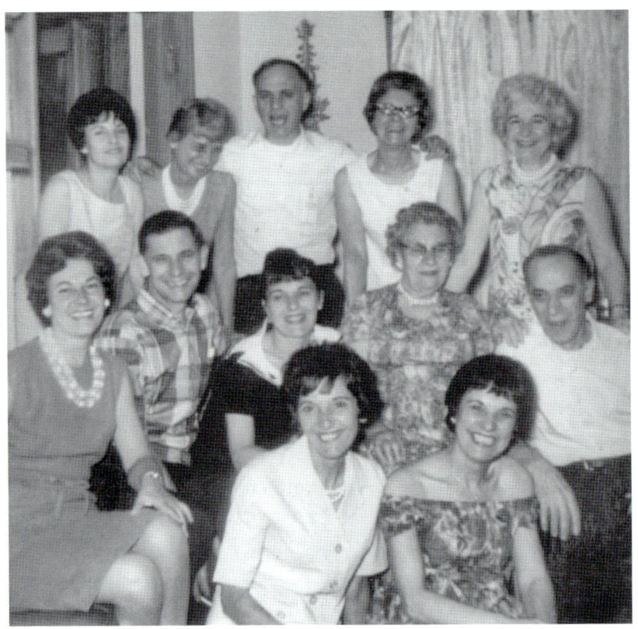

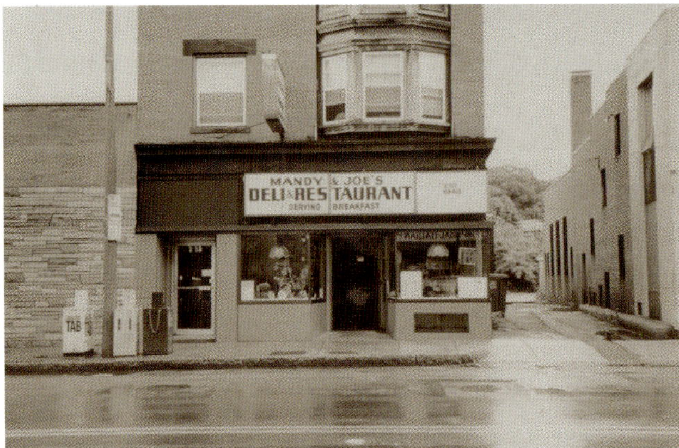

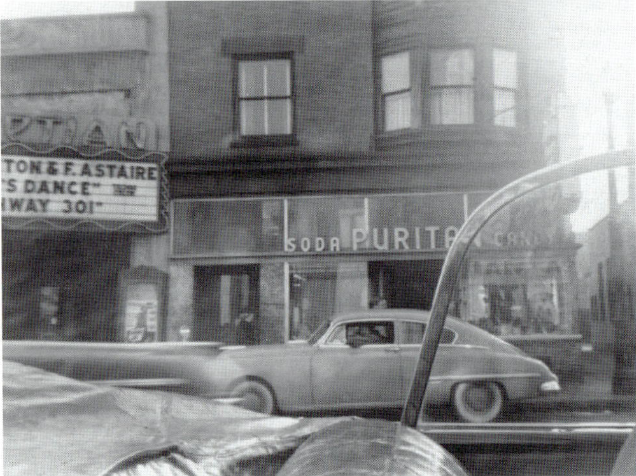

Mandy and Joe's Restaurant

Mandy and Joe's restaurant has been around since 1948. It was founded by members of the Marino family and remains in the family today. Brothers Joe and Armand "Mandy" (pictured above left with their siblings) worked various jobs after leaving military service. Eventually, they both got jobs at Jack and Marion's, a very popular restaurant and deli in Brookline. However, they wanted a place of their own. In 1948, they opened a small deli in rented space in Brighton Center, which they named Brighton Delicatessen. Its nickname, "The Brighton Del," was more commonly used. They opened at 5 a.m. and closed at 11 p.m. In 1962, the brothers bought a building across the street and the business moved and grew. The original deli counter is gone. (The Marino family.)

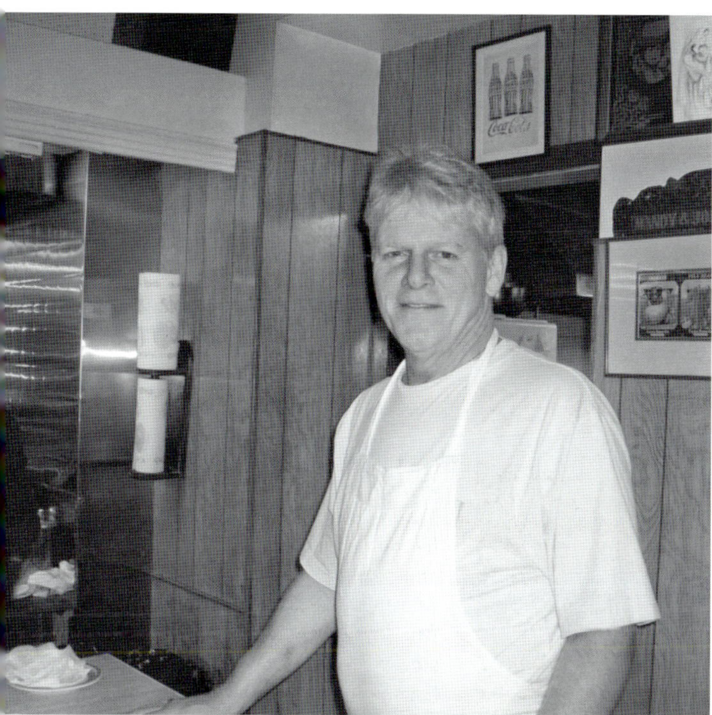

Richard and Ingrid Marino
Joe's son Richard (left) and his wife, Ingrid (below), now own and run the business and are helped by their children. In the 1970s, when supermarkets started selling deli goods, many independent stores had to close or change. Richard decided to focus solely on good, home-style meals. Richard is a longtime collector of historical artifacts, which he displays on the walls and in the front window area. Customers can browse his assortment of memorabilia before digging into their homemade beef stew or freshly baked apple pie. (Photographs by Linda Mishkin.)

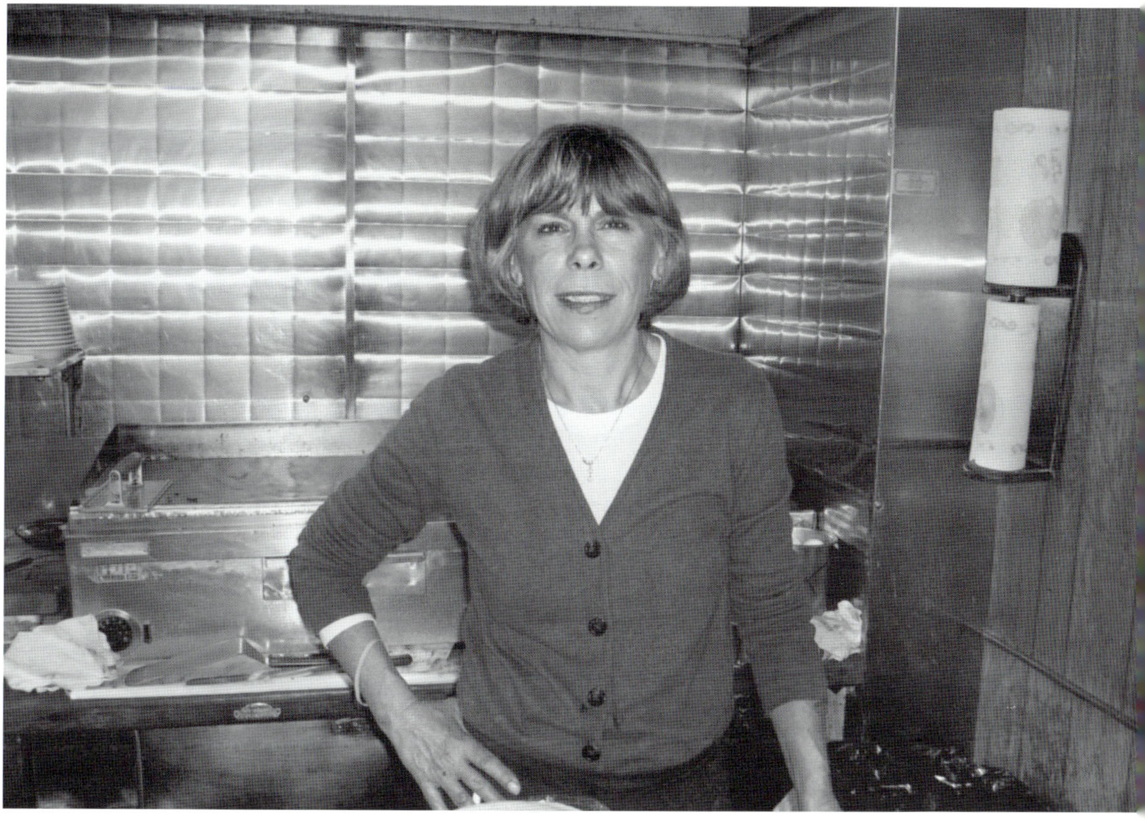

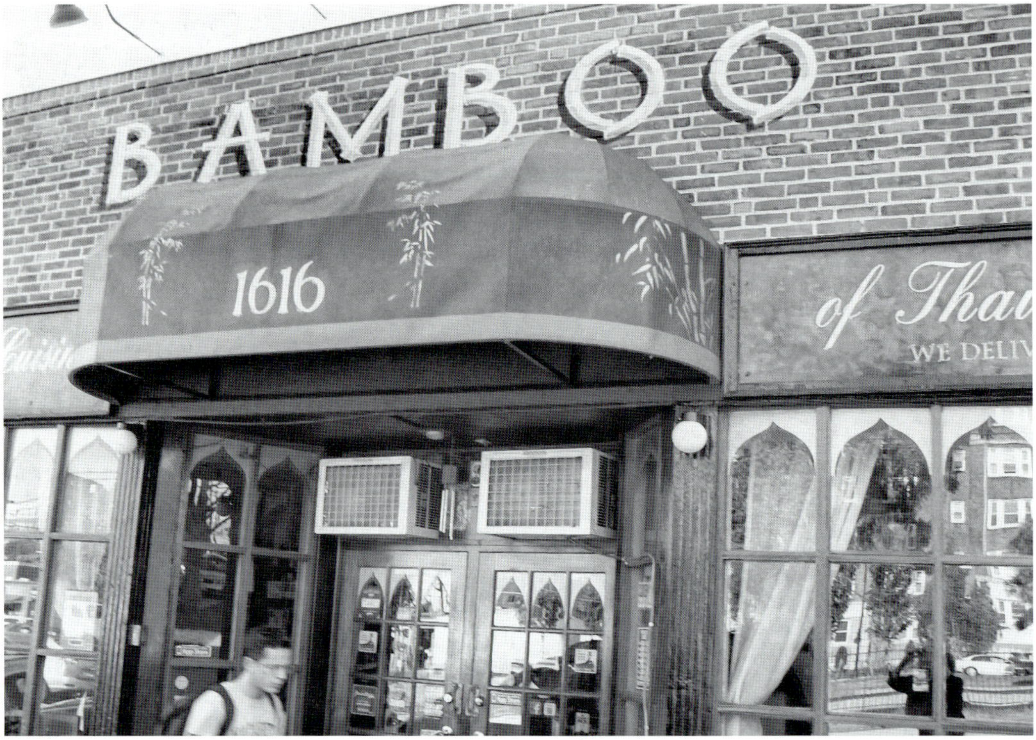

Sam Chindapanich

Sam Chindapanich had been living in California when he came to Boston for a vacation. He never left. Now he is co-owner, along with Well Dinanno, of Bamboo Restaurant in Brighton. Chindapanich manages the restaurant, which opened in 1989. Before he became an owner, he had worked at several restaurants, gaining a lot of practical expertise. His knowledge of Thai cuisine originates in Thailand, where he was born and raised. He describes Thai food as a hearty blend of curry, garlic, chili, and basil, among other things, influenced by Chinese, Indian, Indonesian, and Malaysian cuisines. He inherited his love of cooking from his family, including both of his parents; some of his grandmother's recipes are on the menu at Bamboo. His cultural and family traditions live on in Brighton. (Photographs by Linda Mishkin.)

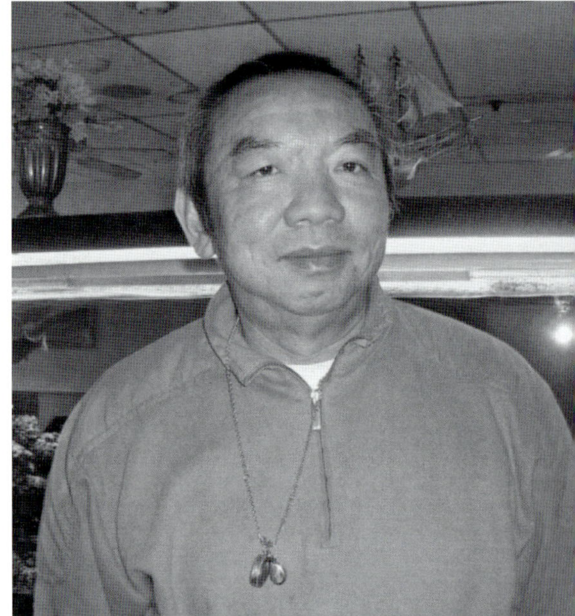

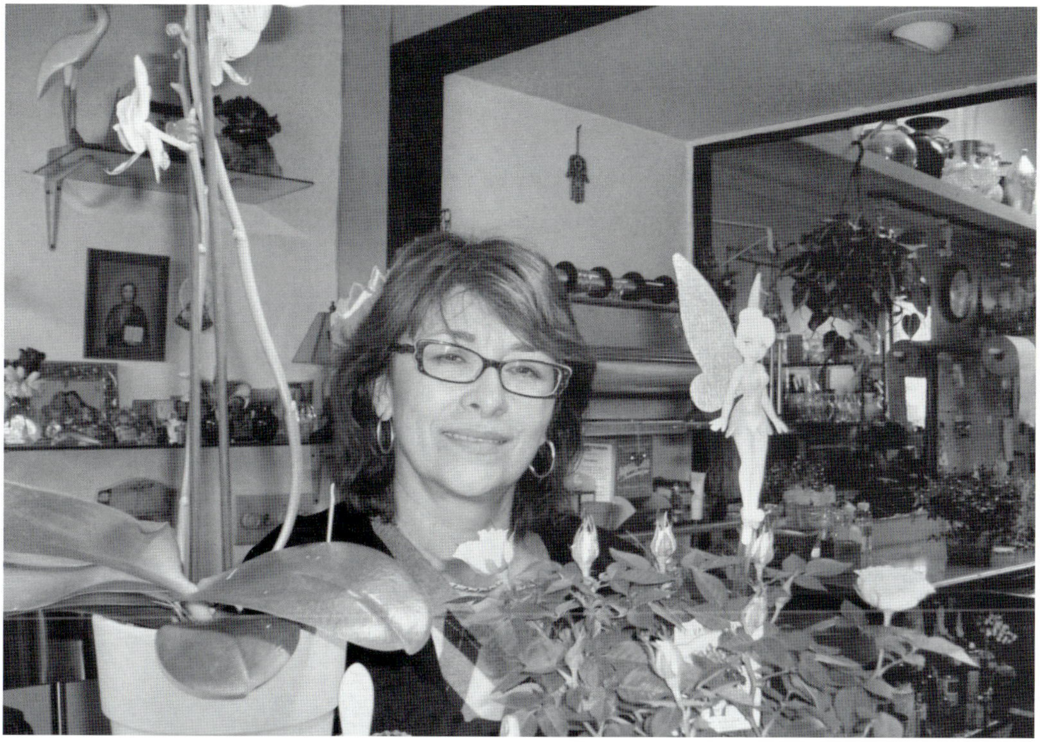

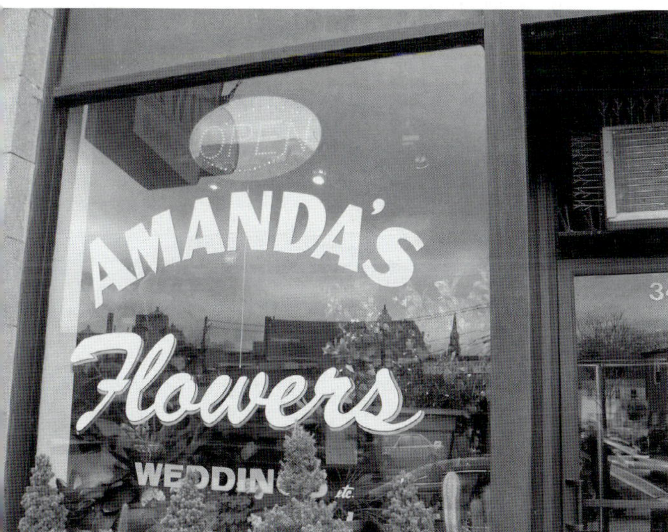

Amanda Rojas

Amanda Rojas opened her flower shop in Brighton Center in 1990. Hard work, family support, community involvement, and willingness to learn contributed to her success. Her mother encouraged her to open her own business and her aunt works with her in the shop. Amanda used networking effectively, including the Latino professional network and monthly meetings sponsored by Brighton Main Streets. Amanda participated in the New England Flower Show and the Art in Bloom exhibit at the Museum of Fine Arts in Boston. Over the years, her inventory changed to reflect the needs of an increasingly sophisticated customer base. She enjoys owning a small business, but cautions new business owners to be patient. With time, as people get to know you and trust you and tell other people about you, you can build a good business. (Photographs by Linda Mishkin.)

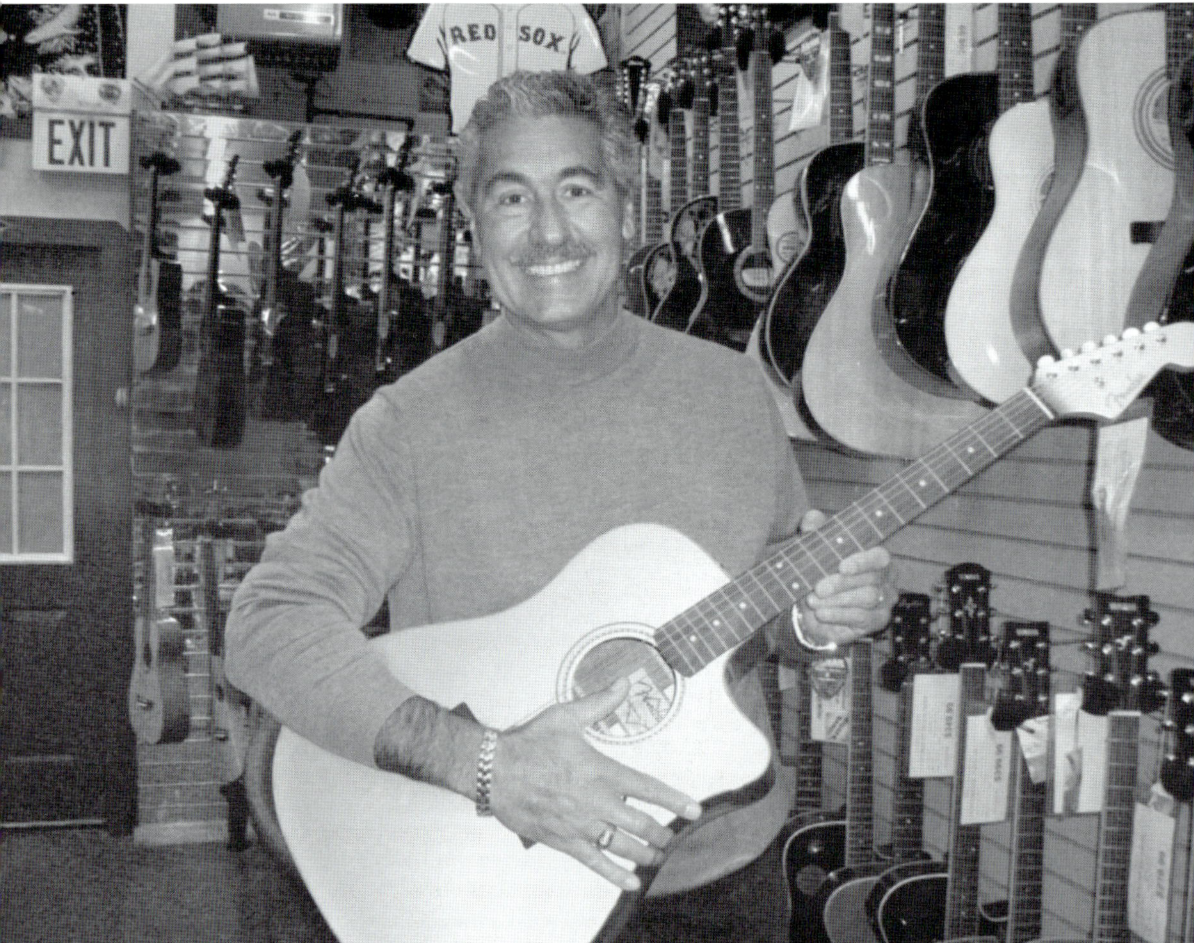

Sal Barone

Sal Barone is owner of Mr. Music in Allston. His brother Tom is the store manager. Since opening its doors in 1973, Mr. Music has evolved from selling records and eight-track tapes to selling musical instruments and accessories. The store's inventory includes new and vintage guitars and amps. Many of the instruments in the store are handmade and cater to a specialized clientele. Mr. Music may be the oldest music store still in existence in Boston. Members of the J. Geils Band and Aerosmith began stopping by in the 1970s. The store has always drawn students from Berkeley College of Music and local musicians, but its online business has expanded the customer base worldwide. As in other niches of the economy, over the years, most of the mom-and-pop music stores have been replaced by big box and chain stores. Mr. Music continues to thrive because the staff is very knowledgeable and caters to the needs of clients from neophytes to experts. Sal's slogan for Mr. Music is "Come Play," which encourages customers to play the instruments right in the store or, for more privacy, to make use of the acoustical room. Longstanding family businesses such as Mr. Music add to the cultural richness of Allston-Brighton. (Photograph by Linda Mishkin.)

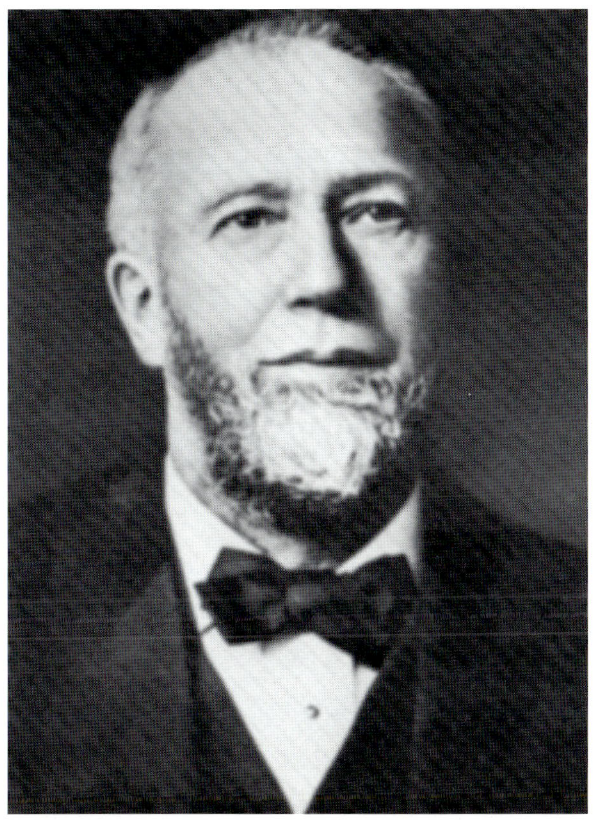

Gustavus Franklin Swift (1839–1903)
Founder of the Swift Meatpacking Company, Gustavus Franklin Swift was born in West Sandwich, Massachusetts. Before emigrating to the west, where he founded the nation's first great meatpacking empire in Chicago, Swift owned and operated a slaughterhouse in Brighton, which was then the most important cattle-trading center in New England. He and his family resided on Brighton's Oakland Street for a time from 1869 to 1872. Swift is credited with having introduced railroad car refrigeration to the meatpacking industry, an innovation that contributed significantly to the decline of the cattle industry in the east and presaged Brighton's transformation into a burgeoning residential suburb of the City of Boston. (Both, BAHS archives.)

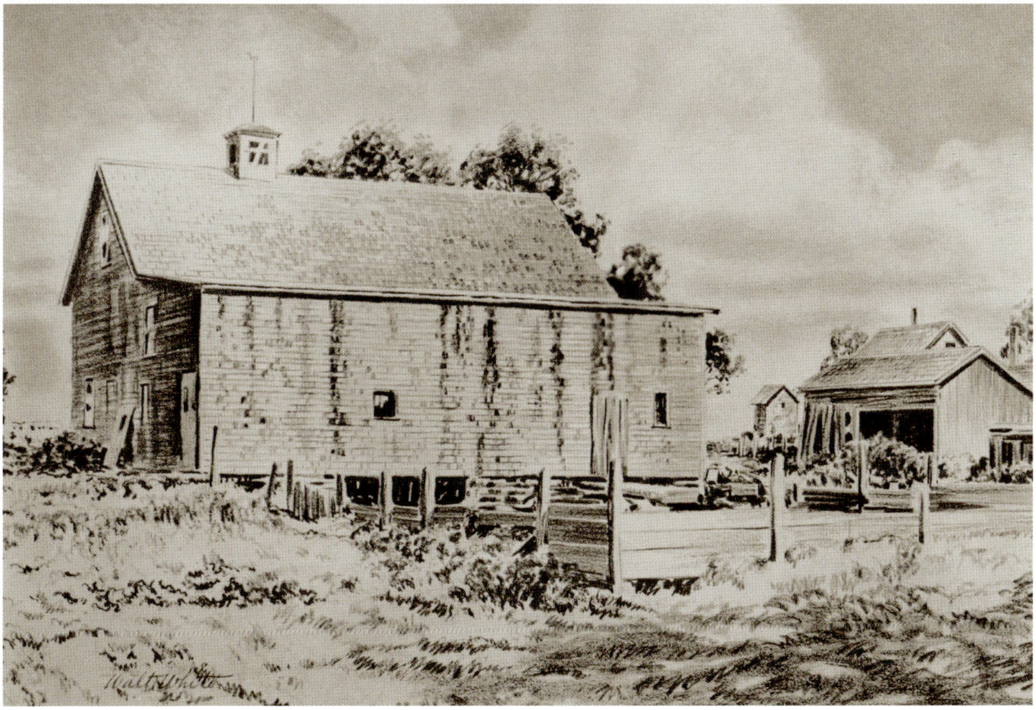

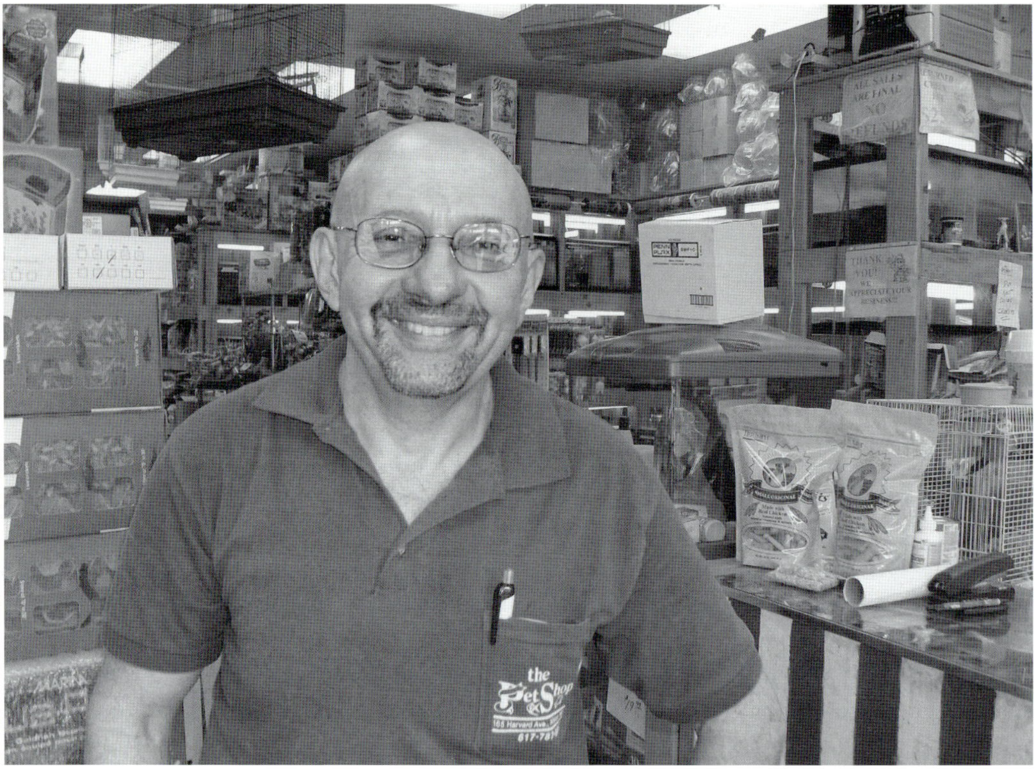

Jim Gentile

Jim Gentile purchased the Pet Shop in Allston in 1975. It had been part of a franchise chain called Big Fish Little Fish. He wanted to sell more than fish, so he changed the name. The store draws a lot of customers from the surrounding area of Allston Village and caters to people with small apartments and condos where dogs or even cats may not be welcome. The Pet Shop is where they can find fish, small birds, a snake, or even a gerbil. Gentile cares about his animals and strives to ensure that the animals and customers are a good match. That feeling is shared by other members of the family. His son works at the store and his daughter helps out occasionally. Even his dogs are part of the business. They accompany him to work and are at the door to greet customers. The Pet Shop is as much a part of the Gentile family as it is part of Allston Village. (Photographs by Linda Mishkin.)

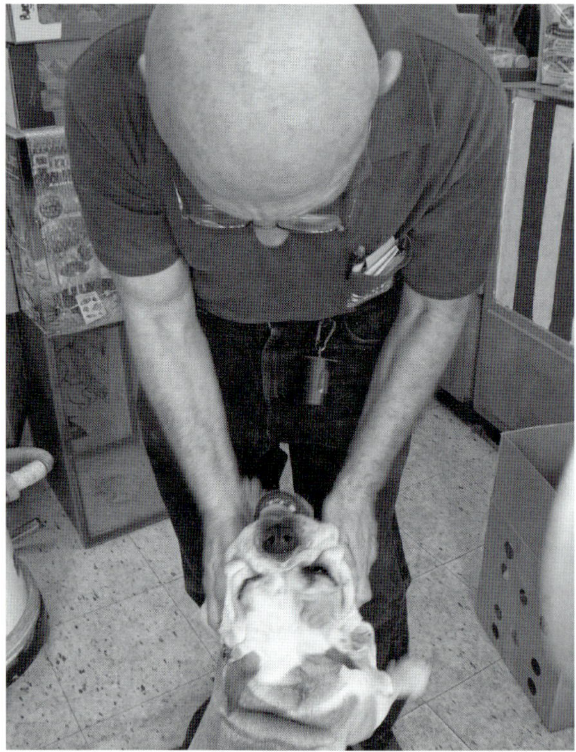

CHAPTER THREE

Builders and Defenders

Residents of Allston-Brighton and beyond are served by people whose impact is often felt only at times of emergency. Here are stories of people who are ready to respond as needs arise. They take risks that are sometimes only appreciated after some dire situation has occurred or is looming. Their work requires specialized skills and involves the ability to work as a team. They take action to ward off what would otherwise negatively impact the community. The builders who are included here have significantly transformed the physical environment, thereby improving the quality of life for residents of Allston-Brighton and beyond.

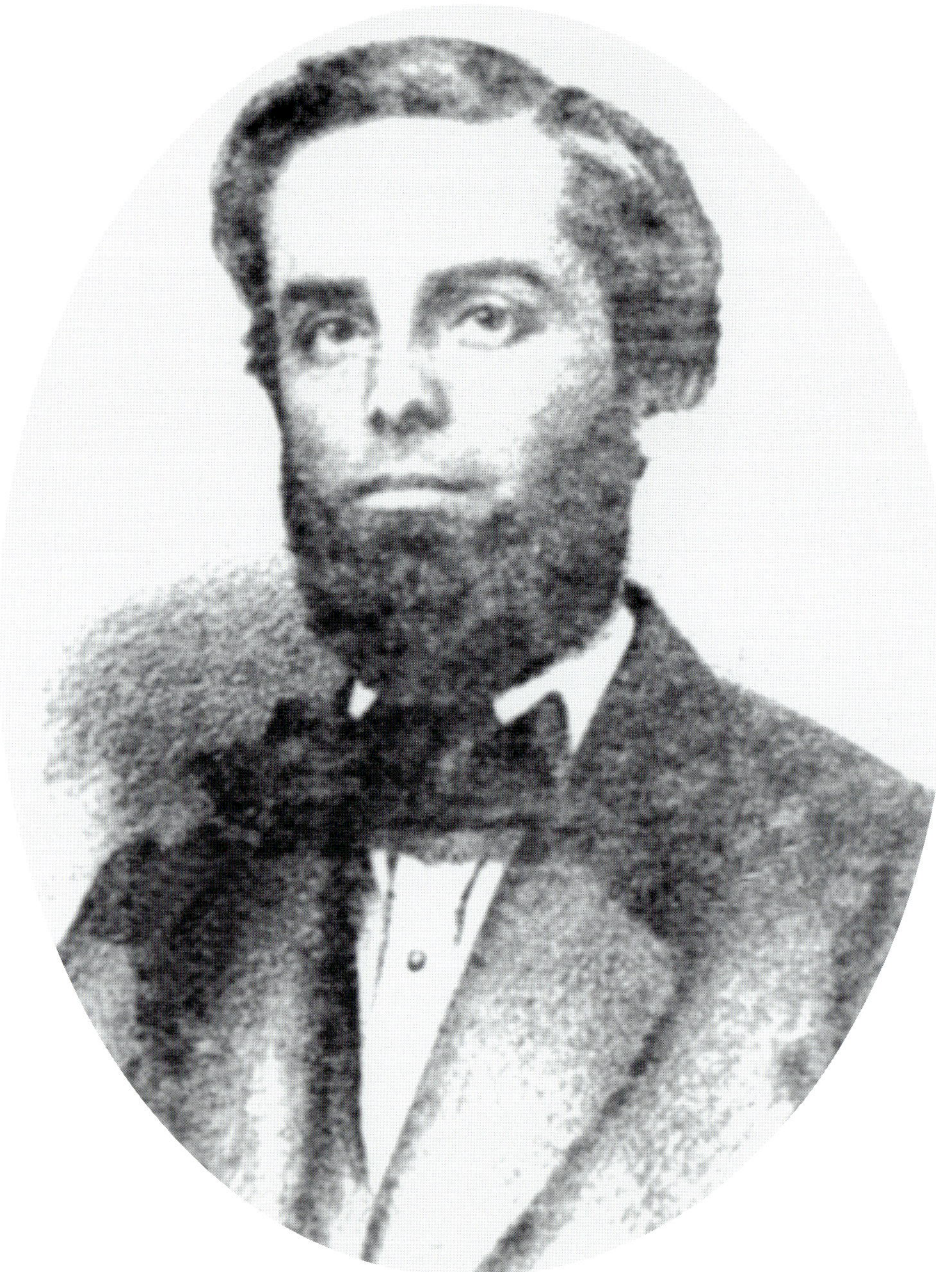

Thomas W. Silloway (1828–1910)

Silloway, a resident of Union Square, Allston, may well hold the record as the architect of the greatest number of churches in the country. He died in 1910 at age 81. This prolific architect also designed schools, academies, colleges, libraries, asylums, town halls, and many private residences over a career that spanned some 60 years. In 1862, Silloway entered upon his second career, that of Universalist minister. He arrived in Brighton in 1863 as pastor of the Universalist Church on Cambridge Street. He retired from the ministry in 1867 when the increasing number of architectural commissions became so burdensome as to preclude his properly attending to his pastoral duties. (BAHS archives.)

Fred Salvucci

Fred Salvucci grew up in Brighton and now lives in the home his father purchased when Fred was seven years old. When Fred was a student at MIT studying to be a transportation engineer, his grandmother's house in Allston was seized by eminent domain. It was one of many torn down to make way for the Massachusetts Turnpike Extension. The poor treatment his grandmother and others received inspired in him a determination to make his career in transportation respectful of residential communities. This was around 1960 and predated laws that have since been enacted that provide better protection for homeowners. Fred joined volunteer groups throughout Boston that opposed plans to install highways through urban neighborhoods. Kevin White, then mayor of Boston, supported their effort. Governor Sargent became supportive as well. This was a public turnaround on Sargent's part that took courage. Fred's volunteer activities led to full-time employment; he became Kevin White's transportation advisor. At that time, Michael Dukakis was state representative and favored putting funds toward public transportation over highway projects. When Dukakis became governor in 1975, Fred was appointed secretary of transportation. Having worked for years to stop transportation projects harmful to communities, Fred now was in a position to develop projects that would benefit communities. One project was the extension of the Red Line to Alewife. Another was the relocation of the old Orange Line from elevated to underground. Burying track opened land; this enabled the development of large park areas that included bike trails and areas for small children. Other projects resulted in the development of buffer parks adjacent to train tracks. Depression of the central artery (the Big Dig) and underground construction of the third harbor tunnel to the airport replaced an earlier plan to put the roadway through the North End. These are just a few examples of successful efforts. Both as a volunteer and government official, Fred was able to work effectively with numerous people and groups to enhance the quality of life for city residents. (Photograph by Linda Mishkin.)

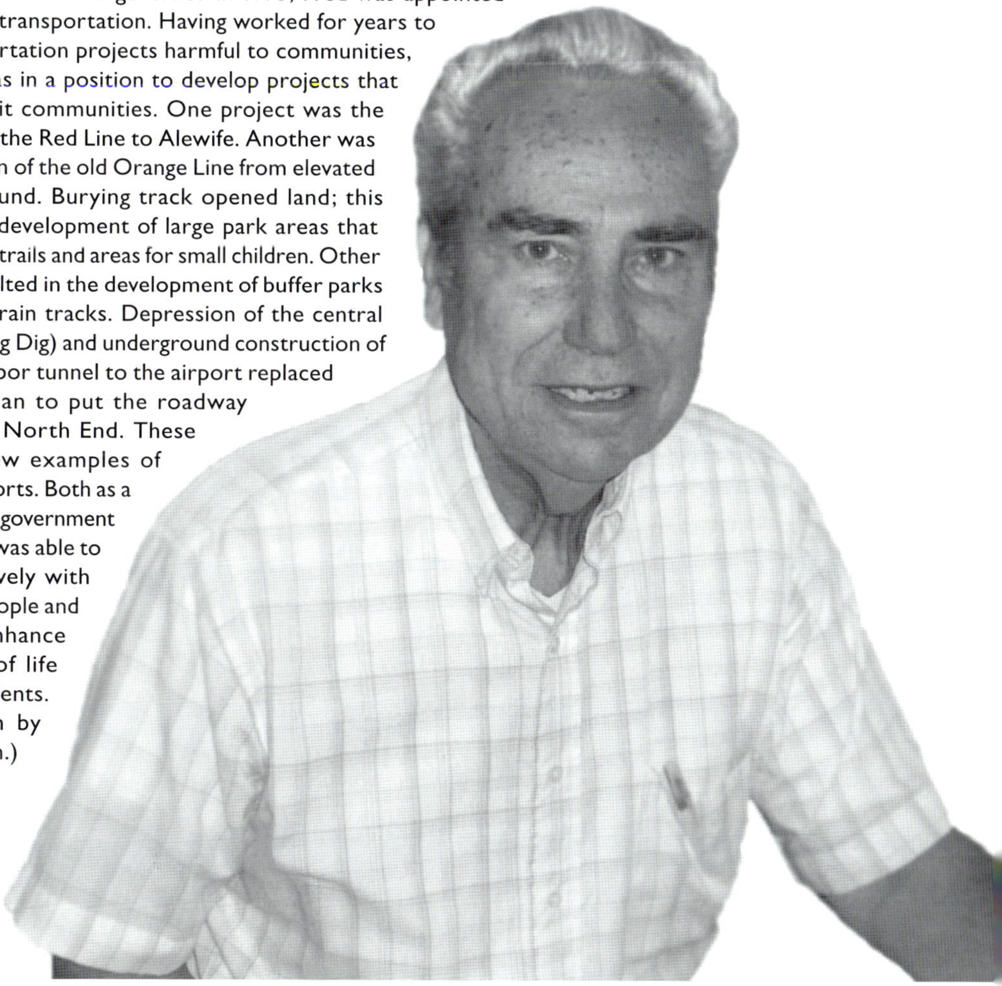

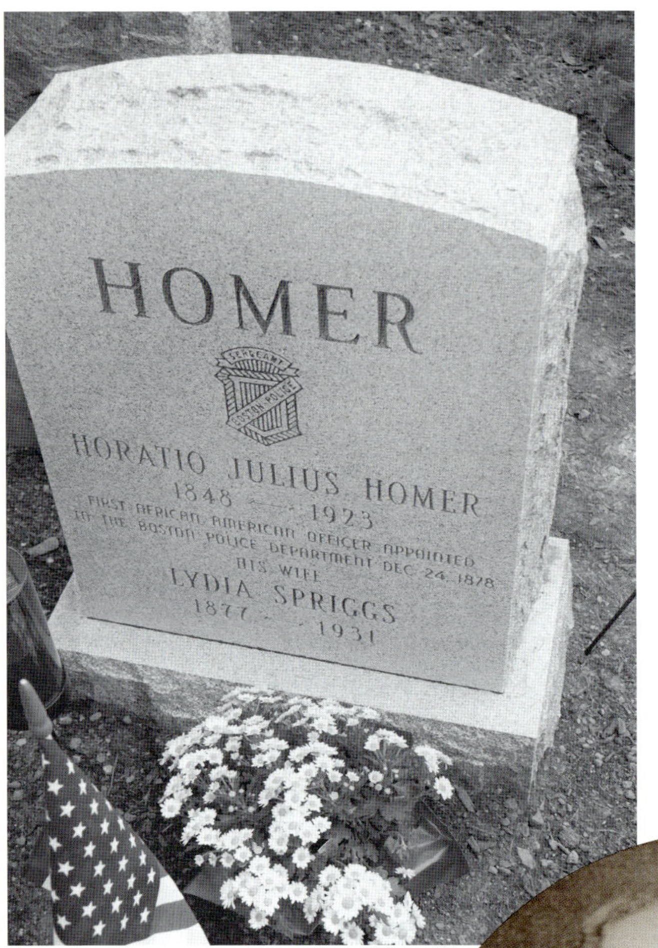

Horatio J. Homer (1948–1923)

In 1878, Horatio J. Homer became the first African American appointed to the Boston Police Department. He settled in Brighton, where he lived from the 1870s until 1903. He was a messenger at Headquarters and had a Sunday walking beat in the Back Bay. He was promoted to sergeant in 1895 and served more than 40 years, retiring in 1919. Homer loved poetry and was highly musical. He played a dozen instruments. He was an active Republican and an officer in a supper club for African American men that hosted prominent elected officials and academics. When Sergeant Homer died, the superintendent of police led the delegation to his burial at Brighton's Evergreen Cemetery. The Homer grave was unmarked for many years. In 2010, the Boston Police Department and unions, Brighton residents, and descendants of Sergeant Homer dedicated a handsome grave marker. (Boston Police Department archives.)

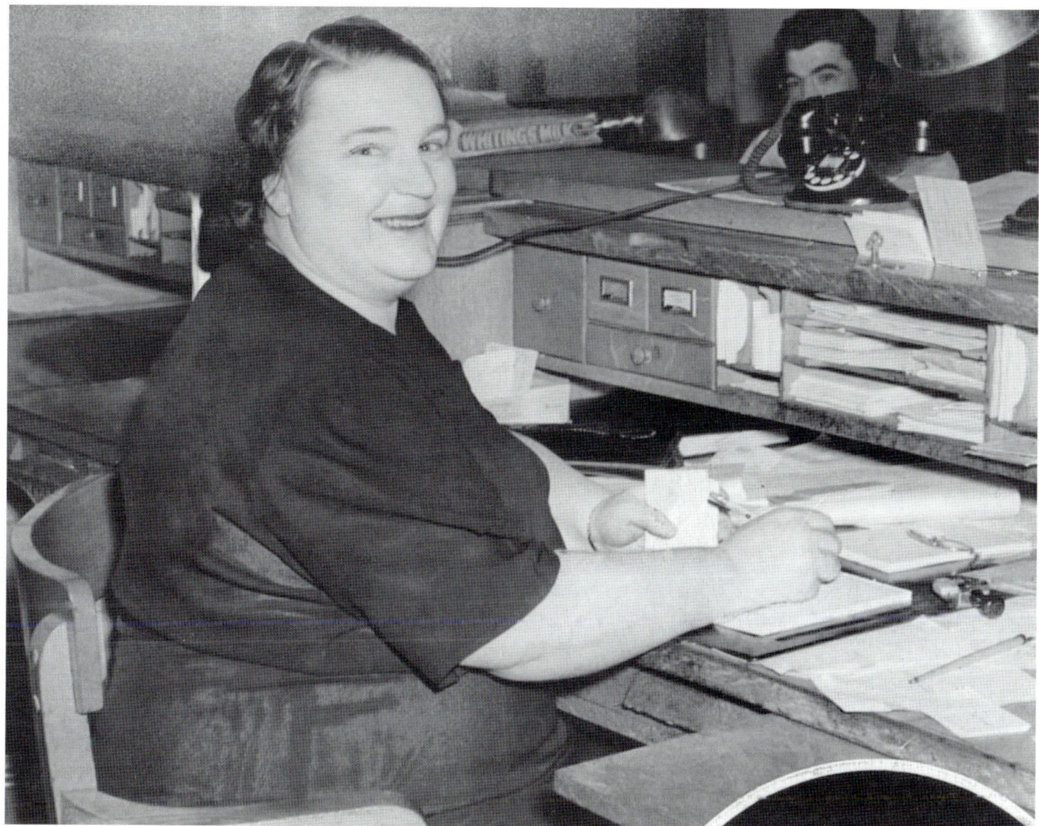

Margaret McHugh

Margaret McHugh was among the first women appointed to the Boston Police Department. Born Margaret Byrne in 1893, she grew up in a large Brighton family. Margaret was orphaned as a teenager and raised her five younger brothers and sisters. She married James McHugh, a Boston police officer who was among the strikers of 1919. As a young woman, Margaret McHugh worked as the chief night operator for New England Telephone and Telegraph Company. In 1920, the Boston Police Department permitted women to sit for a civil service examination. Of the 100 or so applicants, six women were appointed on April 21, 1921. Margaret and the other women were assigned to headquarters and worked particularly with women and children. Unlike their male superiors hoping to make an arrest, the women hoped to steer vulnerable people away from crime. "We're out to prevent crimes—stop arrests if we can," said Patrolman McHugh. McHugh was interested in criminal work and sought an assignment with the pawn squad. She had a sharp memory and could recall descriptions of items stolen years before. Her lieutenant marveled at her skill, saying, "On jewelry Margaret had all the tenacity of Hugo's immortal Javert." She received many commendations for solving high-profile cases. McHugh noted patterns in thefts and where stolen items were pawned, and was sometimes even able to predict which pawnshop a thief would use and arrest him as he walked in the door. Margaret McHugh was made acting-sergeant and supervised the other women police, though she received no pay increase. She saw policing as a service profession and would refer women in trouble to social agencies and often buy them a meal herself. "Help—that's what people need," she often said. Margaret was a leader in her field and in 1948, was elected head of the New England Police Women's Association. The headlines first noted that she could bake a fine Irish soda cake, then in smaller print noted her professional accomplishments. Margaret McHugh retired in 1959 with the rank of detective, first grade. She passed away in 1960, one of Boston's original "cops in skirts." (Boston Public Library.)

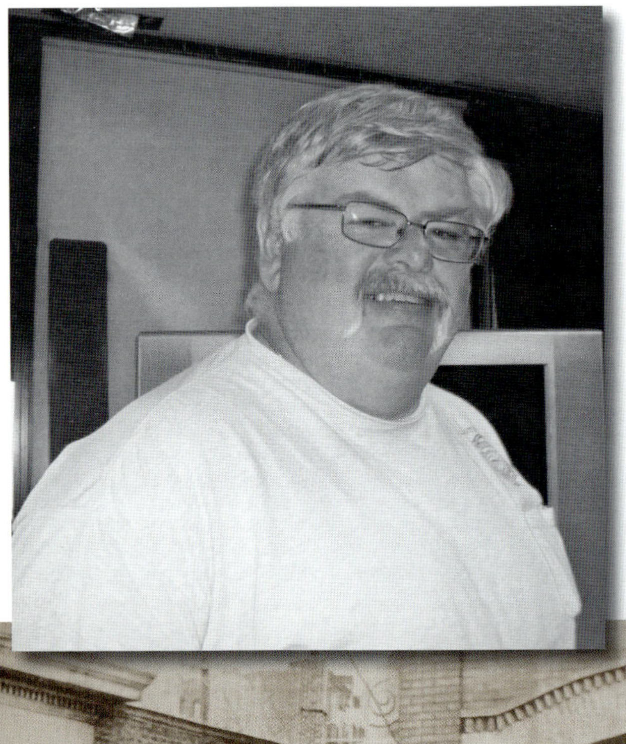

Jim Feeney

Jim "Tapper" Feeney has been both a firefighter with the Boston Fire Department and its historian for 34 years. The son of a firefighter, Tapper's fascination with the profession and related equipment began early on. His dream of becoming a firefighter finally became a reality in 1992. While stationed in Allston, he was promoted to the rank of lieutenant, as his father had been. Tapper's collection of firefighting items is housed in a garage he restyled to resemble a firehouse. He finds that the collection has practical and historical significance. It is a good way to teach young firefighters about the history of firefighting. It helps explain to them what the items are and the evolution of their use. His collection includes items that were used in the 1800s. (Left, Linda Mishkin; below, Boston Fire Department.)

CHAPTER FOUR

Community Supporters, Activists, and Healers

Allston-Brighton is fortunate to have a large number of generous caretakers with broad interests and abilities. They creatively work with segments of the population to build skills and achieve goals. Their work enriches the community by welcoming newcomers and strengthening ties among groups and individuals. In many ways, the resources they provide enable programs and services to be developed and maintained so that the health and welfare benefits extend to those in need. Some of these stories reveal people's dedication to the economic well-being of Allston-Brighton. All of the people here exemplify a spirit that makes the energy of urban life so attractive. Others manage growth and change so that progress and sustained neighborhood life co-exist comfortably.

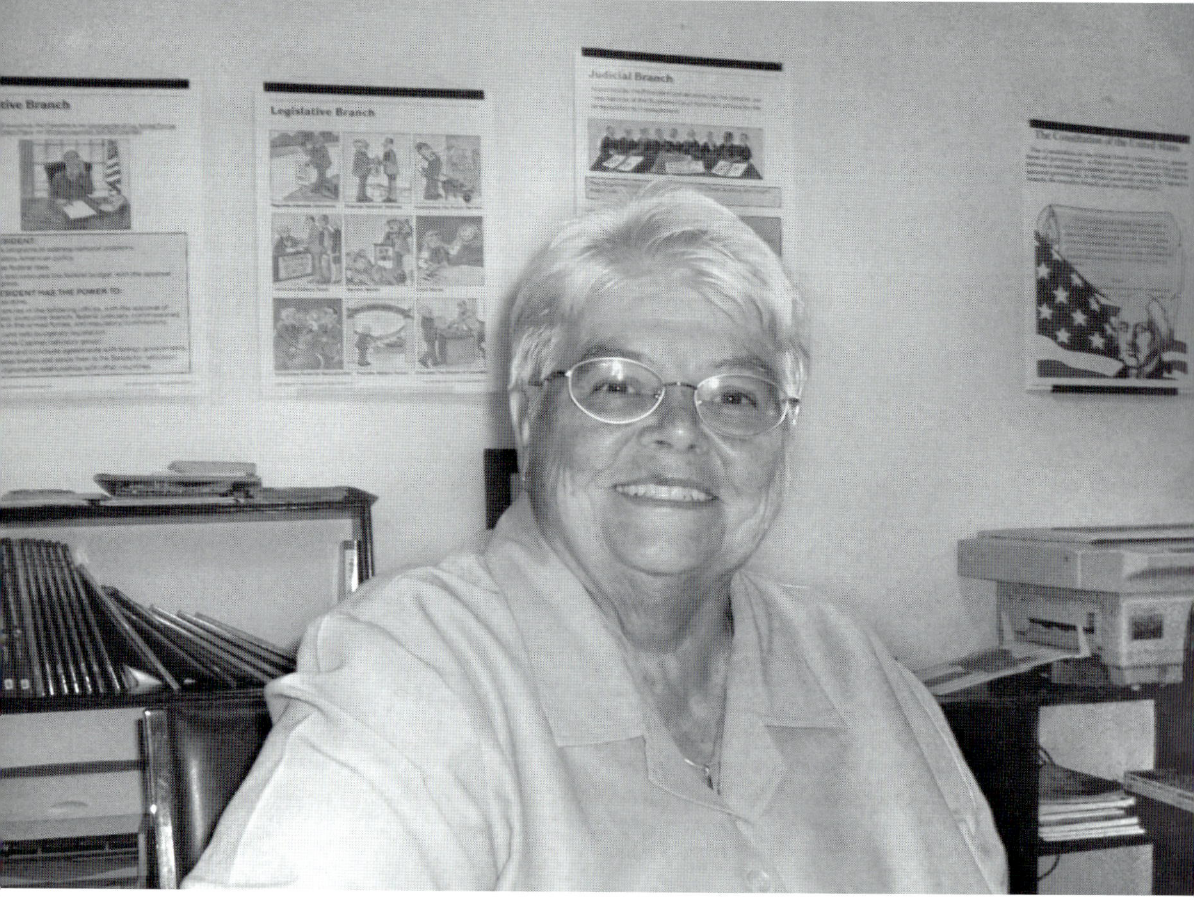

Sister Pat Andrews

Sister Pat Andrews is director of The Literacy Connection (TLC). The program began 25 years ago and continues to be sponsored by the Sisters of St. Joseph in Allston-Brighton. The goal of TLC is to build bridges and to ease tensions that isolate and alienate non–English speaking newcomers to the community. TLC began with a few sisters who had retired from teaching. Beginning with mostly donated material, TLC library is now rich with resources. Over the years, the program has evolved from a sole focus on literacy training to also helping adults earn their General Education Development (GED) degree and achieve other milestones, including US citizenship. The Sisters of St. Joseph have been in Boston for 139 years and have been involved in more than 120 educational institutions that include a religious curriculum. While education has always been part of their heritage, the sisters serve the community in a variety of ways. As they reach out to the neighbor without distinction, the care they provide reflects their mission of reconciliation. During the past few decades, in response to an urging of the Second Vatican Council for Catholics to reflect back on their original calling, the sisters renewed their attention to neighbor and neighborhood. They work in the 360-year tradition of Sisters of St. Joseph, which traces its roots to mid–17th century France. Today, TLC has grown to include about 60 tutors. Instruction is individualized. When new students arrive not knowing a word of English, curricular creativity is required. A tutor's use of pantomime, for example, can be instructive and can also yield peals of laughter. That, too, is part of the process. Trust and relaxation fit nicely into an otherwise arduous curriculum. Sister Pat has been director of TLC for 12 years. Over that time, the program has worked with populations of immigrants from Eastern Europe, Asia, and Latin America. The program welcomes, cares for, and adjusts to the needs of those who seek language training. (Photograph by Linda Mishkin.)

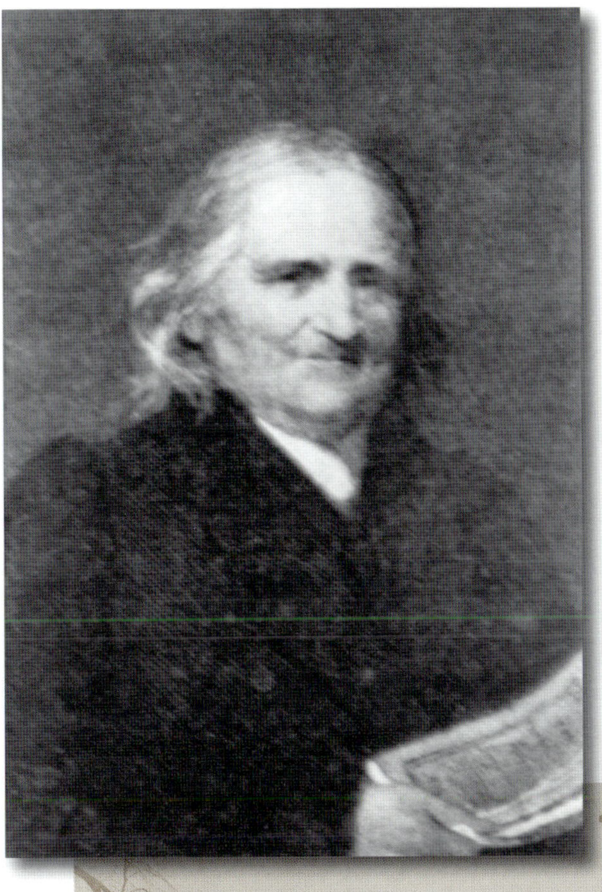

Noah Worcester

Noah Worcester moved to Brighton in 1813 when he accepted the position of editor of the *Christian Disciple*, a monthly journal. He was an ordained minister and one of the founders of the American peace movement. He is known to history as "The Apostle of Peace." In 1814, Worcester published a book titled *A Solemn Review of the Custom of War*, the first antiwar tract published in the United States. It was widely read in the United States and England and was subsequently translated into several European languages. Worcester founded the Massachusetts Peace Society. His Brighton residence was a gathering point for many of the leading Boston intellectuals of his day. In 1815, Worcester established a quarterly journal titled *The Friend of Peace*. In 1818, Harvard conferred upon Reverend Worcester the degree of doctor of divinity. He died in 1837. (BAHS archives.)

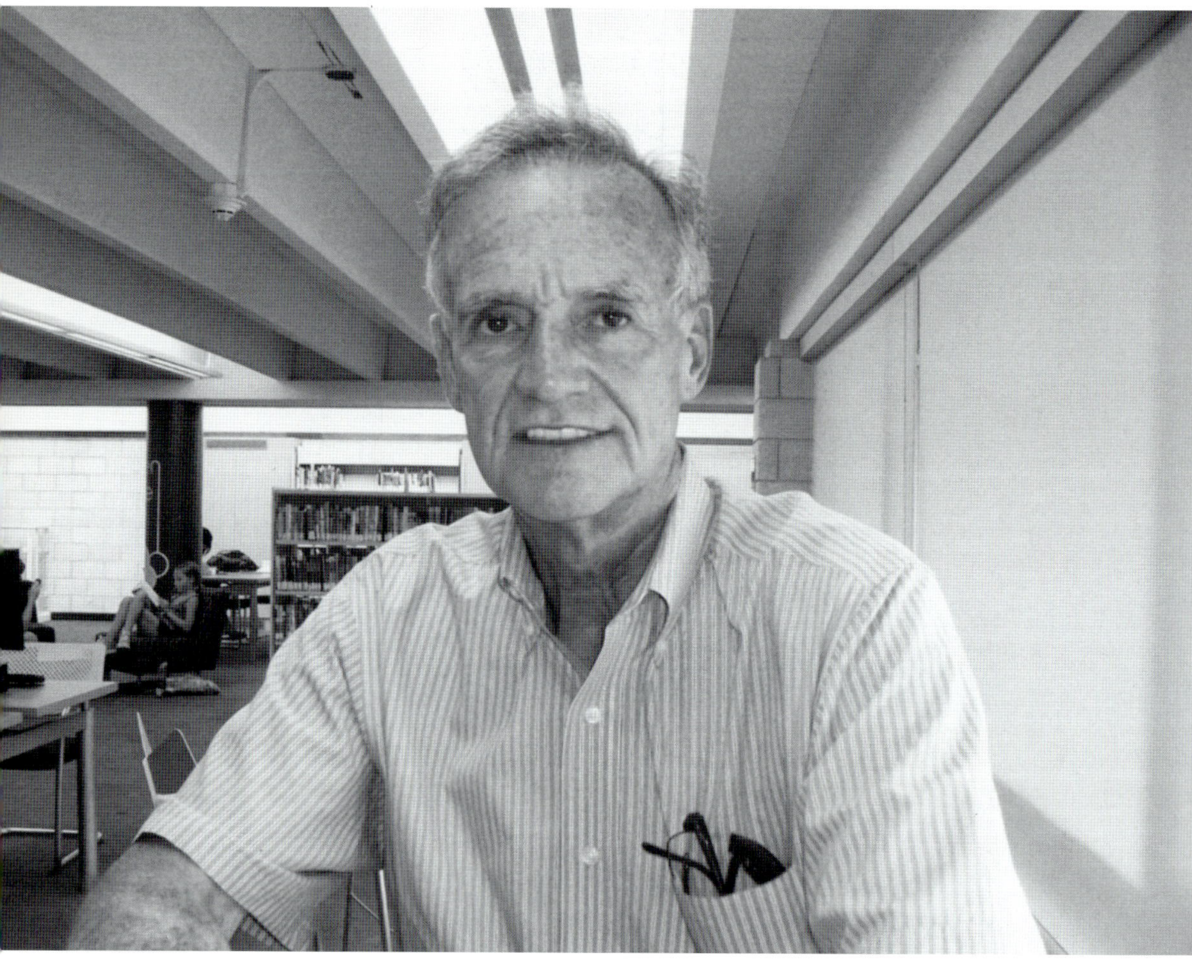

Paul Berkeley

Paul Berkeley is a second-generation, lifelong resident of Allston-Brighton. His grandparents emigrated here from Ireland. Joe Smith (another local legend) was his Boy Scout leader and next-door neighbor. Berkeley started attending meetings of the Allston Civic Association when Joe became president in 1962. He stayed with the organization and has been its president for 18 years. Working closely with many different agencies within the city that affect neighborhood quality of life, the civic association reviews land use and licensing requests. Taken into consideration are such things as noise level and traffic volume. Where there are concerns, the association tries to negotiate with the developer to alleviate perceived problems. Developers are lured to Allston because of its proximity to downtown Boston and its neighborhood setting. It also has the advantage of ample public transportation and close access to the Massachusetts Turnpike. Like many others, Berkeley loves living in Allston. He continues working to keep the close neighborhood feel that is part of Allston's attraction. (Photograph by Linda Mishkin.)

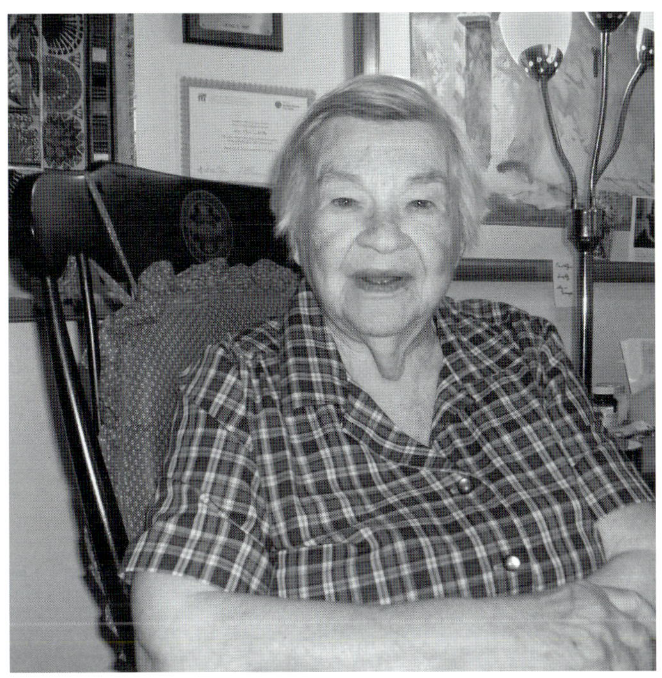

Alice Mills
Alice Mills served as president of Friends of the Faneuil Library, and now, at the Honan Branch Library in Allston, she helps people learn English. For Alice, learning languages has always come easily. She studied Latin from eighth grade through high school. She also studied French and German. Alice graduated from University of Maine at Orono earning membership in Phi Beta Kappa and a degree in sociology. Her mother was a member of the Daughters of the American Revolution (DAR). Her father came (with his father) to the United States from the Ukraine when he was eight years old to escape growing anti-Semitism. (Photograph by Linda Mishkin.)

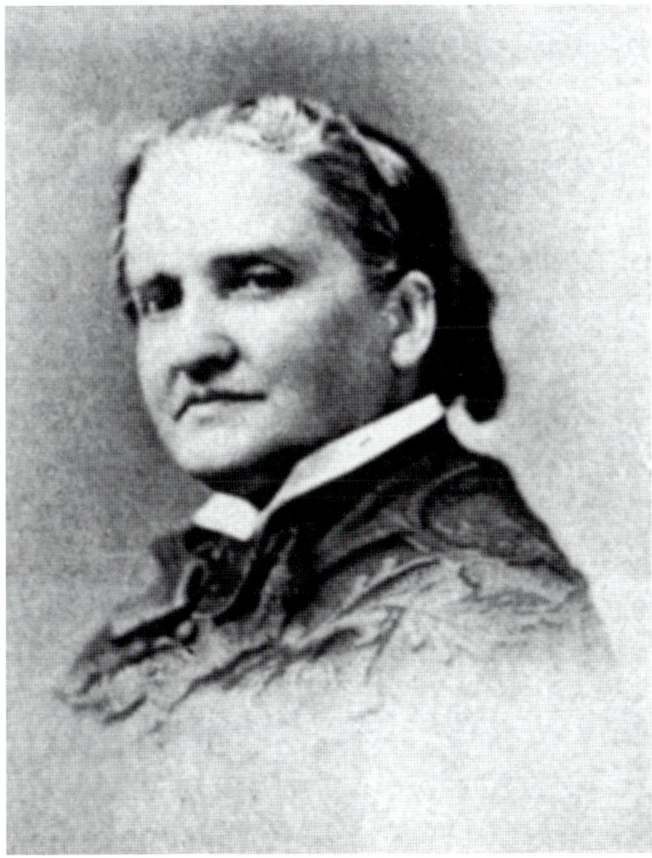

Elizabeth Rowell Thomson (1821–1899)
Elizabeth was one of 12 children of a very poor farmer in rural Vermont. She developed a keen interest in the arts after marrying a wealthy man who was a devoted patron of the arts. After his death, Elizabeth became the dispenser of his vast estate. She gave generously to antislavery causes, helped support wives and children of Civil War soldiers, and contributed funds for research to eradicate yellow fever. (BAHS archives.)

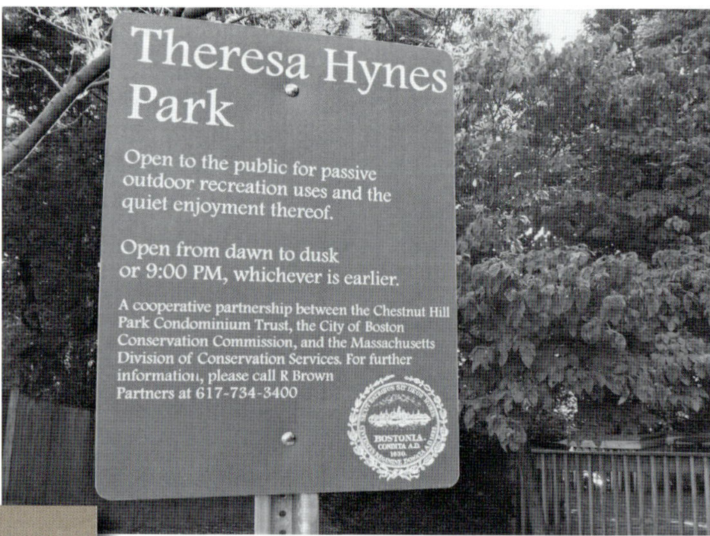

Theresa Hynes
Theresa Hynes was born in Ireland. Marriage brought her to Brighton where she and her husband raised their three children. She has been an active community volunteer for decades. Around 1980, she became a founding member of the Brighton Allston Improvement Association (BAIA) and later served as its president. The organization works to ensure zoning laws are enforced and on neighborhood beautification. For her longtime efforts, a small park has been named in her honor. For 12 years, Theresa has worked with others on the development of Brighton Common with a stage for musical or other events. The project is finally underway. A time capsule has been buried in the park. When it is retrieved and opened 50 years from now, people will learn what it was like to be in Allston-Brighton in 2012. (Photograph by Linda Mishkin.)

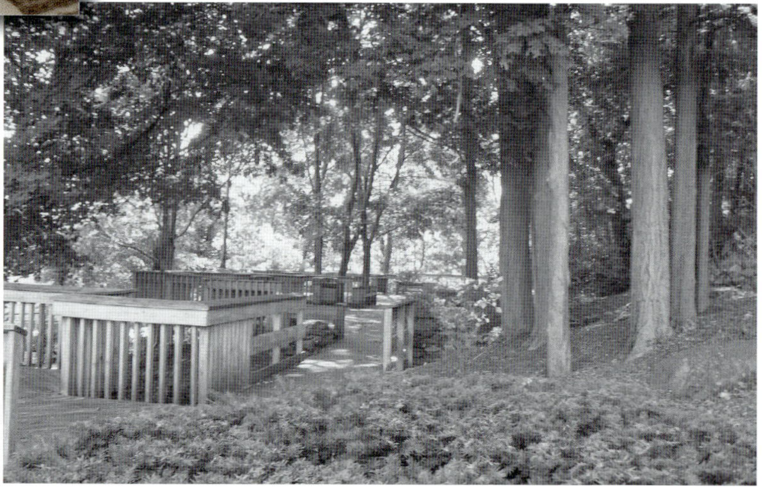

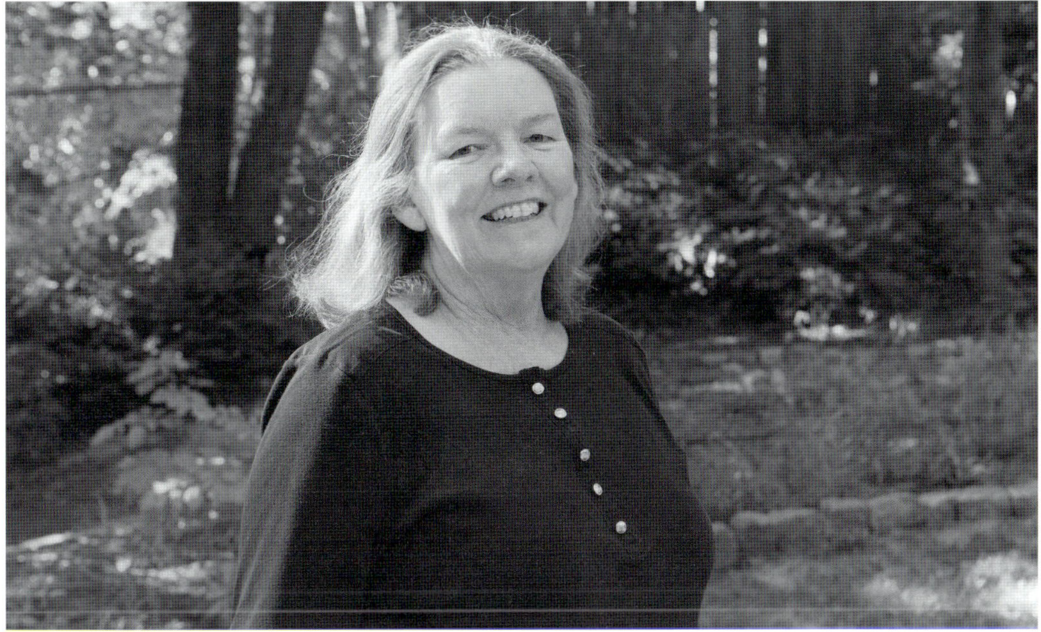

Nancy O'Hara

Nancy O'Hara and her husband, Mike, moved from Newton to Brighton in 1976, a time when many homeowners were leaving Boston due to busing. Nancy was an educator for 36 years in East Boston. She taught high school English and was a school librarian. Knowing how libraries are essential to a healthy neighborhood, Nancy led a group to found The Friends of the Faneuil Branch Library and established its major annual fundraiser, naming it The Funky Auction. Even when raising her son and daughter and pursuing a career, Nancy has always been active in volunteer activities, such as recording books for the blind and tutoring students in Boston Public Schools (BPS). Now retired, Nancy puts her considerable talent and energy toward a wide variety of activities. She serves on the board of the Brighton-Allston Historical Society and is a lector at St. Columbkille Church. Nancy also participates in activities that draw on her athletic and creative abilities. Every Saturday she plays volleyball at the Jackson-Mann Community School with a multiethnic and multigenerational group, many of whom are Latino and Russian immigrants in their 80s. To nurture her creative side, Nancy was a founding member of the Allston-Brighton Community Theatre Foundation and continues working with its precursor, the "57 Readers and Writers," where she serves as emcee and coproducer of three public performances each year. Performances consist of original writings on a selected theme that may include poems, playlets, stories, and essays. The group chose its name from a play titled *The 57 Bus*, written by Pat Walsh, an original member. Nancy successfully strives to promote community building through activities that contribute to the culture of connectedness that makes Allston-Brighton unique. (Photograph by Liane Brandon.)

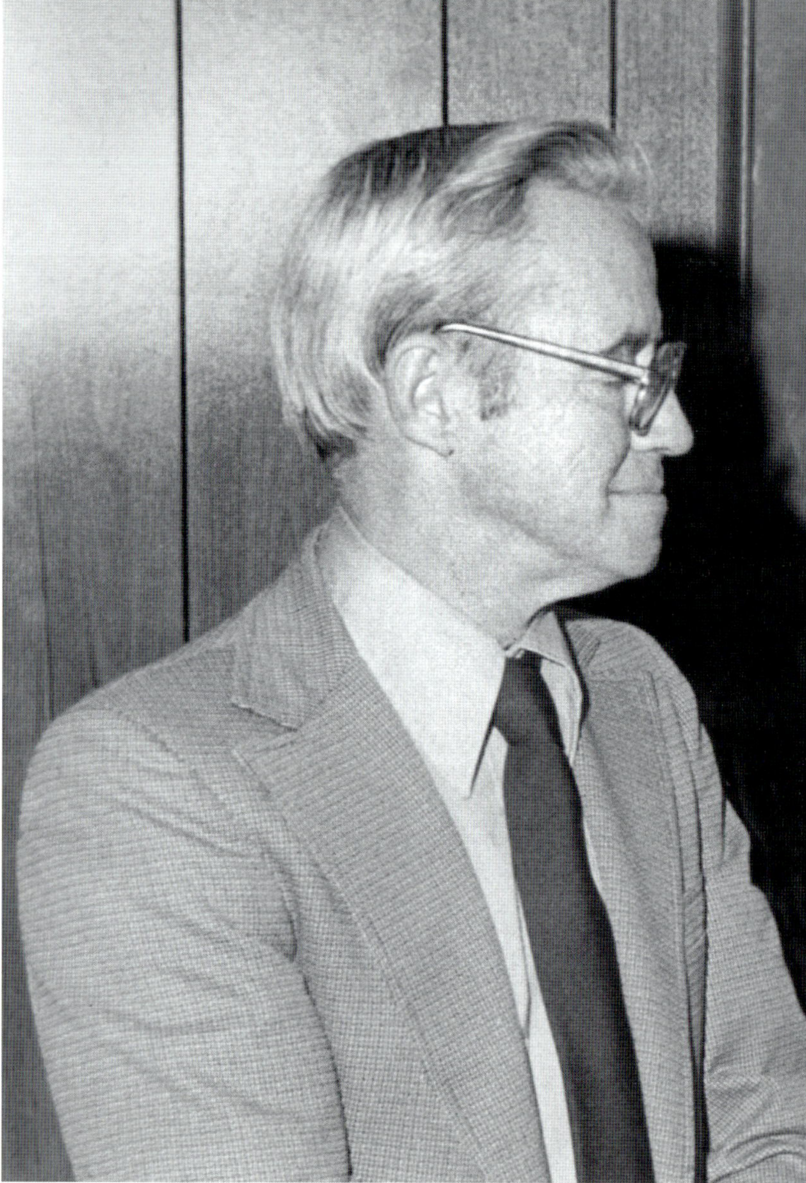

Joseph Smith
Joseph Smith never held public office, but he contributed greatly to the public wellbeing. After starting the Allston Civic Association, he became its first president. He also served as director of the Allston Brighton Citizens Council. Healthcare for local residents was one of his major concerns. When federal funding became available, he successfully rallied the support of the community to obtain funds for a community health center. The first center in Allston was named the Allston Brighton Health Center, but after his death on October 12, 1979, it was renamed the Joseph M. Smith Community Health Center. (BAHS archives.)

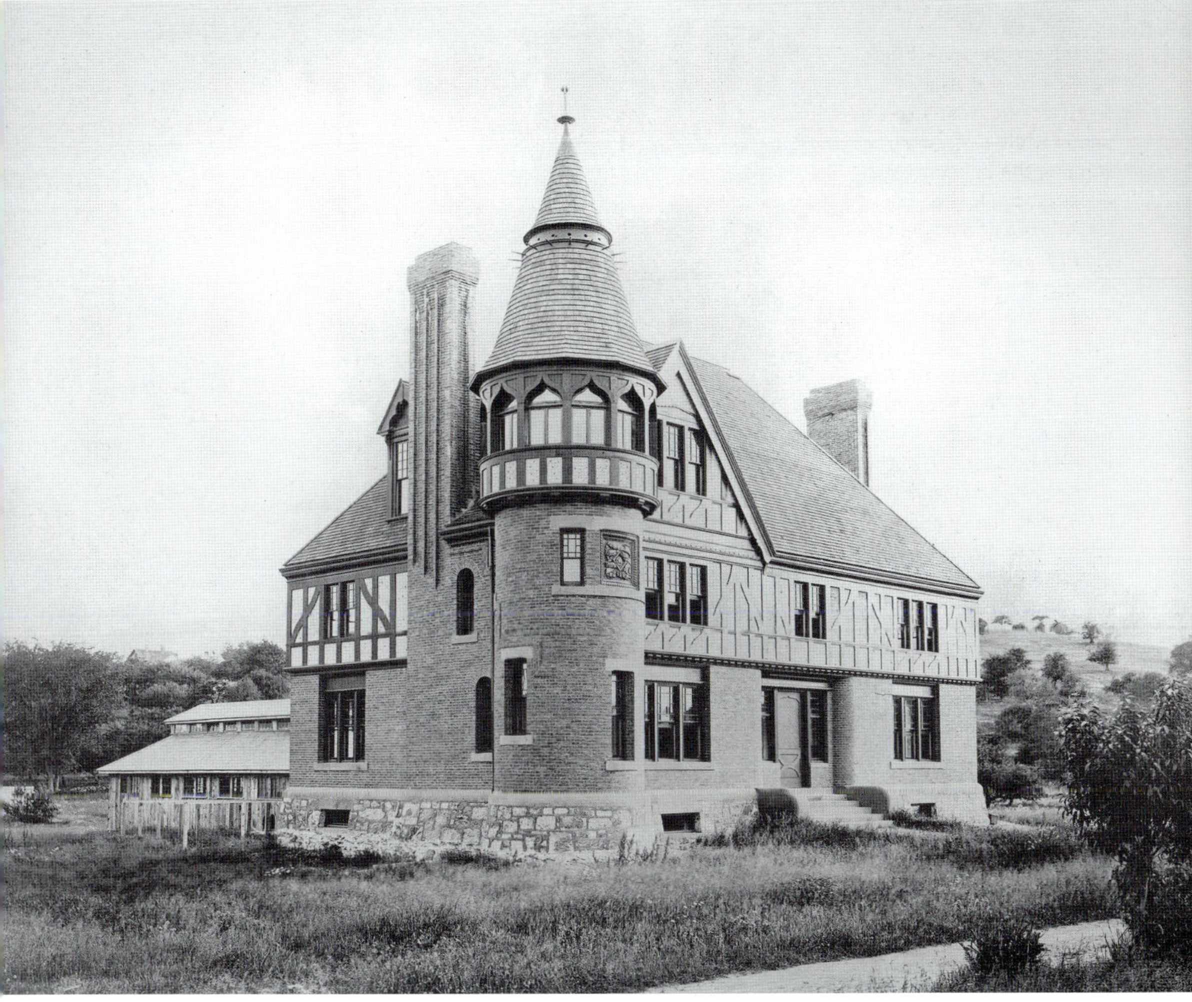

Ellen H. Gifford

Ellen H. Gifford inherited an estate worth several million dollars, much of which she donated to worthy causes throughout her life. Her generosity continued even after her death. When she died in 1889, the residual estate amounted to $93,236.26, which was distributed by her trustees to such institutions as the Women's Charity Club of Boston, New England Hospital for Women and Children, the Sunny Bank Home of Boston, the General Hospital Society of Connecticut, the Home for Aged Colored Women in Boston, and the Home for Children and Aged Women in Roxbury. Her lifelong generosity also extended toward animals in need. She was the founder and benefactor of the Ellen M. Gifford Sheltering Home for Animals in Brighton. The home got its start when, in 1883, she made a donation to the Massachusetts Society for the Prevention of Cruelty to Animals (MSPCA) to build a home for animals that had been abandoned by their owners. In 1884 she wrote, "If only the waifs, the strays, the sick, the abused, would be sure to get entrance to the home, and anybody could feel at liberty to bring in a starved or ill-treated animal and have it cared for without pay, my object would be obtained." The home was built on land donated by Capt. Nathan Appleton Jr. of Brighton. Appleton was the brother-in-law of Henry Wadsworth Longfellow. Gifford left an endowment for the care and shelter of all animals. However, due to hardships during World War II, care at the home was subsequently restricted to cats. The home is now called Ellen M. Gifford Sheltering Home and functions as a cage-free, no-kill cat shelter. (BAHS archives.)

Veronica Smith

Veronica "Ronnie" Smith was a lifelong resident of North Allston and a community activist, especially on behalf of Allston-Brighton's senior citizens. In 1984, she was appointed deputy commissioner of Boston's commission of the affairs of the elderly. It was through community efforts spearheaded by Ronnie that the city established in the early 1980s the Brighton Senior Center. Ronnie served as the center's first director. When illness forced her resignation in the mid-1980s, the city renamed the center in her honor. She died May 1, 1986. (Right, BAHS archives; below, Linda Mishkin.)

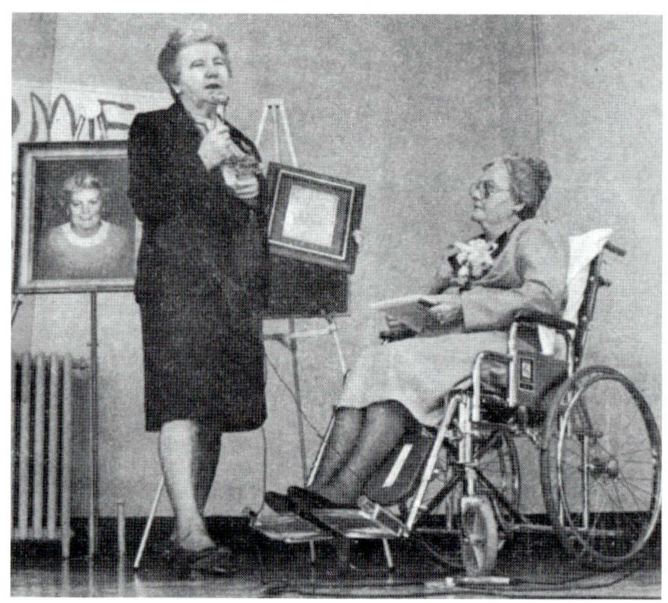

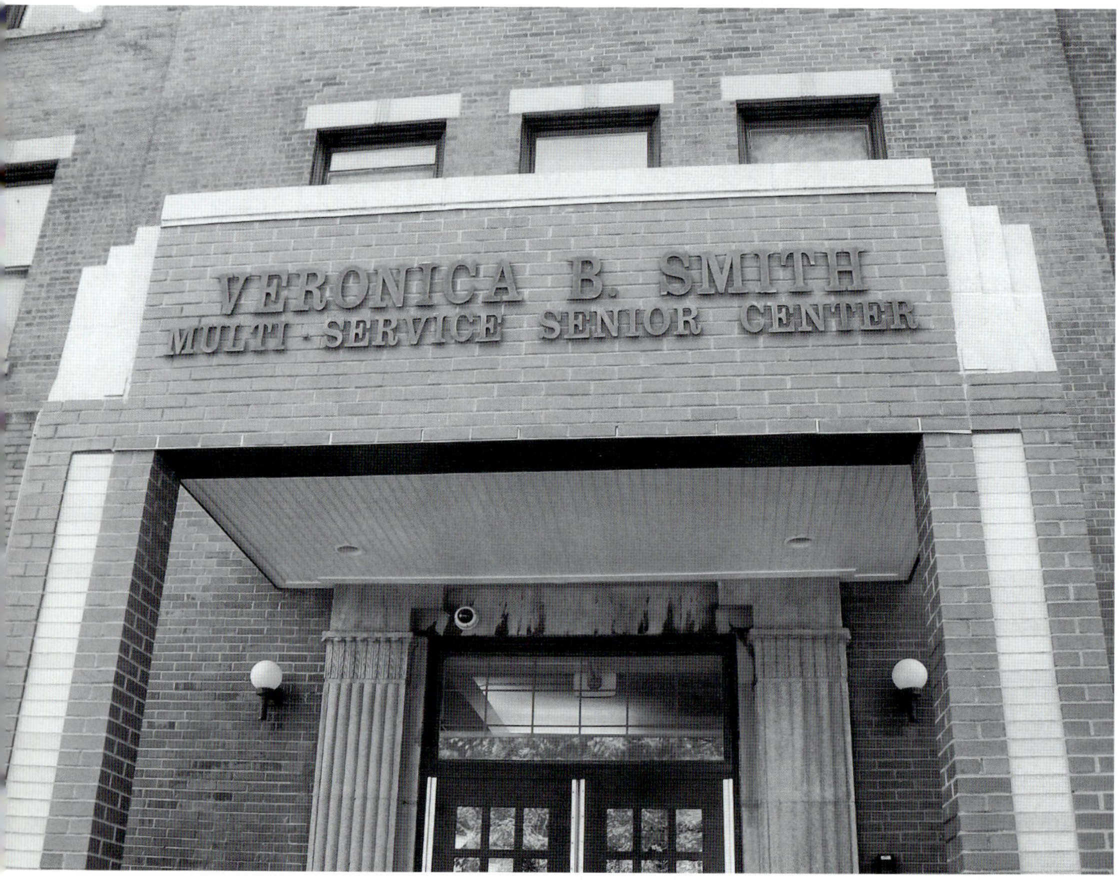

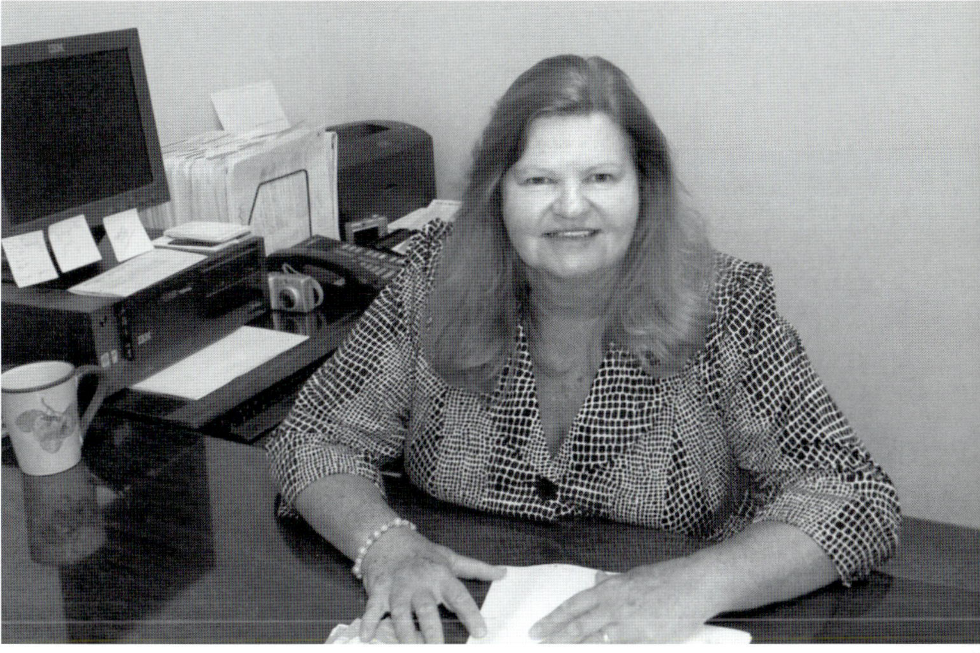

Millie Hollum-McLaughlin
Since 1992, Millie Hollum-McLaughlin has worked at the Veronica B. Smith Multi-Service Senior Center. She became director in 2008. The job brought her back to community work after a self-imposed hiatus to raise her children. The center provides a variety of services, some in connection with other organizations. Over the years, Millie Hollum McLaughlin has had to think creatively about the activities so that they do not become stale. She likes that the center is a home-away-from-home for seniors. It is especially important for those who live alone. People come to the senior center for their own reasons; Millie sees that they can get as much or as little companionship as they need. (Photographs by Linda Mishkin.)

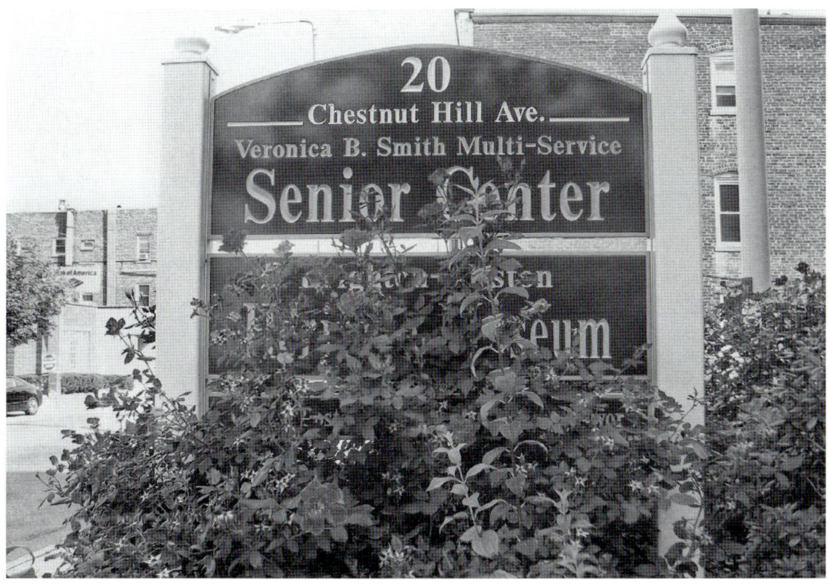

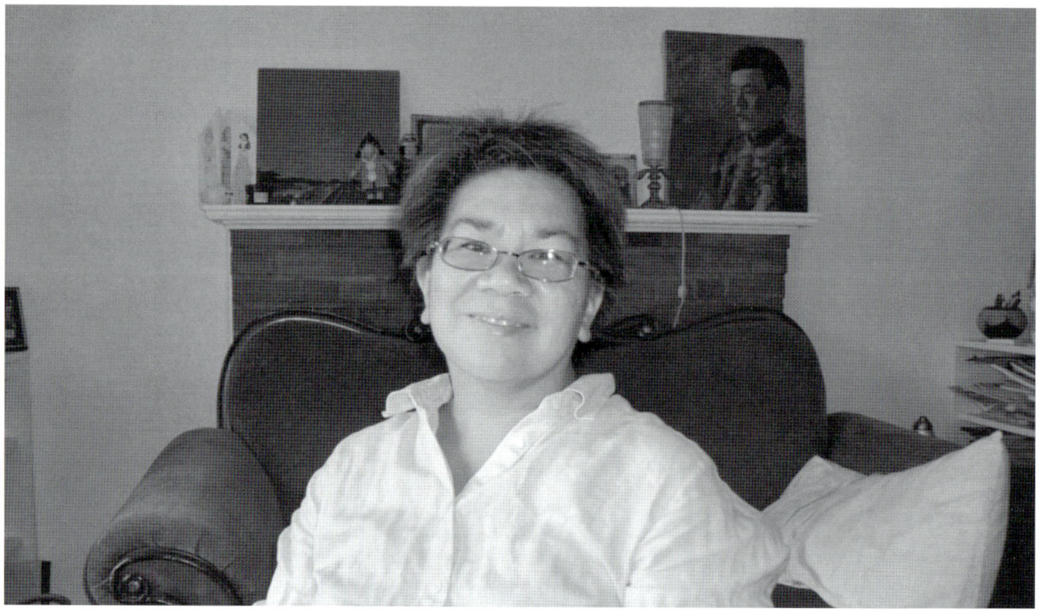

Ava Chan

Since graduating from Boston University 30 years ago, Ava Chan has lived in Allston-Brighton. She was drawn by its low key, straightforward vibe and the Chinese community. For nearly a decade, she worked at the Allston-Brighton Community Development Corporation. Currently, she is a member of the Congregational Church, The United Church of Christ in Brighton Center, where she is volunteer director of the food pantry. Ava is a felt maker and is starting a textile business making such things as rugs, hats, and wall hangings. (Photograph by Linda Mishkin.)

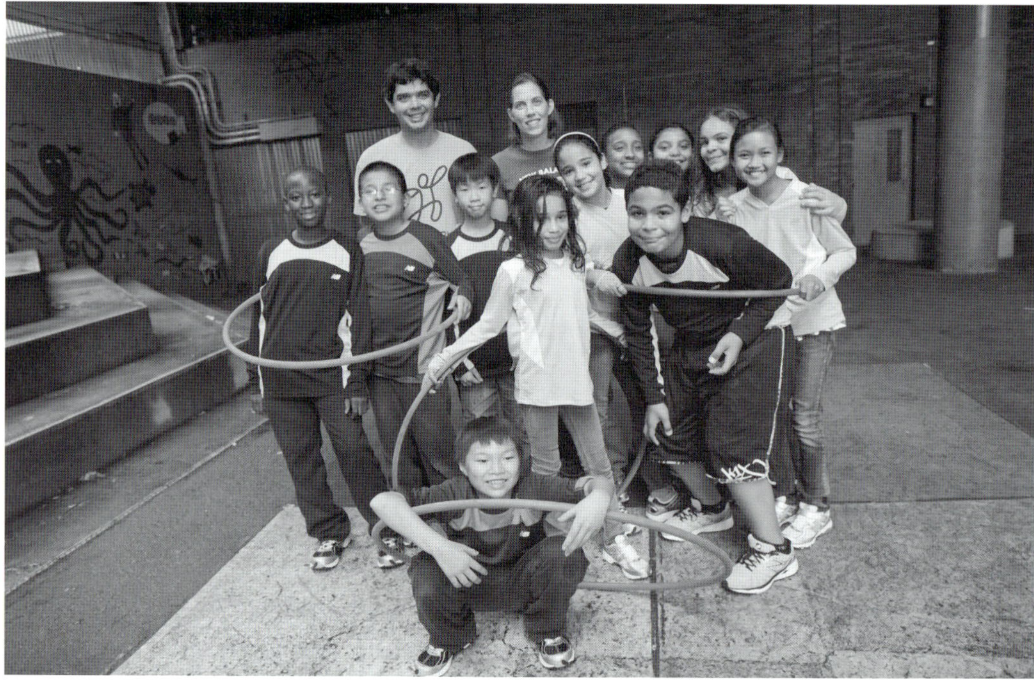

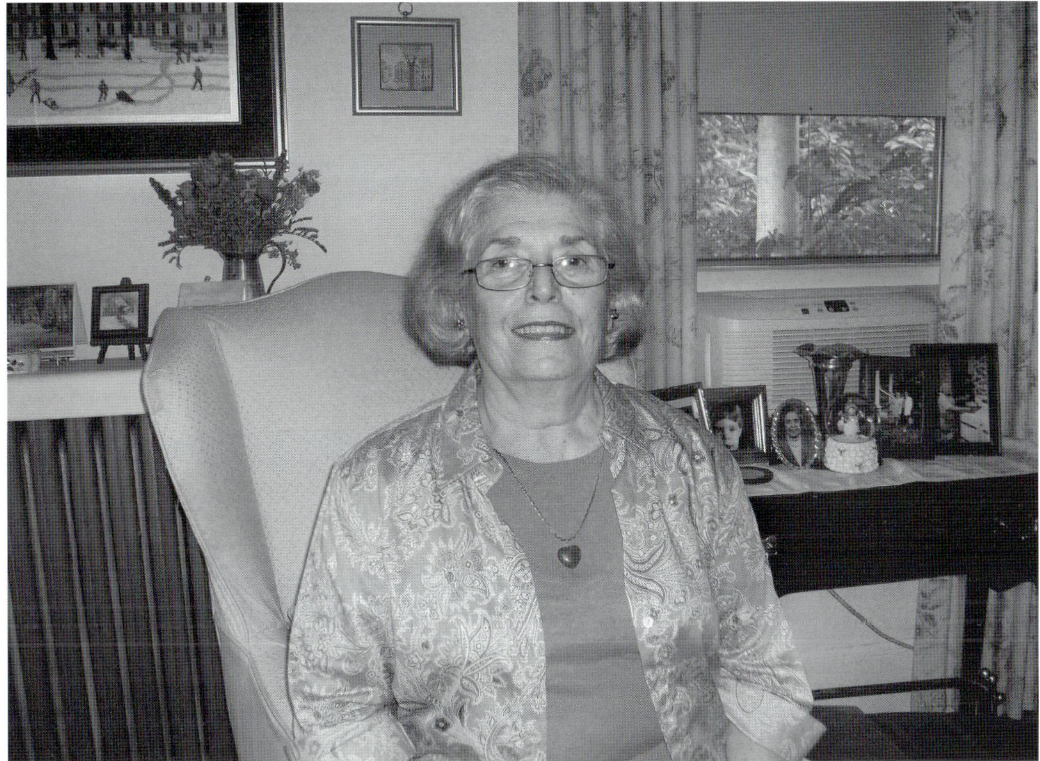

Toni Rossi

Toni Rossi was in the fifth grade when her family moved to Brighton from the North End. They first lived on Market Street and then moved to Lake Street, where she still resides. The house she lives in dates to the early 1800s and is historically significant. It was the home of horticulturist James Lloyd Lafayette Warren when he ran the adjacent Nonantum Vale Gardens. Warren later moved to California where he became known as the "Father of California Agriculture." Toni has been active in Allston-Brighton community work for many years. She first joined the LUCK Neighborhood Association, which sought to protect the area from overdevelopment and to preserve its open green space. Toni was a founding member of Brighton Main Streets. She served as president and is still on its board of directors. She credits Main Streets for improving the storefronts, signage, cleanliness, and lighting of Brighton Center under the guidance of Rosie Hanlon, who served as executive director of Main Streets for many years. In addition to improving the physical area, the organization encourages new businesses to start up in Brighton Center by providing key economic and demographic information. Toni's devotion to the Allston-Brighton community exemplifies good citizenship. (Photograph by Linda Mishkin.)

Molly Santry (OPPOSITE PAGE, BACK ROW)

Molly Santry is charitable programs manager for the New Balance Foundation, which distributes approximately $6.5 million annually to some 70 nonprofit organizations. New Balance has kept its corporate headquarters in Brighton since 1976. James Davis, chairman, and his wife, Anne, vice chairman and executive vice president of administration, feel it is important to thank and support the people and communities that sustain the company's success and support areas where the company's associates live and work. Molly is proud to be part of the important work of the New Balance Foundation in helping to build a healthy community and future for the children of Allston-Brighton. (New Balance.)

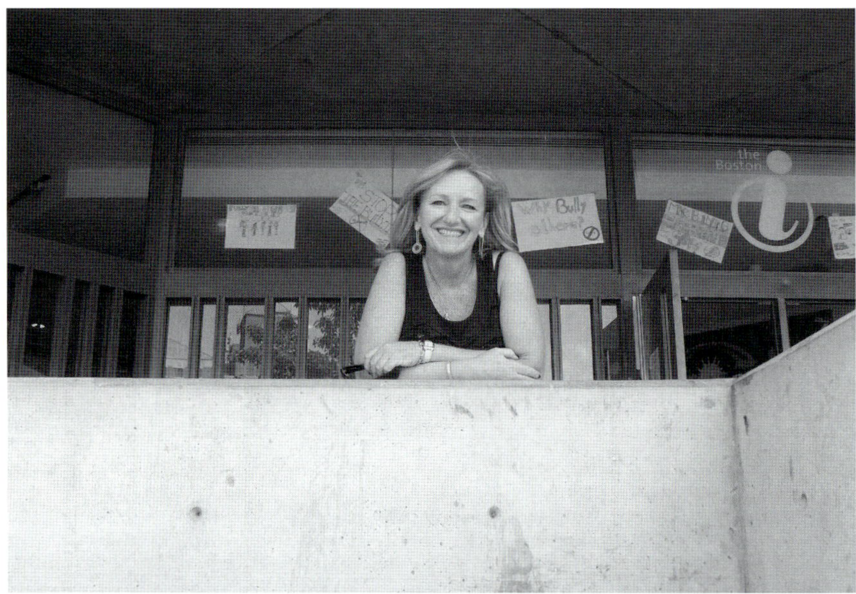

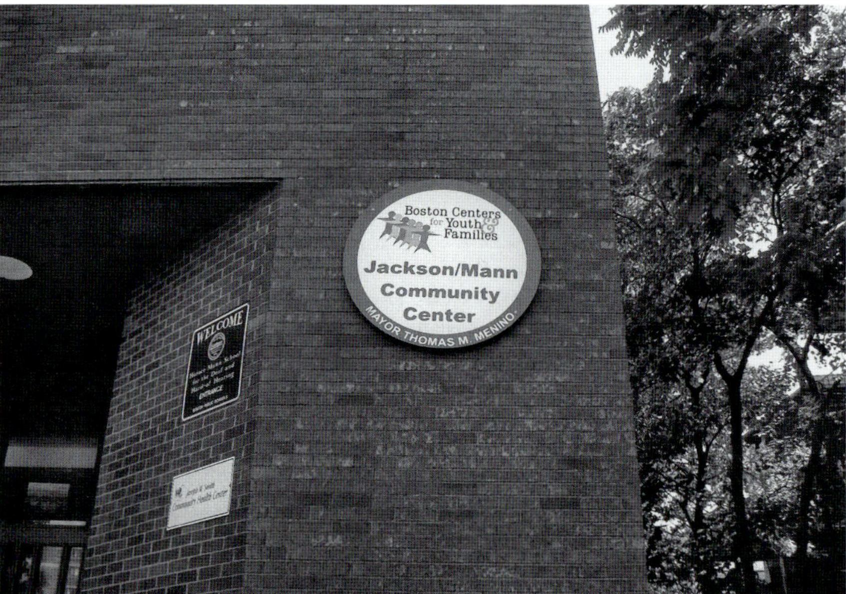

Rosie Hanlon

For 15 years, Rosie Hanlon was involved with Brighton Main Streets, including 13 years as executive director. During that time, there was significant improvement in the look, cleanliness, and safety of the Brighton Center business area. Now Rosie has taken on a new role. She is administrative coordinator of the Jackson-Mann Community Center in Allston. Her vision for the future is to expand services to appeal to a greater cross section of the 75,000 residents in Allston-Brighton. The center will continue to offer its popular before-and-after-school programs, the adult education programs, and computer lab programs. Rosie would like to see instruction that also nurtures creativity, including classes in art and handcrafts. She hopes to involve the local business community in planning new activities. (Photographs by Linda Mishkin.)

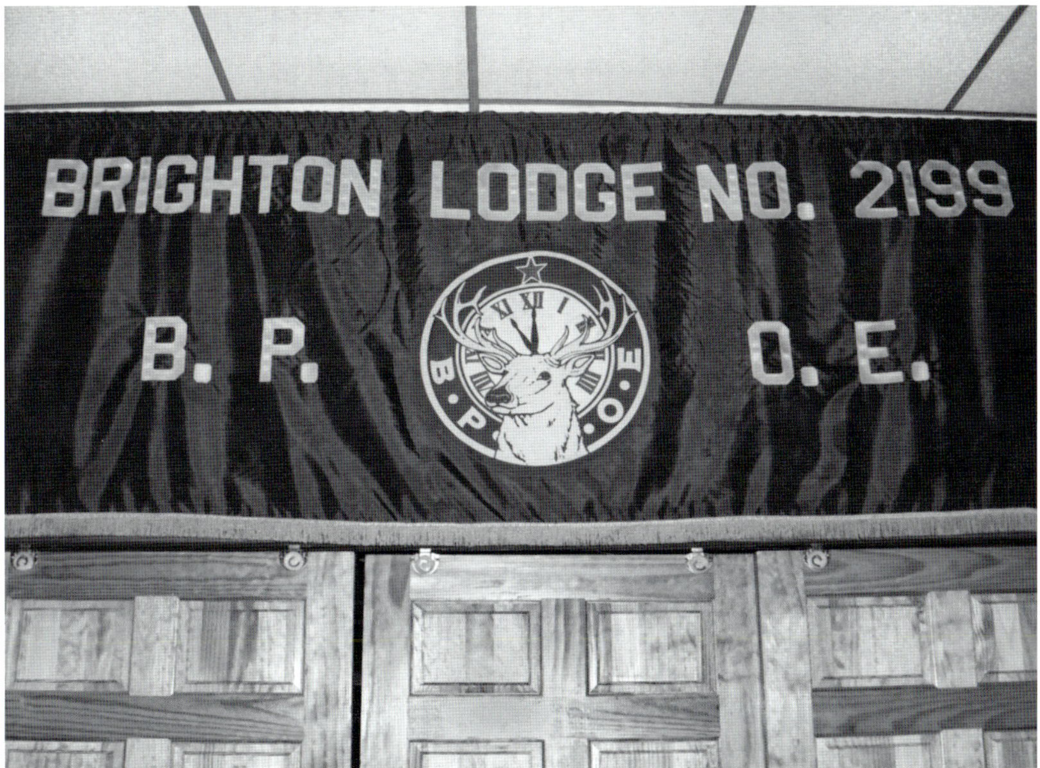

Tom Hogan

Tom Hogan has written history for the Benevolent and Protective Order of the Elks and is a member of the Brighton lodge. Currently, there are 2,000 lodges with 850,000 members across the United States, Puerto Rico, Philippines, Virgin Islands, Canal Zone, and Guam. It is the largest veteran's support group in the United States. The Elks opened the first veterans' hospital in the United States and upon dedication, turned it over to the government. The total amount of awards through its student scholarship program is more than that of the US government. Hogan's wife, Claire, manages that program in Brighton. The Elks are totally self-funded and welcome both men and women and people of any religious faith or ethnic background. The Elks has no political affiliation. The Brighton Elks lodge was chartered in 1961 and soon moved to the building that previously held the Egyptian Theatre. (Photographs by Linda Mishkin.)

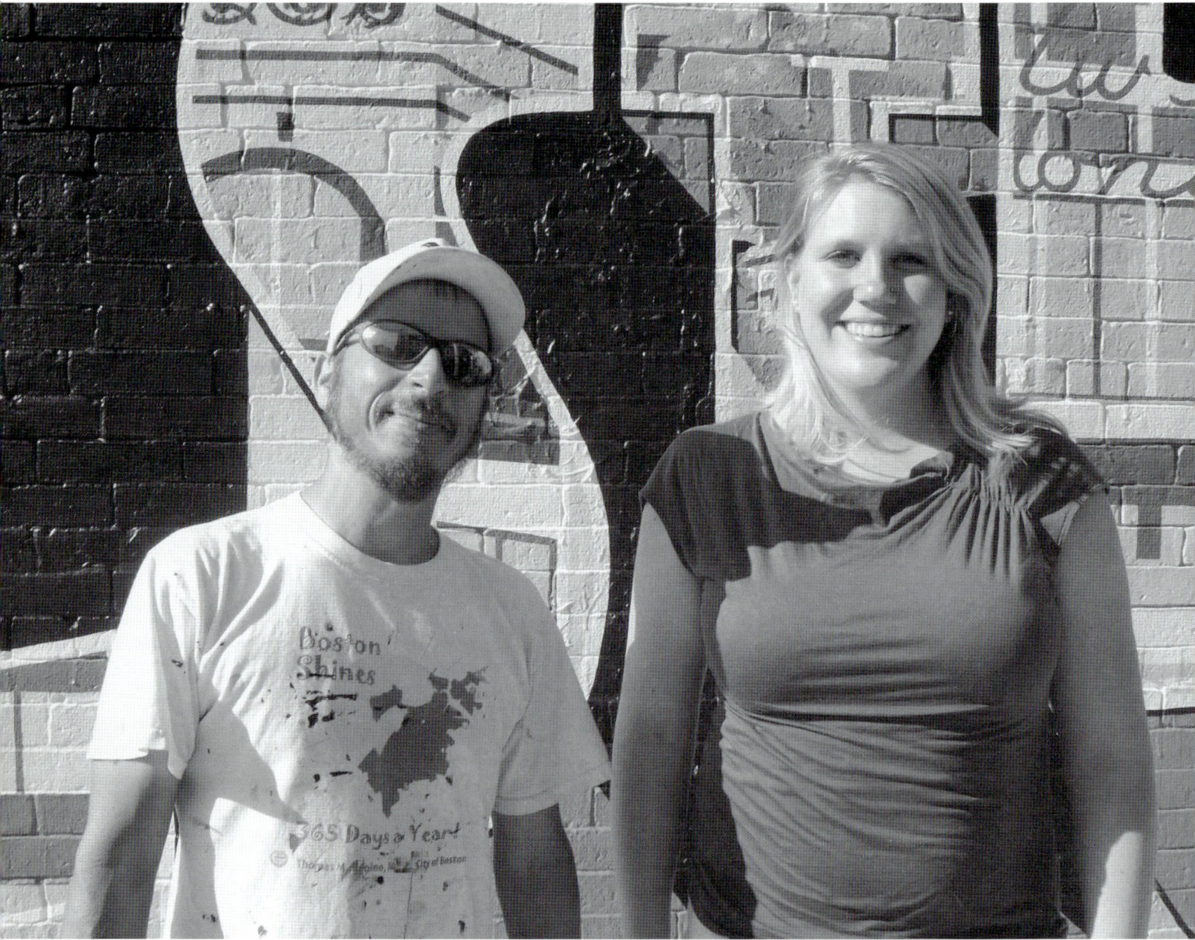

Alana Olsen and Gregg Bernstein

Alana Olsen has been involved with Allston Village Main Streets since 2010 and became executive director in 2011. In that role, she manages all the volunteers and programming and works closely with the board of directors in carrying out the organization's mission to make Allston Village a better place to live, work, dine, and shop. A lot of her work has centered on coalition building. Allston Brighton Community Development Corporation, a recent collaboration, led to the creation of the Allston Village Farmer's Market in Union Square. (Photograph by Linda Mishkin.)

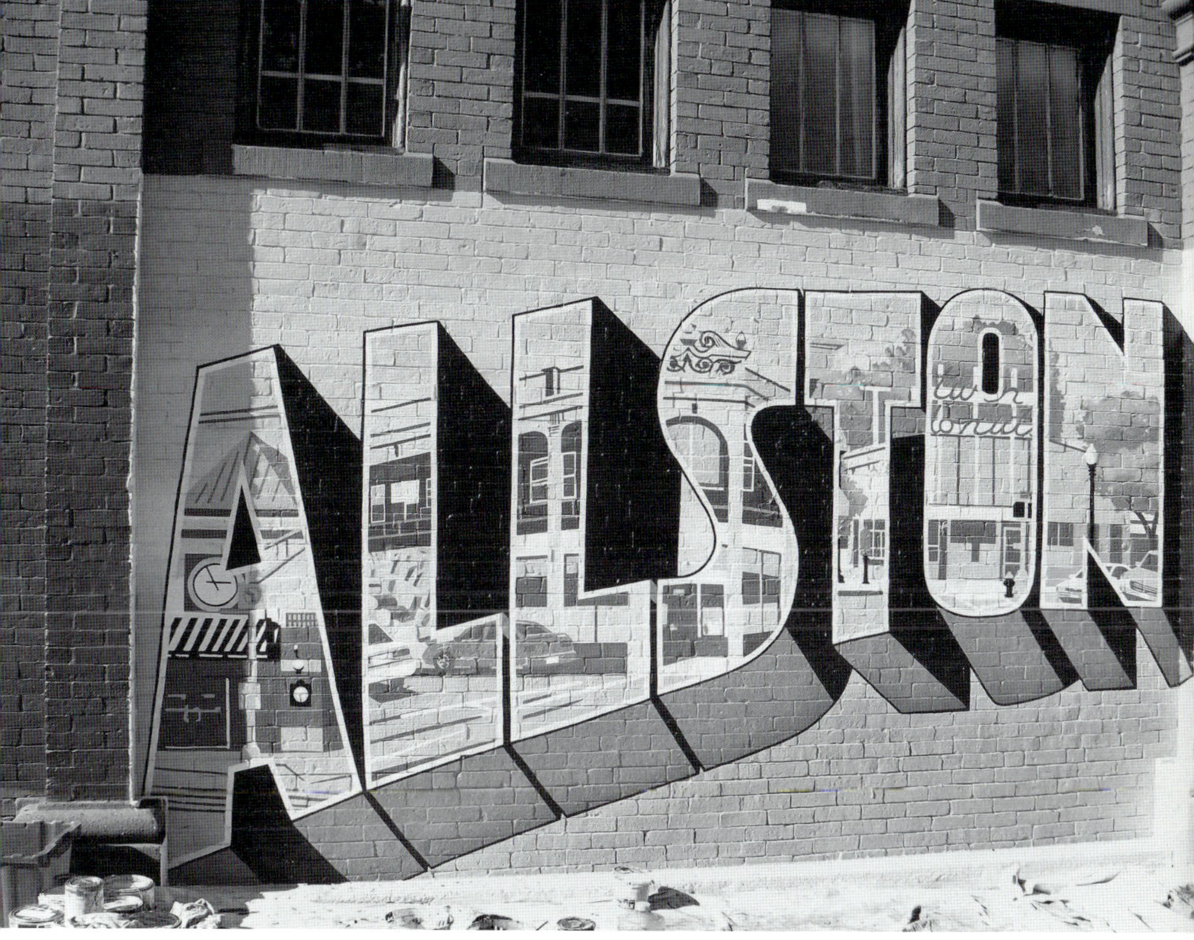

Allston Village Farmer's Market

The market brings in farmers and bakers from around the state as well as local craftspeople. Another of Alana Olsen's projects focuses on public art. It is part of a program called Mayor's Mural Crew. Artist Gregg Bernstein, who was formerly director of the program, is finishing a mural that will make a total of eight commissioned murals in Allston. Alana is an important contributor to the lively cultural activities in Allston Village. (Mural by Gregg Bernstein.)

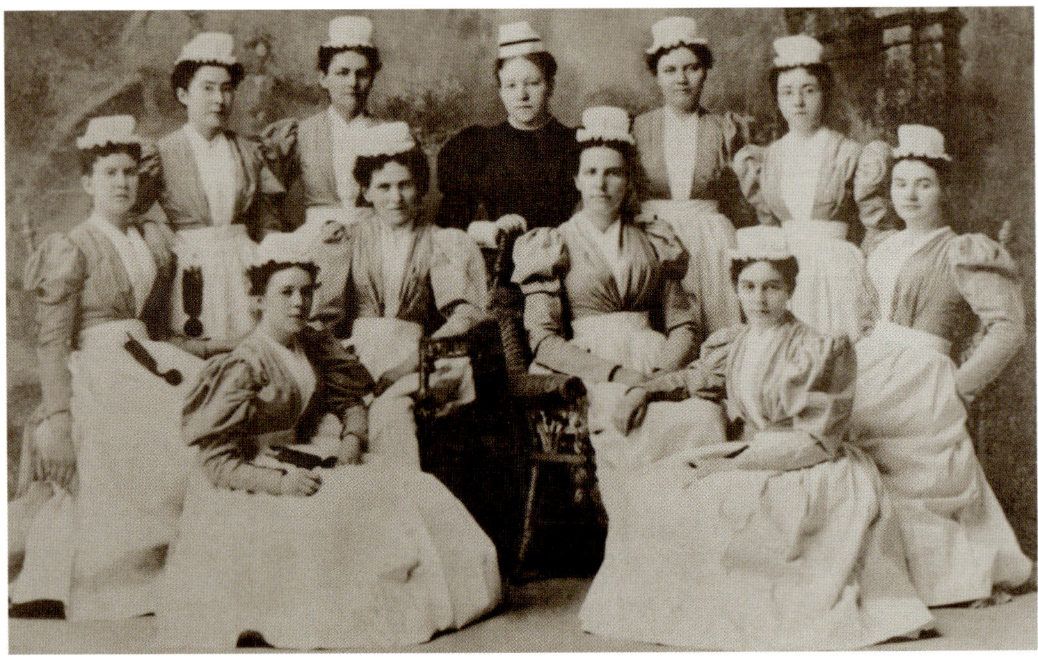

St. Elizabeth's Hospital

St. Elizabeth's Hospital was started by five lay Franciscan women in 1868 for the purpose of providing medical care and shelter at reasonable rates for "retired or feeble women who had grown old in domestic service." The hospital was incorporated in the Commonwealth of Massachusetts in 1872 as St. Elizabeth's Hospital for Women. In 1914, the hospital moved from downtown Boston to Brighton, continuing to focus on its three-pronged health concerns of patient care, research, and teaching. Over the years, services extended to include men, and the charter was amended. In 1951, the hospital was licensed by the department of mental health, the first general hospital in Massachusetts to be so licensed. In 1953, St. Elizabeth's became a teaching affiliate of Tufts University School of Medicine and is now part of the Steward Health Care System. (BAHS archives.)

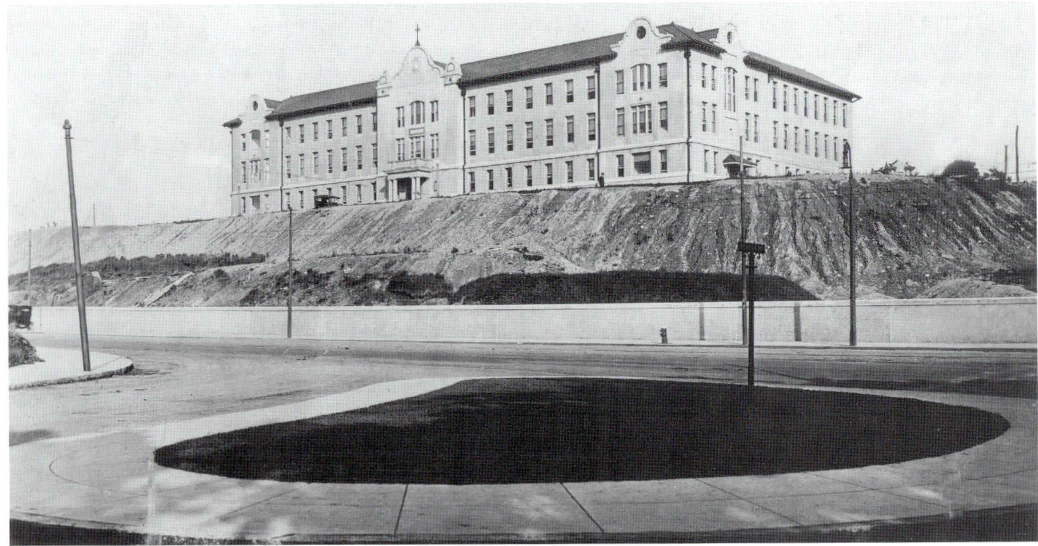

CHAPTER FIVE

Historians and Preservationists

Included in this chapter are stories of people who ensure that the history of Allston-Brighton is not lost or forgotten. Their work includes maintenance of historical facades, overseeing renovations of historical buildings, and creating or maintaining green space. This group also includes historians who recollect or research and record Allston-Brighton's distant and recent past. Current residents are better able to reflect upon and appreciate the community in which they live when reminded of all that went before. As part of a continuum, knowledge of the past guides more thoughtful plans for the future.

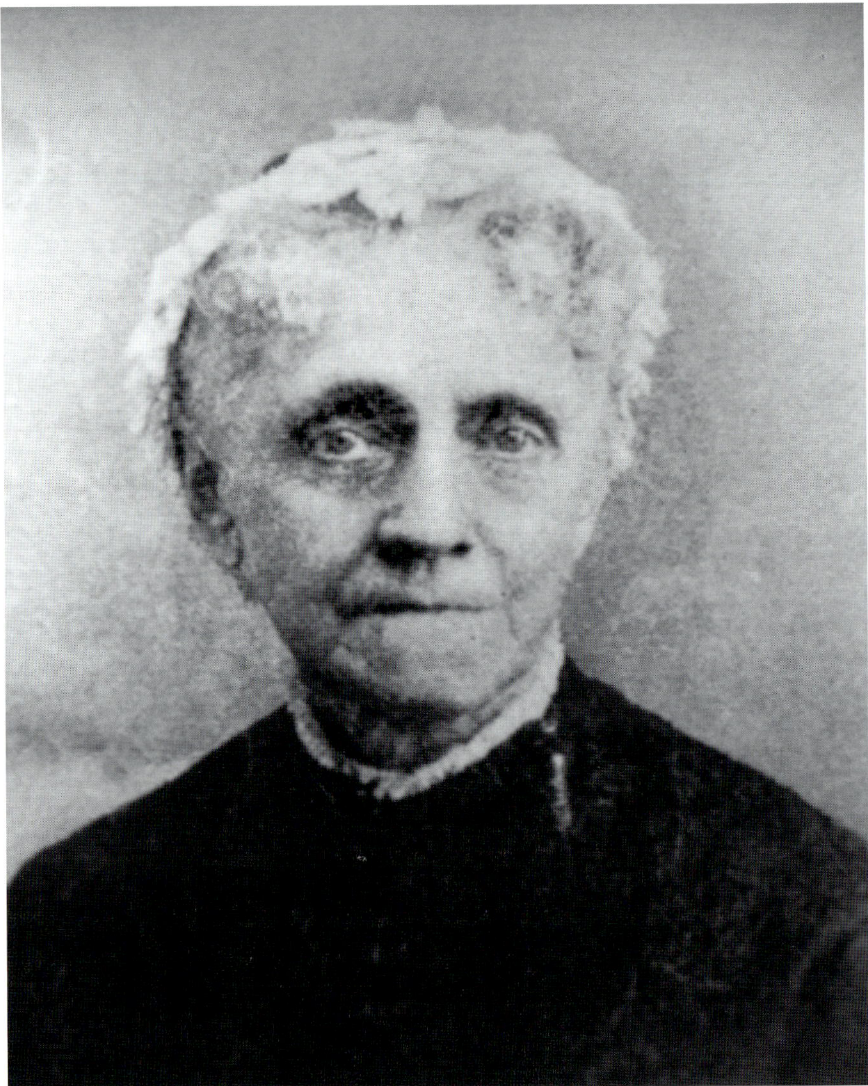

Mary Jane Kingsley Merwin (1814–1911)
Mary Jane Kingsley was raised in a family of six children in a house located near the Cattle Fair Hotel and Brighton Stockyards. She contributed significantly to the preservation of the history of early Brighton by writing a series of reminiscences of her girlhood during the period of 1825 to 1835. That was a time when Brighton's cattle and slaughtering industries were at their height. Over 20 of her lengthy articles were published in the *Brighton Item* in 1886 and 1887 under the title, "Personal Recollections of Brighton Many Years Ago." The articles described what it was like living in Brighton at that time and included detailed descriptions of physical changes occurring in Brighton. These included the building of new roads and bridges and the introduction of rail service into the town in 1834. Her articles constitute the earliest lengthy historical account of Brighton and provide invaluable insights into its unique character. Later, when J.P.C. Winship published his two-volume history of the town in 1899 and 1902, he paid special tribute to her as the first systematic historian of Brighton. (BAHS archives.)

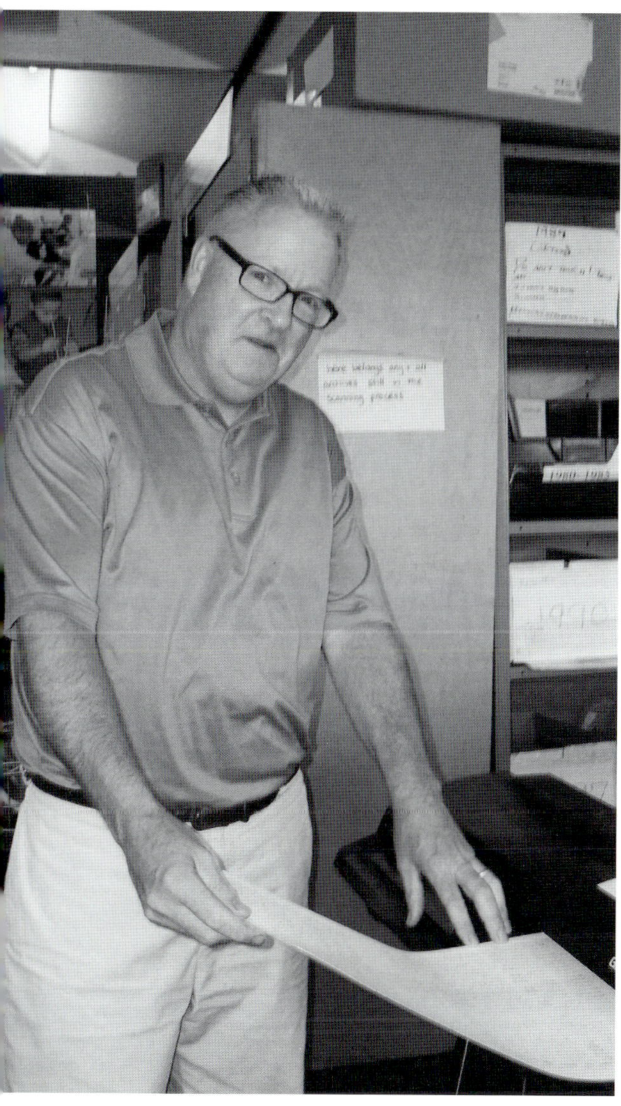

Tom Lally

Tom Lally and his students at the Horace Mann School for the Deaf are digitizing several years of local newspapers. They are scanning all the pages and converting them to a format that will be accessible on the Internet and can be downloaded. This will protect the information in the newspapers from environmental damage that would otherwise occur and preserve it for future generations. The issues hold a lot of historical information about Allston-Brighton. The project includes issues of the *Allston-Brighton Tab*, *Allston-Brighton Citizen Tab*, and the *Allston-Brighton Citizen* between the years 1977 and 1984. Lally is working with students between the ages of 15 and 22. His lab is considered to be vocational training that prepares them for jobs when they leave. The students at the Horace Mann School for the Deaf come from countries around the world. They all learn American Sign Language and use that to learn English. Sarah Fuller, former director of the school, was Helen Keller's private tutor when Keller was about 16 years old. When Lally started his job, he was not able to sign. To learn as quickly as possible, he entered an immersion program for a master's degree in deaf education at Western Maryland College. He is now providing a service in historical preservation as well as vocational training for deaf students. (Photograph by Linda Mishkin.)

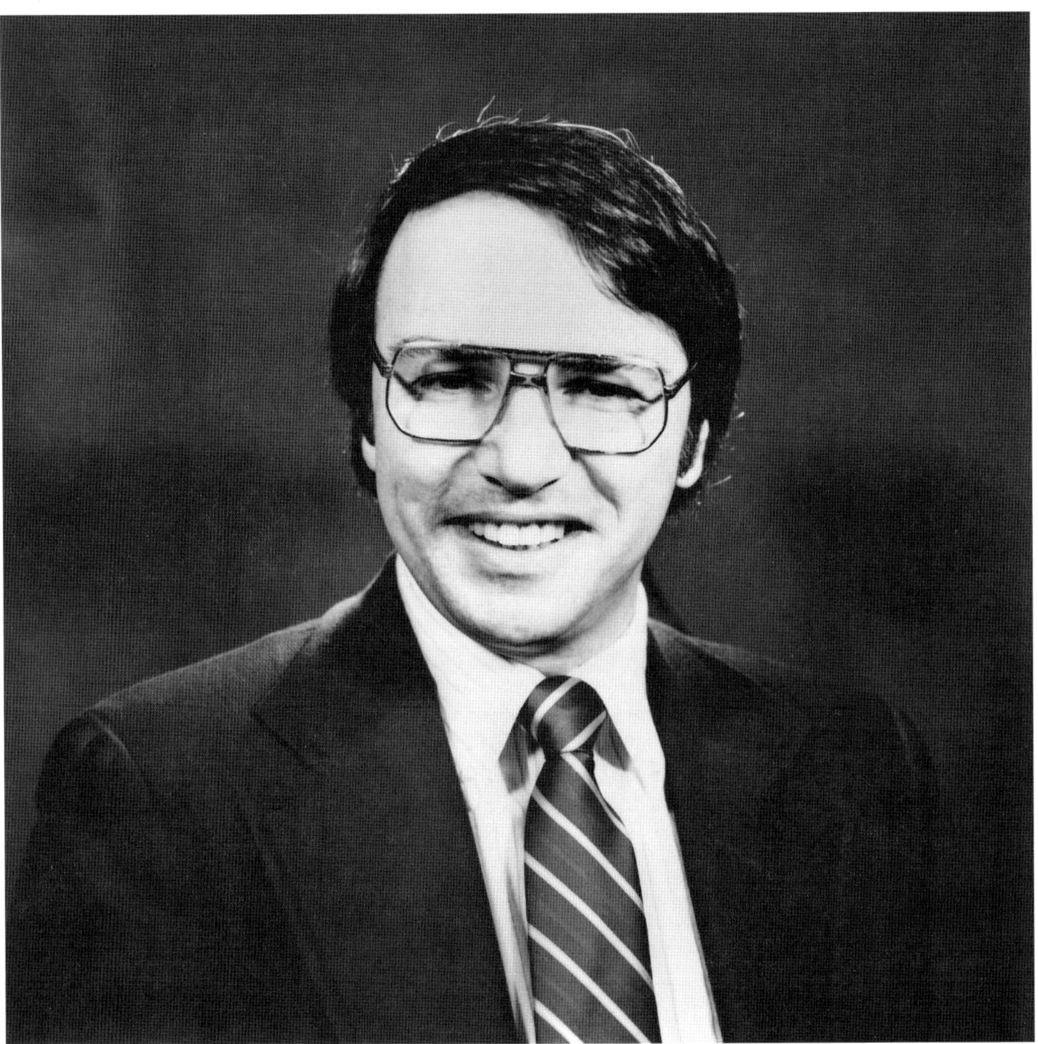

William Marchione

William Marchione was born in Brighton, where he functioned as the community's local historian for over 30 years, engaging in researching, teaching, writing, and giving public lectures and walking tours of Allston-Brighton. The first of his six books, *The Bull in the Garden*, was the first modern history of Allston-Brighton, published in 1986. Marchione held the office of president of the Brighton-Allston Historical Society 11 times over the years. As president, his goal was to expand the community's knowledge of its past through systematic research and public programs. Under his leadership, historical society membership grew substantially, and the BAHS became one of the most proactive preservation advocacy groups in the city. He was also active in the establishment of the Brighton-Allston Heritage Museum, the community's unique local history museum, which opened in 2007 and played a key role in the foundation of the Metropolitan Museum of the Waterworks, also located in Brighton. In the 1980s, Marchione served as an elected member of the Boston School Committee. From 1995 to 2008, he was a commissioner of Boston Landmarks Commission, wrote regular newspaper columns on Allston-Brighton and Boston history, and lectured widely on Boston area historical topics. His last two books comprised collections of these informative newspaper columns. During the time he was Boston landmarks commissioner, a city of Boston architectural conservation district was created in Brighton's Aberdeen neighborhood, and two national register historic districts were established in Allston-Brighton principal commercial areas, Brighton Center and Allston Village. A recipient of many awards for his work as an educator, historian, and preservationist, Marchione was elected a fellow of the Massachusetts Historical Society in 2008. He now resides in Atlanta, Georgia, but maintains contact with the BAHS, serving as an honorary board member. (William Marchione.)

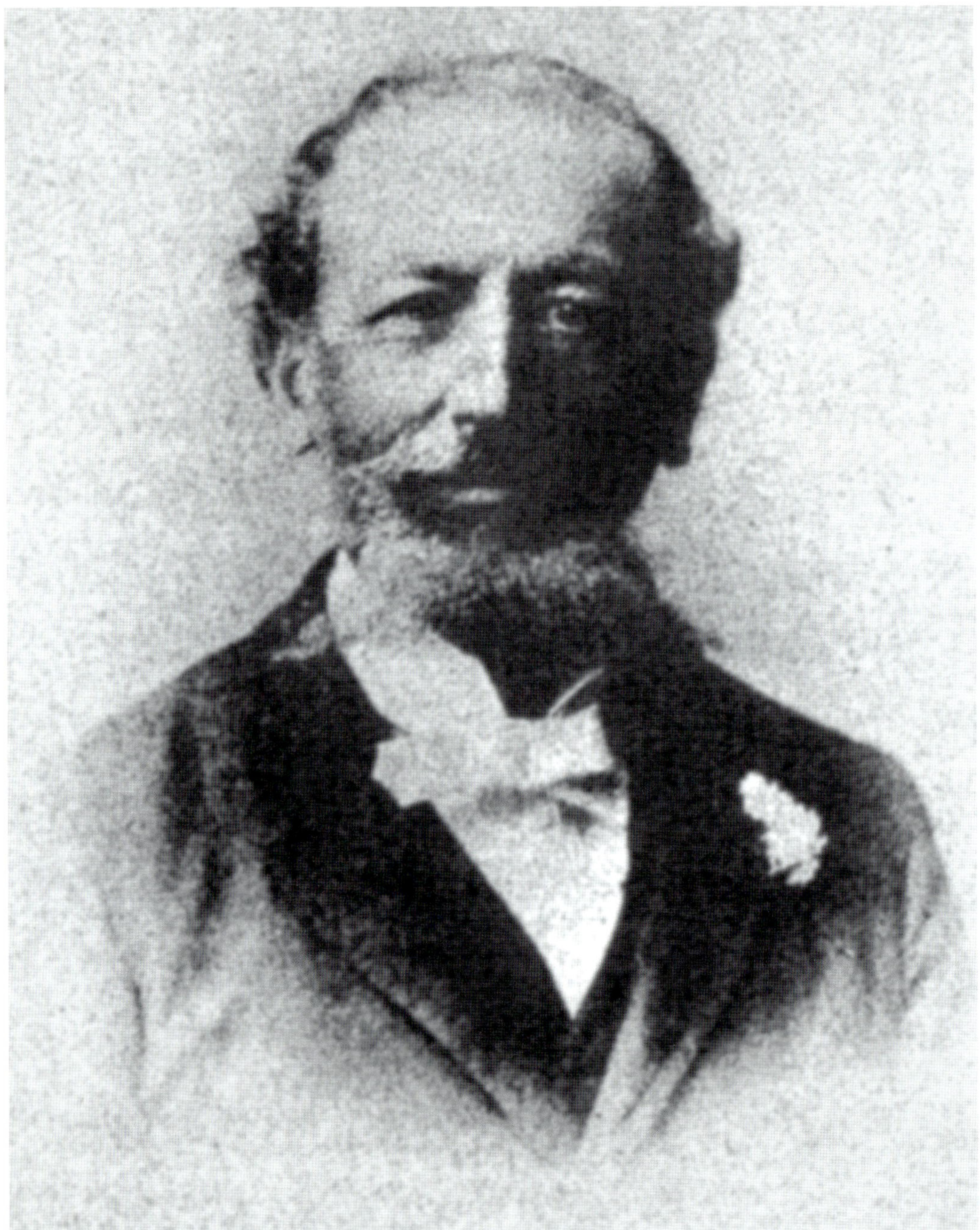

J.P.C. Winship

J.P.C. Winship is the author of *Historical Brighton, An Illustrated History of Brighton and Its Citizens*. Volume I was published in 1899, and Volume II was published in 1902. The history begins with Brighton's early connection with Cambridge and its earliest settlers in the 1600s and continues through the late 1800s. (BAHS archives.)

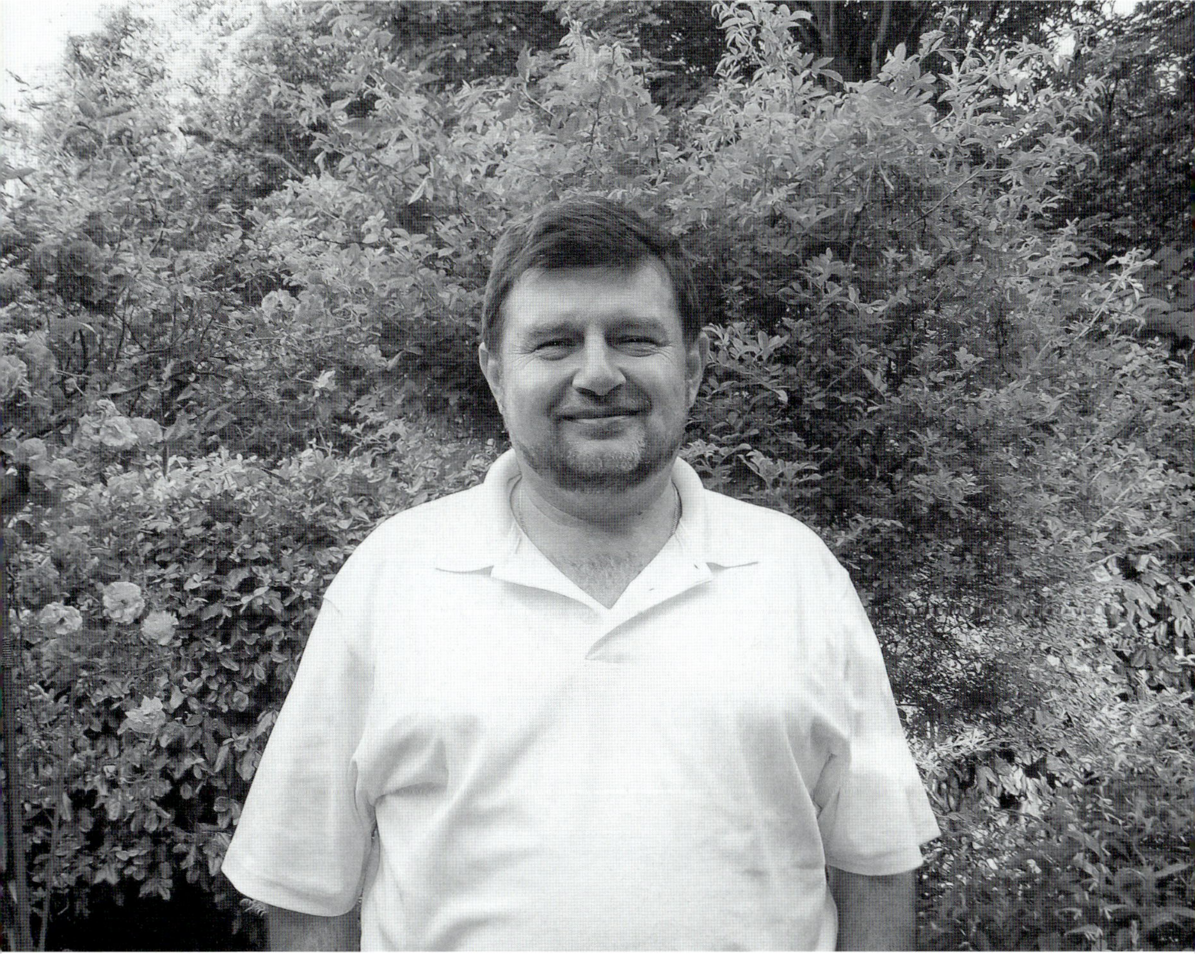

Charlie Vasiliades

For decades, Charlie Vasiliades has fought to preserve the fabric of the Allston-Brighton neighborhoods, with a focus on both buildings and landscape. An avid gardener, he was a founding member of the Brighton Garden Club. When the city of Boston made plans to close the Oak Square School building, he worked with residents and community organizations in spearheading the effort to preserve the structure. The interior of the building was successfully reconfigured for condominiums, but the exterior looks like it did when he attended the school as a young boy. Vasiliades was active in the effort to retain the Faneuil Branch Library when the city considered closing it. Another large successful project he worked on involved preserving the building that previously held the Presentation School, also in Oak Square. Again, the exterior remained, but the building was repurposed as a community center. Grateful residents in the area often refer to him as the Mayor of Oak Square. He has been at the forefront of just about every major preservation project in Allston-Brighton. This includes many efforts to save the so-called "urban wilds," such as the Cenacle/EF property. He is vice president of the Brighton-Allston Historical Society and a member of the Landmarks Commission. (Photograph by Linda Mishkin.)

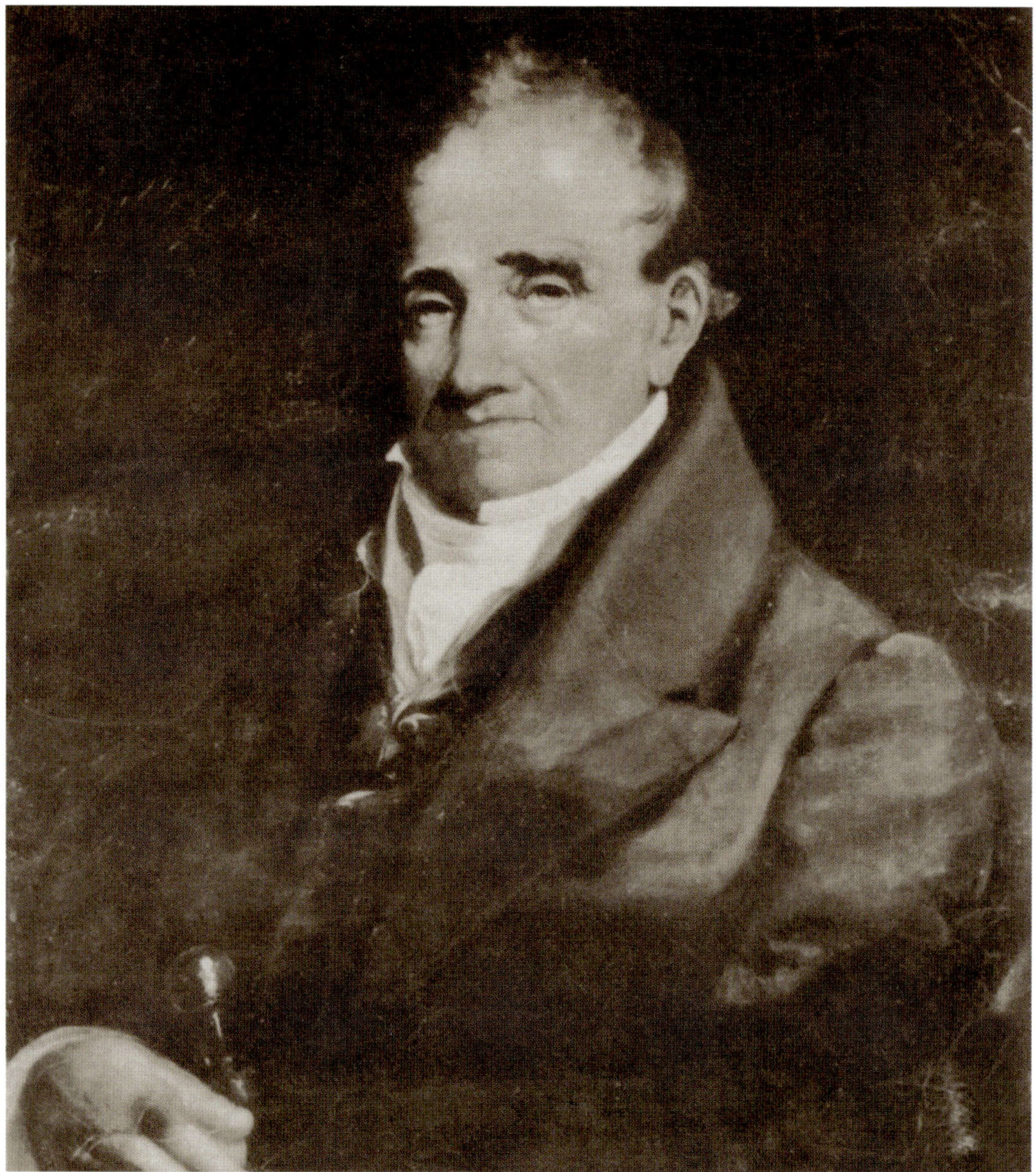

Daniel Bowen

Daniel Bowen relocated to the Boston area from Philadelphia in 1791 to open a museum. He was a close friend of the nation's pioneer museum-keeper, Charles Willson Peale, and it was said that Bowen moved to Boston to avoid competing with his friend. Soon after his arrival, Bowen purchased a nine-acre estate in the part of Cambridge that, in 1807, became the town of Brighton. His local estate, called Lime Grove, was situated in the Oak Square section of the community. His Brighton household included nephew Abel Bowen, the highly talented engraver. Daniel Bowen's Boston museum, called the Columbian Museum, had a modest beginning, initially comprising some wax figures and a few paintings that he laid out in a popular Boston tavern. He later moved this collection, which he had greatly expanded, to more commodious quarters. Art historians credit Bowen's art collection with influencing major painters, including the great Romantic painter Washington Allston. (BAHS archives.)

CHAPTER SIX

Authors and Academics

The creative and intellectual life of Allston-Brighton is revealed through the stories of its writers, poets, and academics. Their pursuits have wide appeal. In some cases, their work reflects worldwide achievements. The community and its residents may provide inspiration for their work, a jumping-off point, or a quiet place of refuge. Existing among fine schools and universities, Allston-Brighton lures talented people who in turn add to the appeal of the community. Local and widespread recipients of their ideas are challenged to think differently or to become more aware of other lives and experiences. Their works entertain, inspire, and inform.

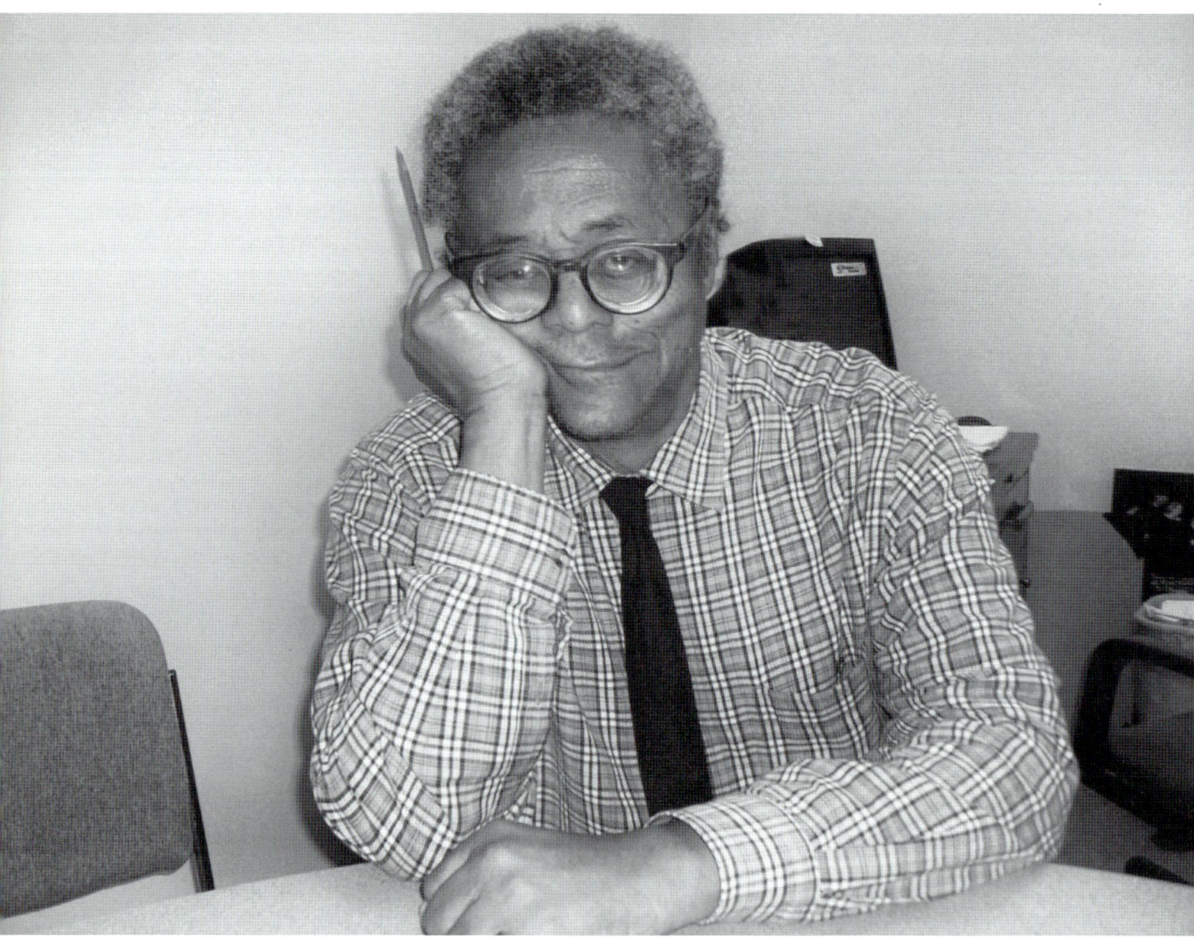

Sam Cornish

Sam Cornish is poet laureate of Boston. His generosity in both spirit and talent enriches the cultural life of the city. Reading, film, and city life inspire his writing. As a youngster growing up in Baltimore, he frequented the local library and bookstores. One that was especially dear to him became the model for a bookstore he co-owned in Brookline with his wife, Florella Orowan, years ago. Cornish reads broadly, which is reflected in his work. He is intrigued by psychological mystery novels that explore themes of human motivation. He enjoys realistic fiction that emits the sense and sound of its characters. As a keen observer of urban multiculturalism, he appreciates that different races, cultures, and even neighborhoods have their own sound. Sound is integral to his poetry. Film also inspires his imagination. He appreciates the classic films of John Ford for their exploration of the immigrant experience. Similar to film, poetry consists of images tied together by a theme. His early reading of T.S. Eliot's *The Waste Land* and *The Hollow Men* influenced his decision to write poetry. It was the recognizable imagery in those poems that ignited his ability to see and smell the city, and it is the immediacy of those senses that create a certain spiritual urgency. He enjoys living in Brighton and gives generously with his time through poetry readings at local venues. He also offers poetry workshops free of charge at the Boston Public Library. His most recent book of poetry, *Dead Beats*, was published by Ibbetson Street Press. A theatrical production based on Sam's writing is currently running in Boston. *An Apron Full of Beans* is directed and choreographed by Marshall Hughes and stars a multiracial group of actors. The production portrays movement from an African American narrative to a universal poem. His work both takes from and gives to the urban community of Allston-Brighton. (Photograph by Linda Mishkin.)

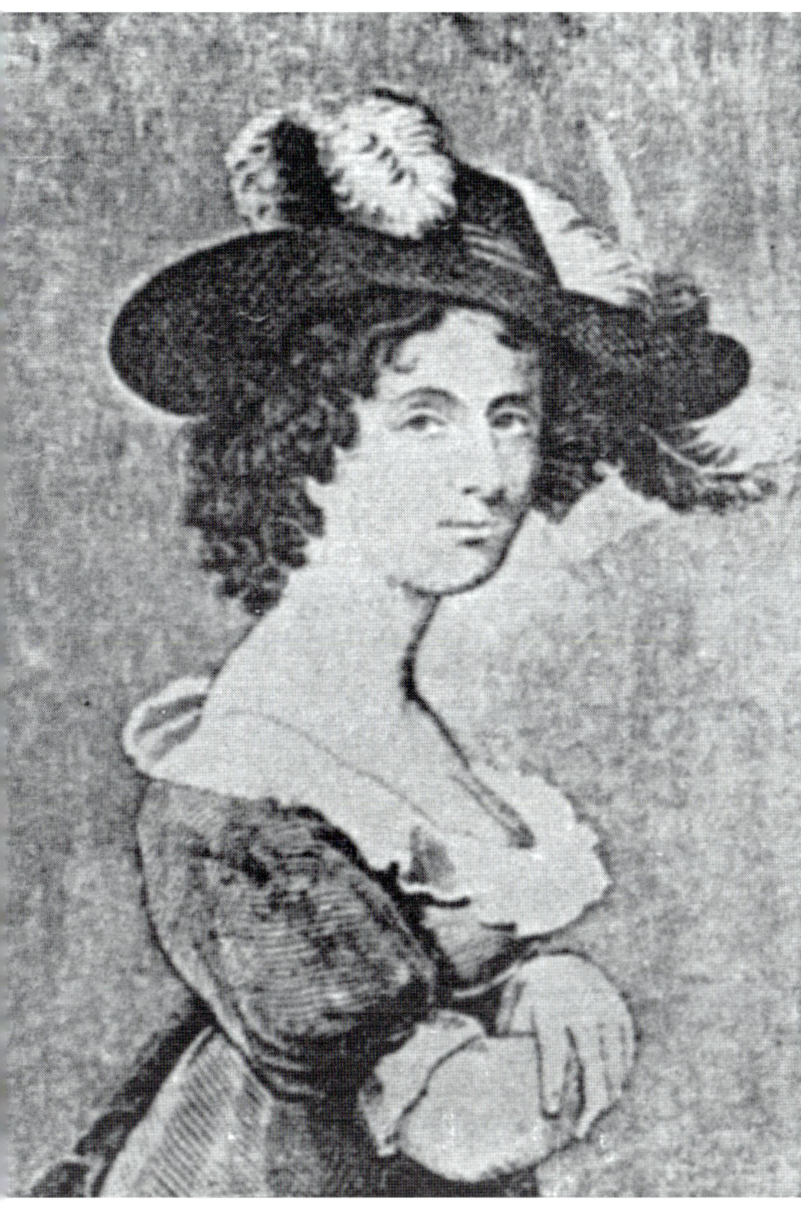

Hanna Webster Foster
Hannah Webster Foster of Little Cambridge was the first American-born woman to write and publish a novel. *The Coquette, the History of Eliza Wharton,* which appeared in 1797, was a thinly veiled actual account of the seduction, betrayal, and eventual death in childbirth of Elizabeth Whitman. Then, as now, a scandal exerted a powerful attraction upon the reading public. The *Coquette* was said to have been, next to the Bible, the most popular reading material of early 19th century New England. By 1840, it had appeared in some 30 editions. (BAHS archives.)

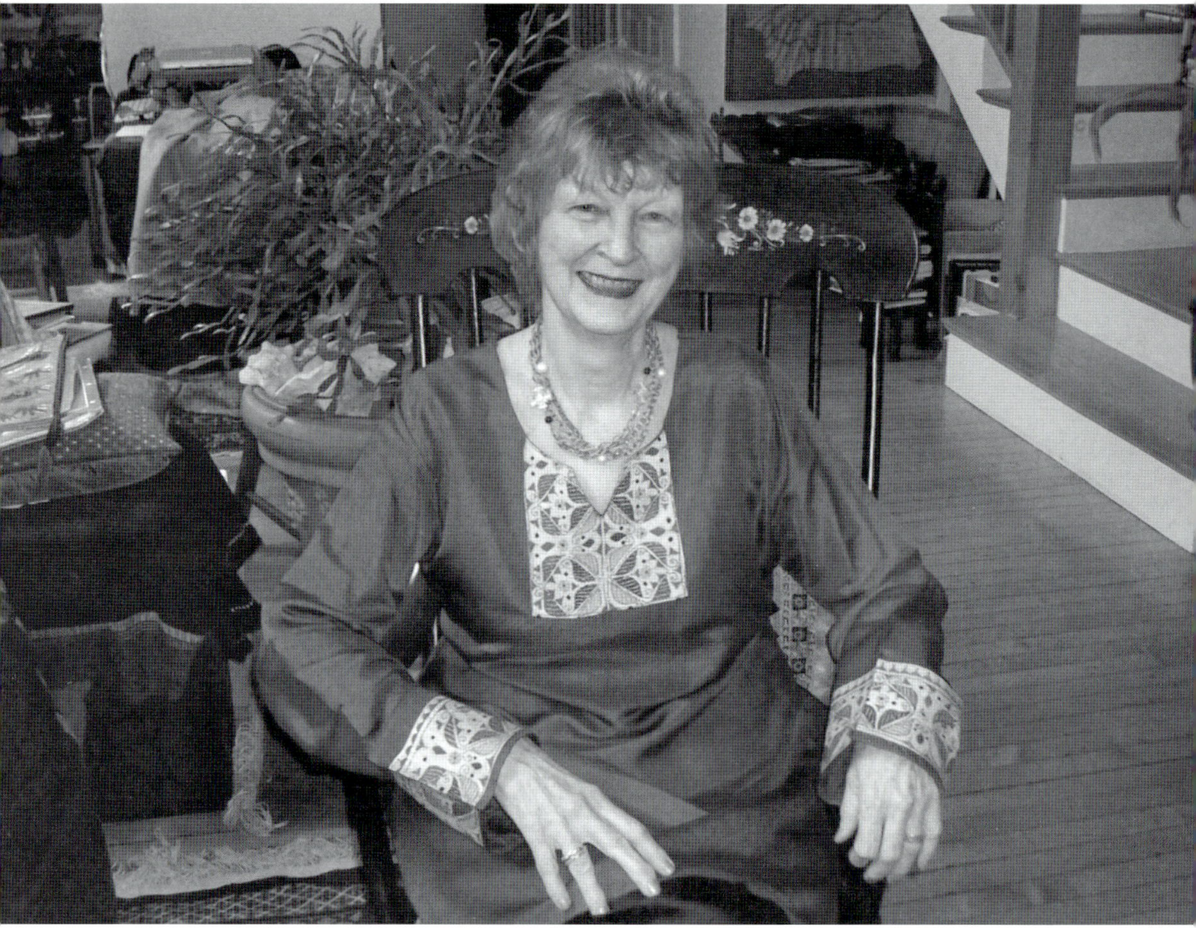

Brenda Gael McSweeney

Brenda Gael McSweeney returned to her native home of Boston upon completion of her 30-year career with the United Nations. She lived and worked with the United Nations in many parts of the world. Her endeavors had a consistent theme: helping the least advantaged, notably women and girls, live better lives. She oversaw development projects in India, Africa, and the Caribbean. From Geneva, then Bonn, she was in charge of the global UN Volunteers program. Now she continues her work in academia. She began teaching at the Women's, Gender, and Sexuality Studies Program at Boston University. As resident scholar at the Women's Studies Research Center at Brandeis University, Brenda continues her research and writing. She lives in a landmark building in Brighton that once was the Oak Square School, designed in 1894 by renowned Boston architect Edmund March Wheelwright. Now that Brenda is living in Brighton, it is the local community that benefits from her intelligence, enthusiasm, and creativity. Upon joining the board of directors of the Brighton-Allston Historical Society, and in keeping with her interest in women's issues, she immediately noticed that there was no committee focused on the history of women in Allston-Brighton. She rallied support that resulted in the society's formation of its Women's History group, which she chairs. She also helped instigate the Brighton-Allston Women's Heritage Trail and its accompanying guide, "Women of Vision." While focusing on local issues, Brenda never loses sight of the world at large. Through her outreach, the Women of Vision idea has spread to parts of the developing world and is a prototype for a UNESCO e-learning tool for African youth. It is important for Brenda to create lasting products. She has done that. Brenda has innovated improvements for women and girls and thus whole communities around the world and here in Allston-Brighton. (Photograph by Linda Mishkin.)

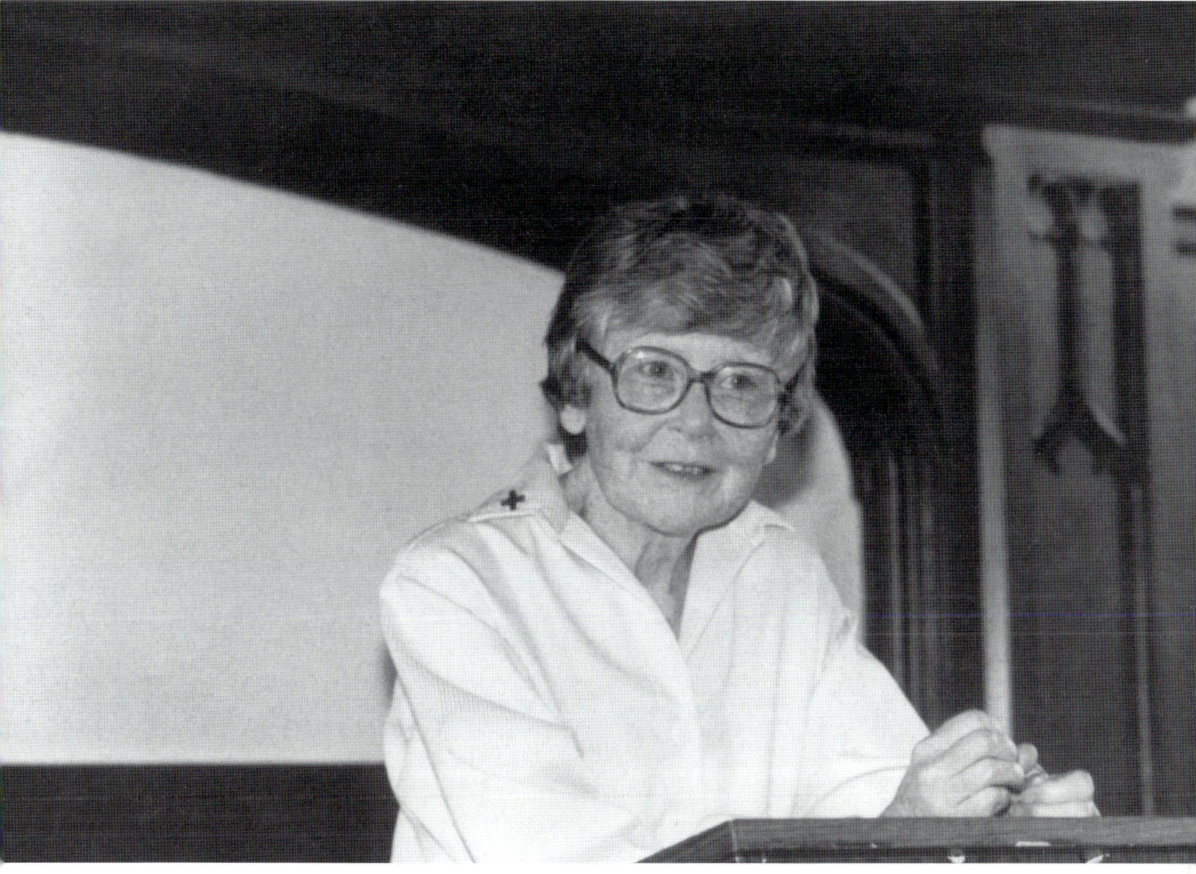

Mary Augusta Neal
Mary Augusta Neal, a sister of Notre Dame de Namur, was a distinguished sociologist and educator who had a lifetime association with Brighton. She earned scholarships to the Notre Dame Academy and Emmanuel College. She received a master's degree from Boston College and a doctorate of philosophy from Harvard University. She became a professor at Emmanuel College in 1963. She was one of two religious representatives on the governor's Commission on the Status of Women in 1965. In 1966, Sister Marie Augusta conducted the National Sister Survey of 130,000 Catholic religious women across the United States. This study provided profound insights that challenged the traditional role of women in the church. She was passionate about social justice. At the height of the civil rights movement in 1967, at a National Catholic Education Association conference, Sister Marie Augusta urged the church to improve the education of Catholics in matters of peace, poverty, and civil rights. (BAHS archives.)

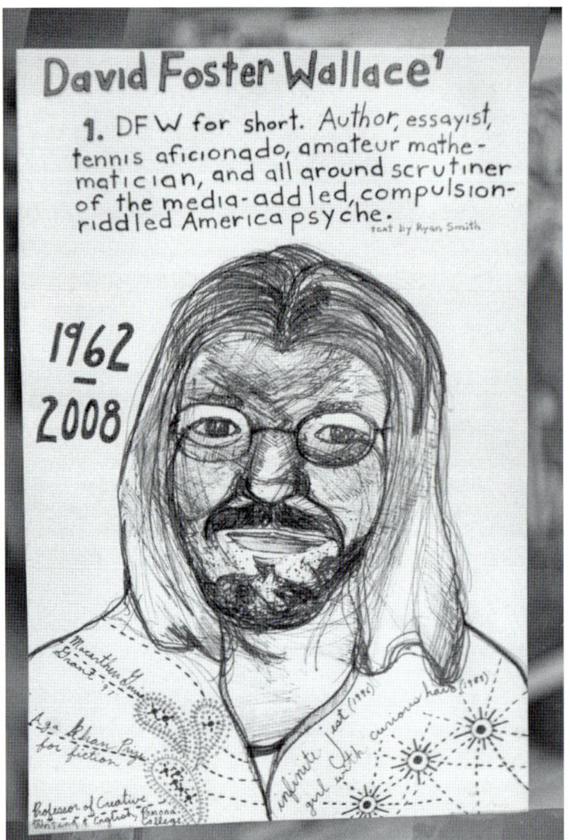

David Foster Wallace (1962–2008)

Acclaimed as a brilliant author and one of the most important writers of his generation, David Foster Wallace struggled with depression and self-doubt his entire life. His second novel, *Infinite Jest*, published in 1996, was partly written while the author resided in Brighton at a drug and alcohol rehabilitation halfway house. The book contains many allusions to Brighton personalities and locations. It is often considered a "Boston story," especially in terms of setting and dialect. Wallace reminisced: "Boston made a big impression on me, because linguistically it's very different than where I'm from." The writer grew up in Illinois and attended Amherst College, majoring in English and philosophy focusing on logic and mathematics. Wallace's first novel, *The Broom of the System*, was based on his senior English thesis. In 1987, he received a master of fine arts in creative writing. Wallace's career is rich in short story and novel writing as well as essays, articles, and criticism on subjects from tennis to the significance of rap music in American culture. He believed he was a "fairly traditional, conservative kind of writer [who] tended to think of fiction as being mainly about characters and human beings and inner experience." Wallace had a wonderful imagination and breadth of knowledge. He believed that "there's really only one basic problem in all writing—how to get some empathy with the reader." He felt that it was important to know who your audience was and to challenge its ideas. In 2002, he was professor of creative writing and literature at Pomona College in California. He was a kind, committed, and engaging teacher. Wallace married painter Karen L. Green in 2004. He ended his life in 2008 while struggling to control his depression. (Steve Rhodes.)

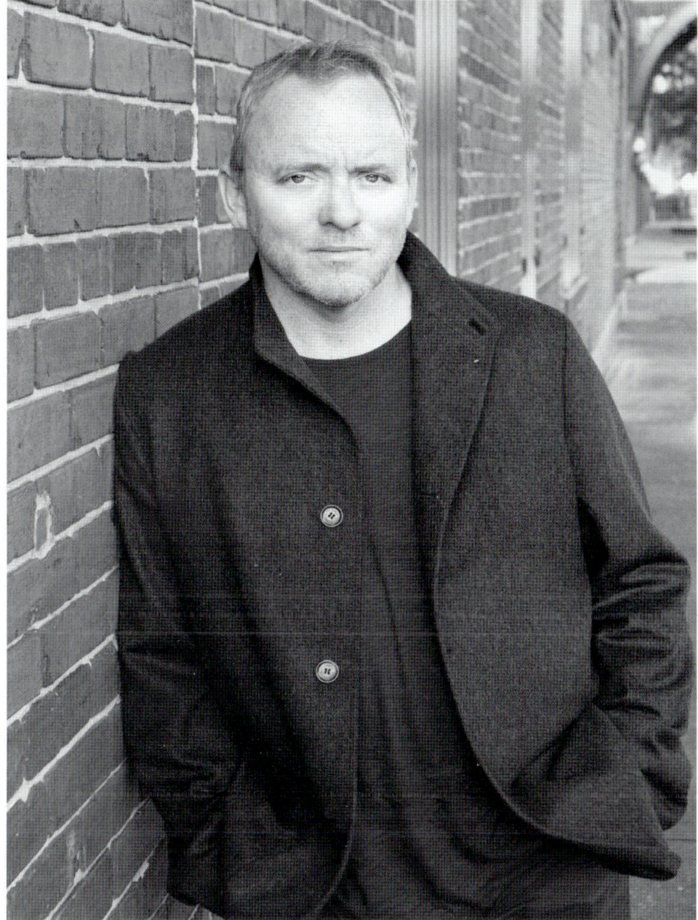

Dennis Lehane

He "would not be a writer," says Dennis Lehane, if he "had not grown up in Dorchester, Massachusetts." He attributes the multiethnic, working-class environment in Dorchester (and later in Brighton) and its bar culture to his success. "People told stories in bars and premiums were placed on how well you could tell a story, how funny you could make it, and how authentic it was," explained Lehane, factors that he has brought to his story telling. The author also grew up with a sense of class distinction that gave him a strong interest in social issues, especially how children are treated in the home and in society. These issues he addresses in his writing, such as his work *Gone Baby Gone*. Often, Lehane creates characters reflecting the duality of his own personality so that he can address an issue from different viewpoints. He hopes that the experience he has as a writer translates to the reader. He is eager to tell the best story he knows so that his work is "the book you most want to read." Yet, he always tries to hold his writing to a certain aesthetic standard. Lehane holds a master of fine arts from Florida International University and is the writer-in-residence at Eckerd College in St. Petersburg, Florida, where he is co-director of the Writers in Paradise writers' conferences. He also serves as writer-in-residence at Pine Manor College in Chestnut Hill, Massachusetts. Before becoming a full-time writer, Lehane worked as a counselor with mentally handicapped and abused children, waited tables, parked cars, drove limos, worked in bookstores, and loaded tractor-trailers. The award-winning author is one of the most popular writers of our day. Three of his thrillers, *Mystic River*, *Shutter Island*, and *Gone Baby Gone*, have been made into acclaimed movies. Lehane lived in Brighton from 1995 to 2002. He purchased his first house on Bigelow Hill near Oak Square. (Ashleigh-Faye Photography.)

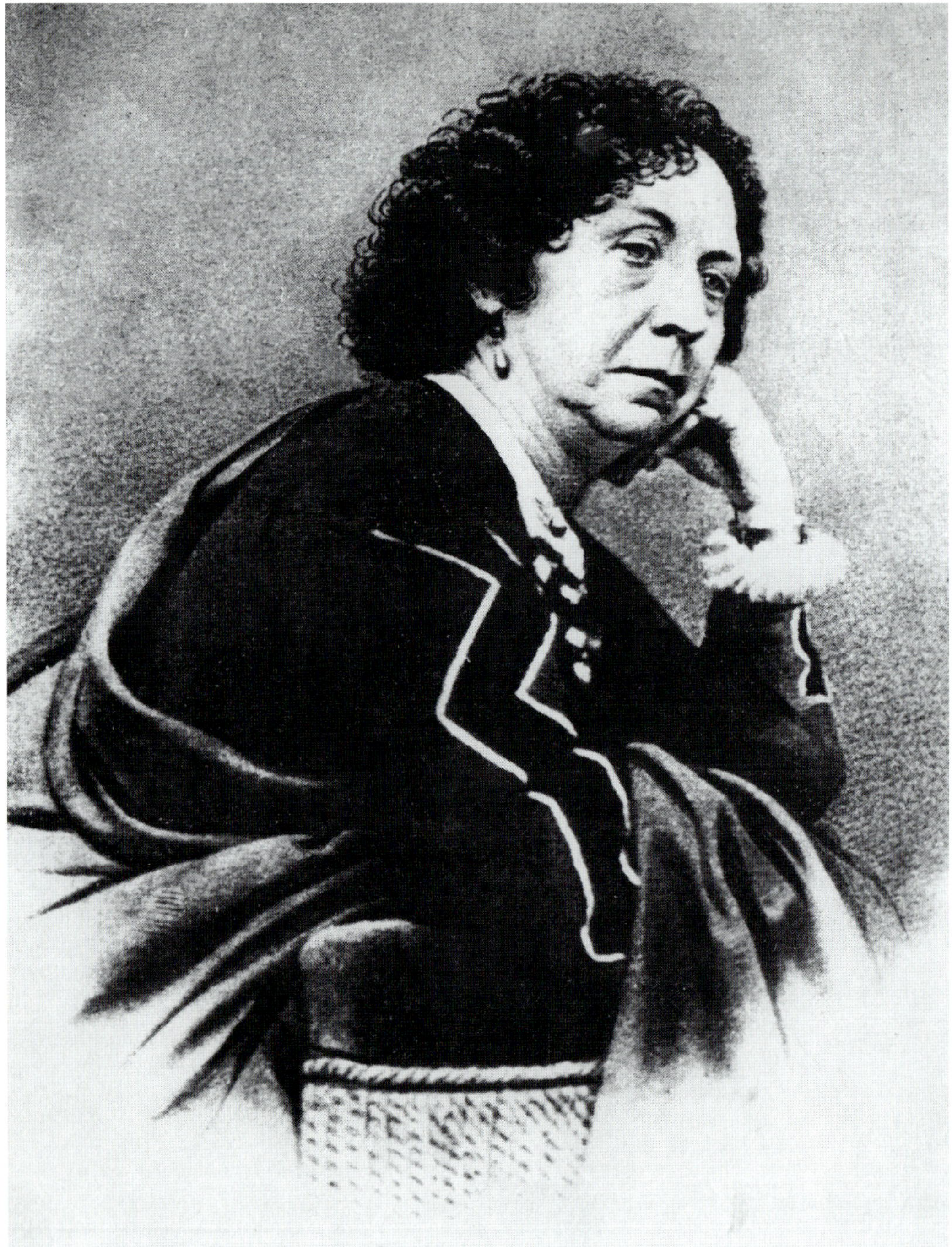

Sara Willis Eldredge "Fanny Fern" (1811–1872)

"Fanny Fern" was one of the most widely read and influential American journalists and novelists of the 19th century. At the height of her career, in the 1850s and 1860s, her columns, which appeared in the *New York Ledger*, reached over a half-million readers weekly. She was one of the highest paid columnists in the United States. She wrote two novels, *Ruth Hall* and *Rose Clark*. (BAHS archives.)

CHAPTER SEVEN

Lawyers, Jurists, and Clergy

The stories of those who serve in various professions demonstrate the diversity of Allston-Brighton's talent pool and mission. The dedication of these people to their community and its underlying principles enriches the lives of residents and visitors alike. Whether administering justice, advancing religious thought and education, or providing solace to those in need, these narratives show commonality in their diversity. People included here improve the lives and well-being of others, both within their local community and beyond.

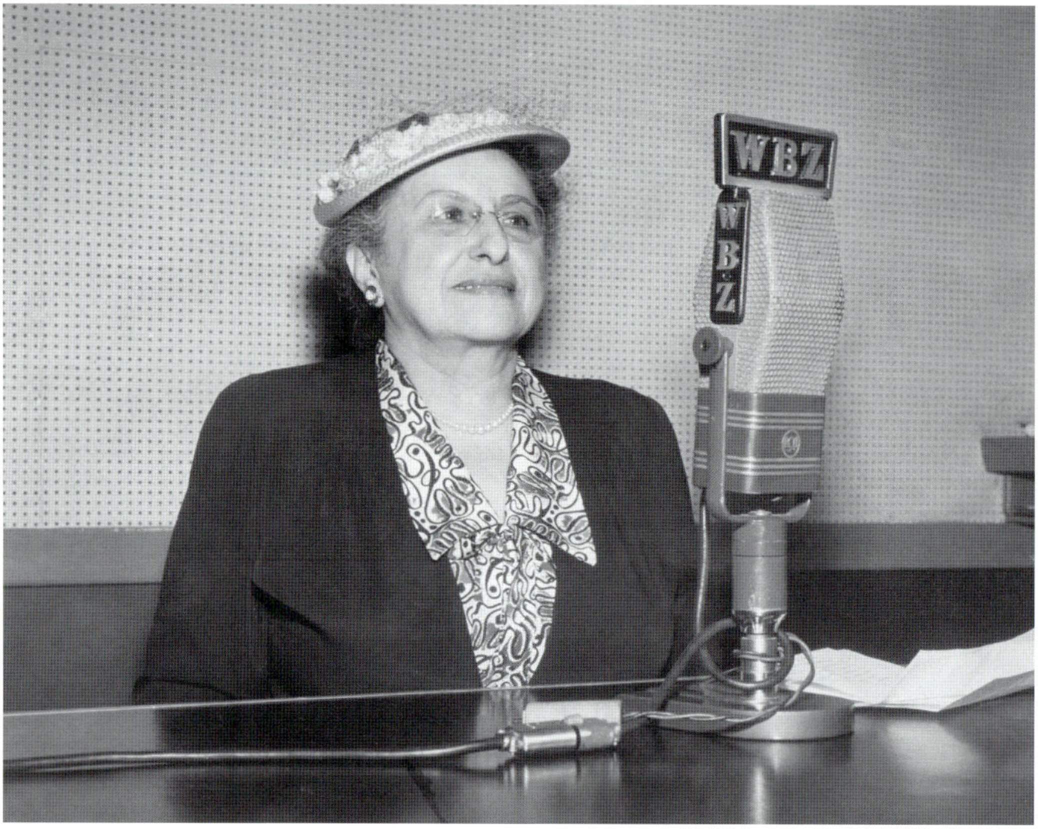

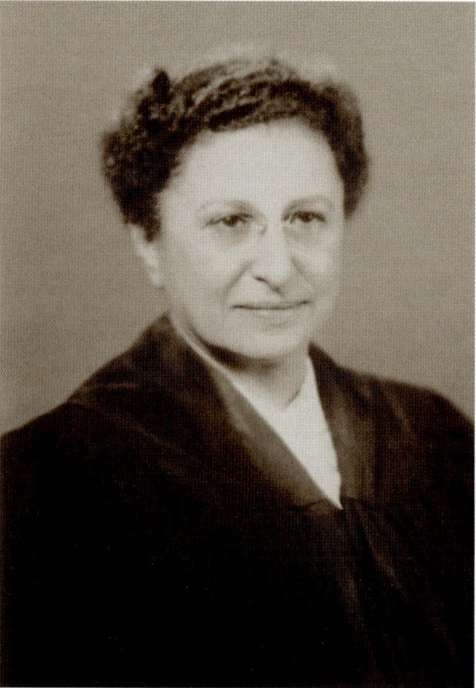

Jennie Loitman Barron (1891–1969)
Jennie Loitman Barron was a longtime Brighton resident who became the first woman to serve as a full-time judge in Massachusetts. She attended Boston University, where she was the first president of the Women's Suffrage Association. Despite her vigorous women's rights activism, she completed her undergraduate education in three years. At Boston University School of Law, she completed her law degree in two years and was admitted to the bar in 1914. In 1918, she married Samuel Barron Jr. and with him formed a Boston law firm. In 1926, while living in Brighton, Jennie was elected a member of the Boston School Committee. While serving as assistant attorney general, she was the first woman to present a case before a grand jury and the first to prosecute major criminal cases. She was appointed to the Boston Municipal Court in 1937 and to the Massachusetts Superior Court in 1959. (Schlesinger Library, Harvard University.)

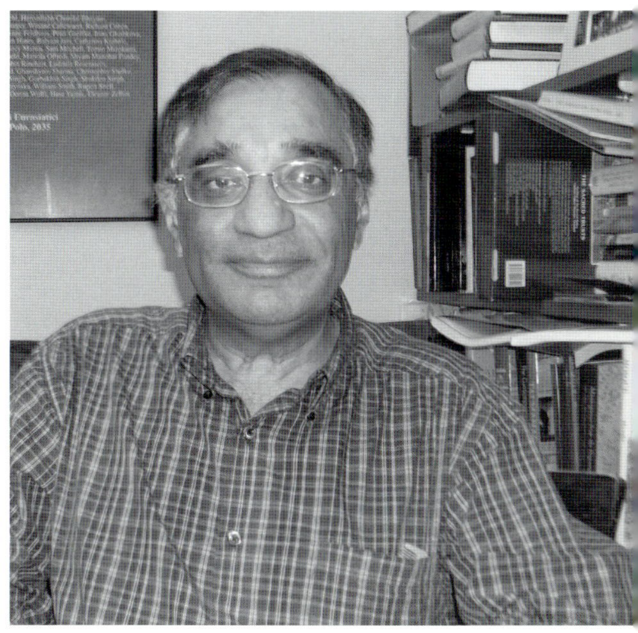

Ali Asani
Ali Asani is a member of the Nizari Ismailis, a division of Shia Islam. The group's prayer space, called a *jamat khana,* which means "house of community" is located in Packards Corner. The jamat khana has a rotating system of lay leadership. Asani has served as leader, called *Mukhi,* intermittently over the last 10 years. The leader takes responsibility for coordinating religious services and classes, visiting the sick, and setting up necessary support systems for those in need. The leader also oversees the welcoming of newcomers and celebrations of milestones, such as student graduations. As with other religious and civic organizations in Allston-Brighton, the members of the Ismaili community contribute to a variety of causes at the local, national, and international level. The Ismailis are happy to have found a home in Allston-Brighton and to be part of its vibrant community. (Photograph by Linda Mishkin.)

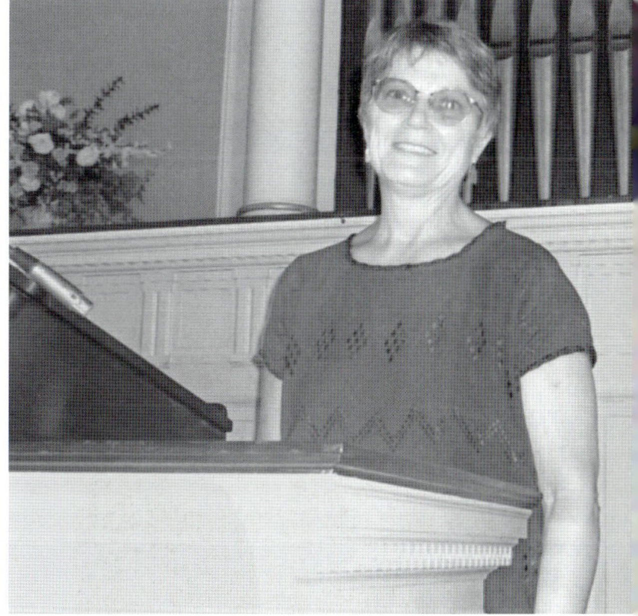

Rev. Karen Fritz
Rev. Karen Fritz has served at the Brighton-Allston Congregational Church since 1998. The congregation reflects the culture and ethnic diversity of the community and has 10 to 12 nationalities among its members. The church not only addresses the spiritual needs of the community but their social and physical needs as well. Over 30 years ago, the church opened a food pantry and soup kitchen and more recently began a movement and meditation class to relieve stress. The class is followed by a supper and draws people who are homeless or live in shelters, and some community residents who live alone and just want the companionship that a communal meal provides. The dinners also provide a sharing of ideas and suggestions as helpful resources to those gathered there. The church sponsors a thrift shop that sells donated clothing and household items at low cost. (Photograph by Linda Mishkin.)

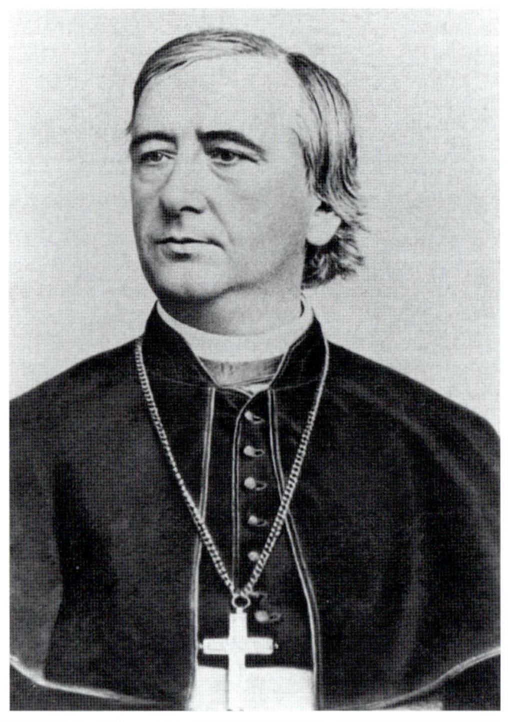

John Joseph Williams (1822–1907)

Fourth bishop and first archbishop of Boston, John Joseph Williams, the son of Irish immigrant parents, was born and raised in Boston. He received his training as a priest at the Sulpician College in Montreal and the Seminary of St. Sulpice in Paris. Williams served as curate of Boston's Cathedral of the Holy Cross from 1845 to 1855, as rector of the Cathedral from 1855 to 1857, and as pastor of St. James Church in Boston's Old South from 1855 to 1866. He was named fourth bishop of Boston in 1866, and became the city's first archbishop in 1875, a post he occupied until his death in 1907. Though Archbishop Williams never resided in Brighton, he is credited with having laid the foundation of Brighton's "Little Rome" with the establishment of St. John's Seminary on the hills of Brighton in 1884. (Both, BAHS archives.)

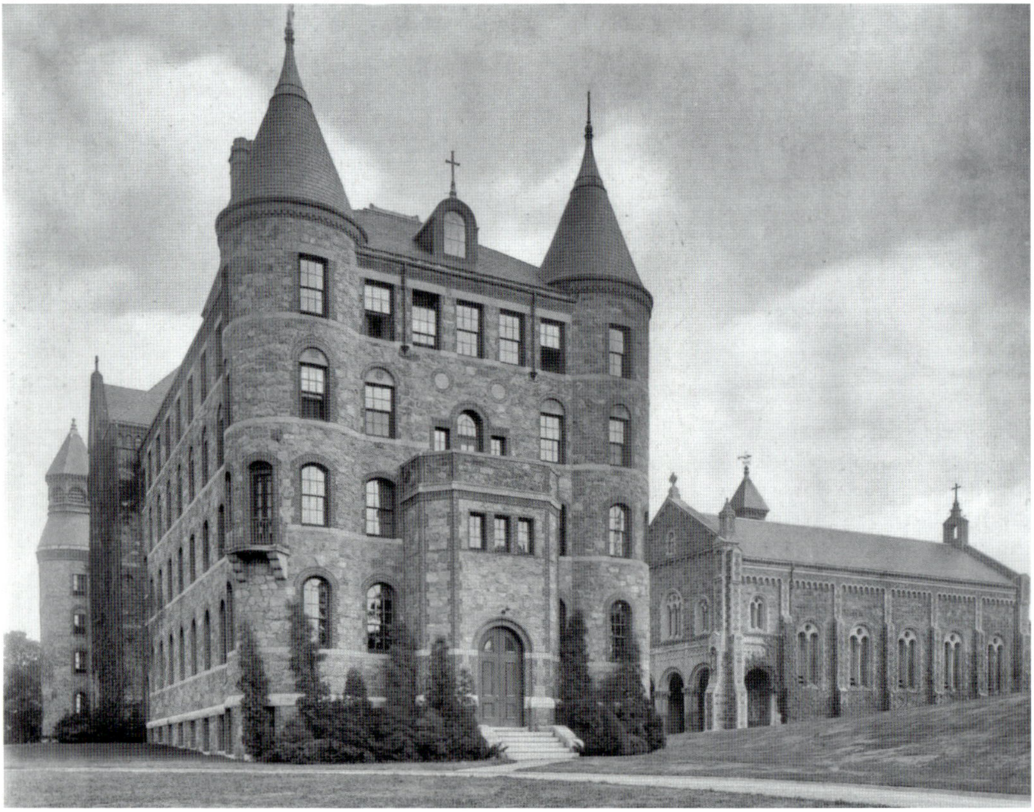

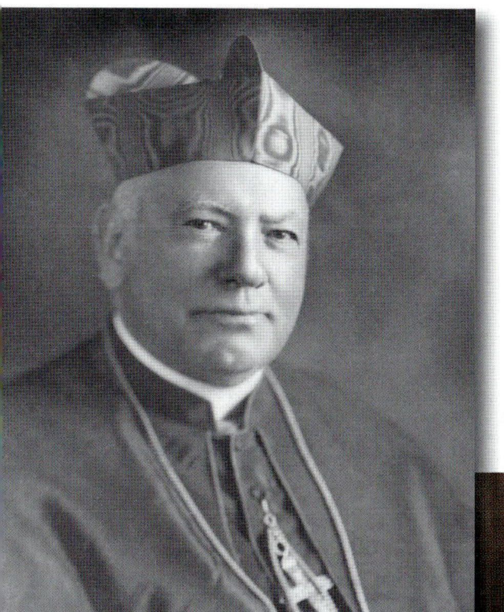

William Henry O'Connell (1859–1944)
William Henry O'Connell was born in Lowell, Massachusetts, to Irish immigrant parents. Educated at Boston College and the Pontifical North American College in Rome, O'Connell was named bishop of Portland, Maine, in 1901 and archbishop of Boston in 1907. In 1911, he became the first archbishop of Boston to be appointed a cardinal. In the 1920s, he moved the headquarters of the Roman Catholic Church in Boston to the grounds of St. John's Seminary in Brighton. (Photograph by Bachrach.)

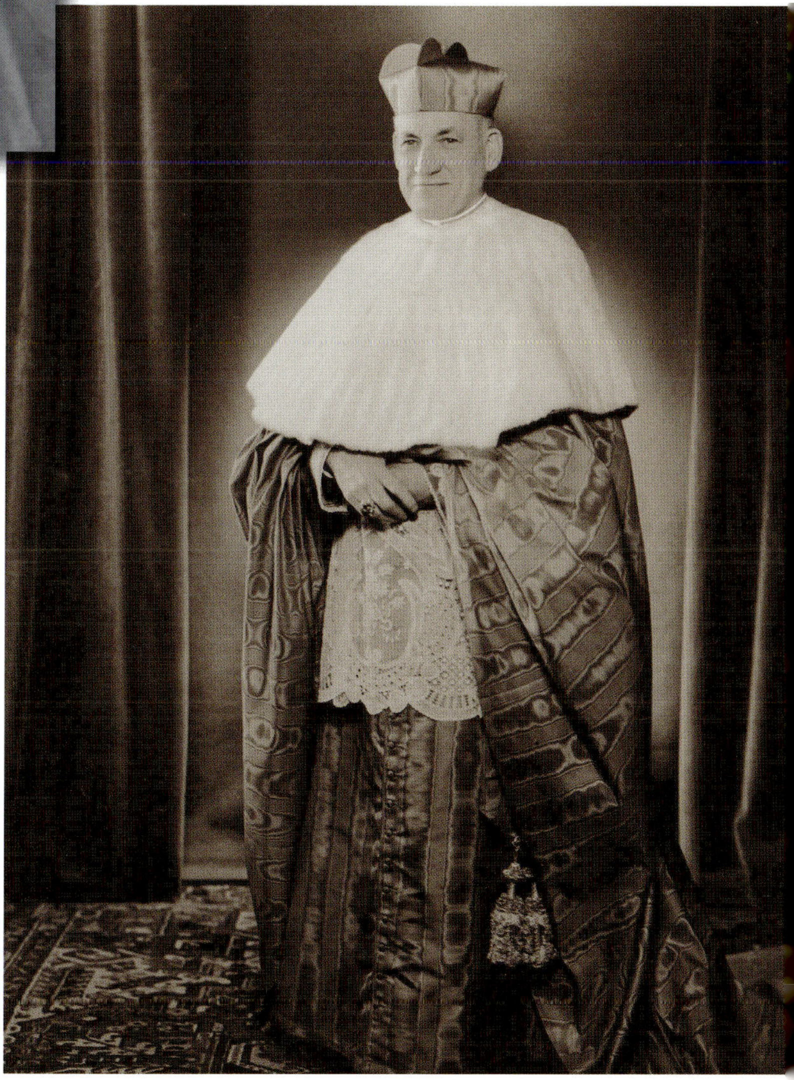

Richard Cushing (1895–1970)
The son of Irish immigrants, Richard Cushing was born in South Boston, Massachusetts, and was educated at Boston College and St. John's Seminary. From 1929 to 1944, he held the position of director of the Society for the Propagation of the Faith. In 1939, Cushing was appointed auxiliary bishop of Boston and in 1966 elevated to the post of archbishop of Boston, following the death of William Cardinal O'Connell. (Photograph by Bachrach.)

Humberto Madeiros (1915–1983)

The son of a farmer and storekeeper, Humberto Madeiros was born in the Portuguese Azores in 1915. He immigrated to the United States with his parents at age 16 in 1931. In 1946, he earned a master's degree from Catholic University and entered the priesthood. He added a doctor of sacred theology degree in 1952. Madeiros was named a monsignor in 1958. Named archbishop of Boston in 1970, he was elevated to the rank of cardinal in 1973. (Photograph by Bachrach.)

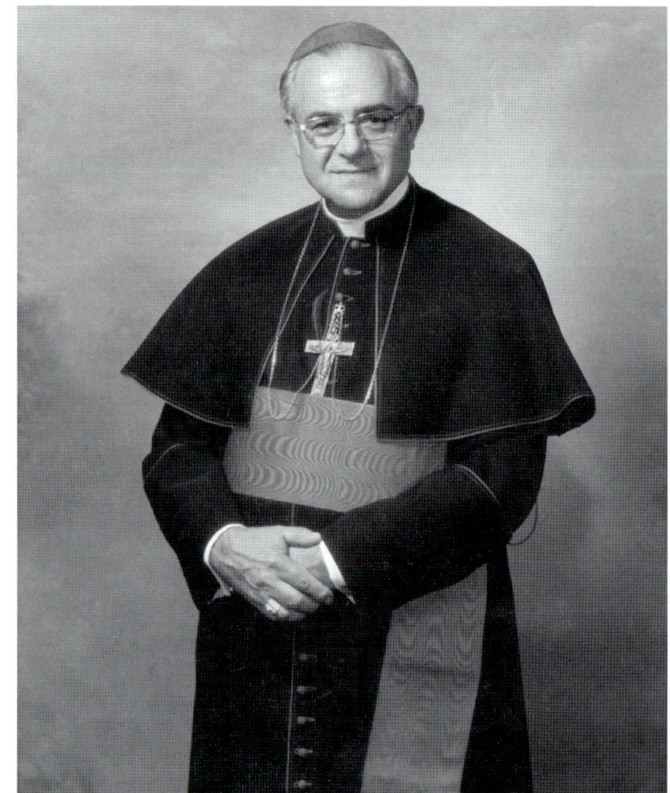

Bernard Law

The son of an airline executive, Bernard Law was born in Torreon, Mexico, in 1931. He graduated from Harvard University in 1953, then entered St. Joseph's Seminary in Louisiana and the Pontifical College Josephinum. He became a priest in 1961. In 1984, he was named archbishop of Boston and a cardinal in 1985. In 2002, when church documents came to light suggesting that he had covered up sexual abuse committed by priests in the Boston diocese, he resigned. He was subsequently appointed archpriest of the Papal Basilica of Santa Maria Maggiore in Rome. He resigned in 2011. (Photograph by Bachrach.)

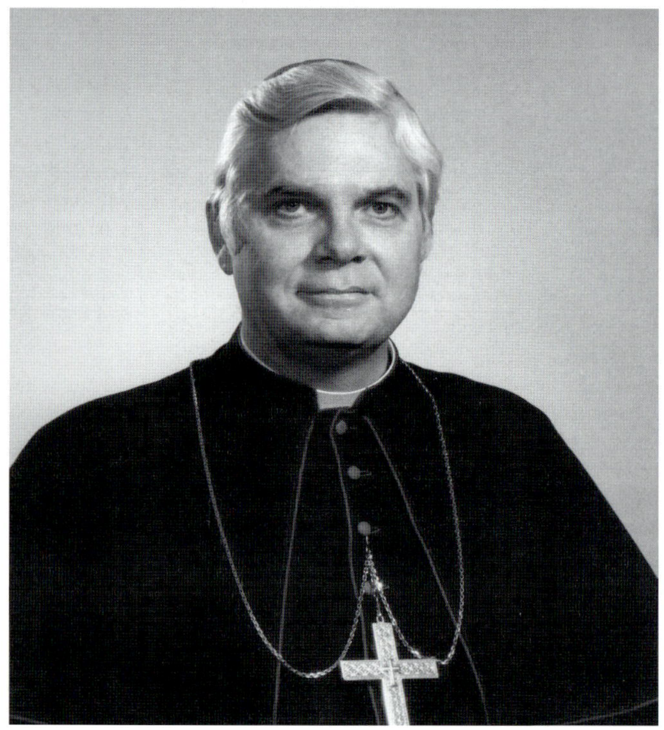

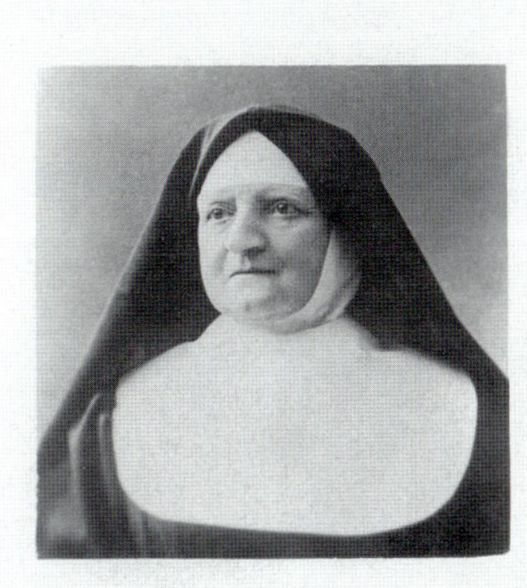

Foundress
of
The Sisters of Saint Joseph
Boston
Massachusetts

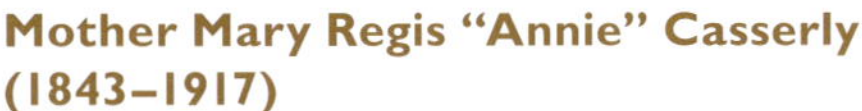

Mother Mary Regis "Annie" Casserly (1843–1917)
A leading educator in the Archdiocese of Boston, Mother Regis established Mount St. Joseph's Academy in 1885. In 1891, the academy moved from Cambridge to its current site in Brighton. At the same time, she established the motherhouse of the Boston Sisters of St. Joseph in Brighton and became the first general superior of the Boston congregation. Regis College in Weston, founded in 1927 by the Sisters of St. Joseph, was named in her memory. (Sisters of St. Joseph.)

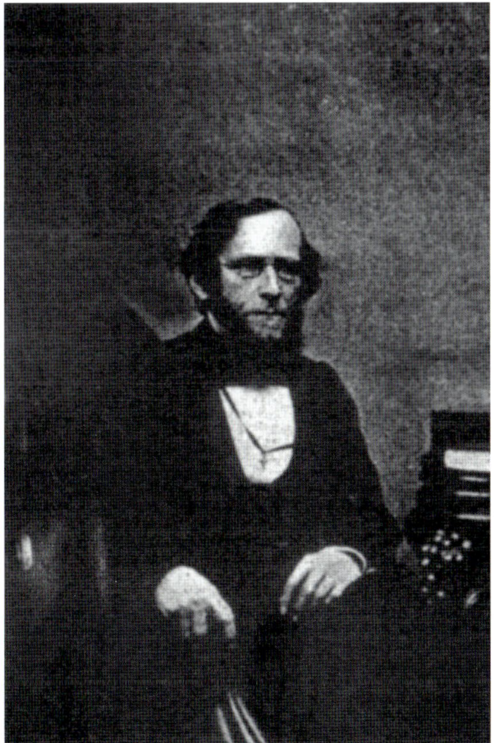

Frederic Augustus Whitney (1812–1880)
Rev. Frederick Augustus Whitney was a longtime minister of the First Church of Brighton. He graduated from Harvard College in 1833 and continued his studies at the Cambridge Divinity School, graduating in 1838. It was while attending Harvard that he became acquainted with the painter Washington Allston, who maintained a studio in nearby Central Square. It was Whitney who suggested in 1867 that the name Allston be applied as a postal address to the eastern half of the town of Brighton. (BAHS archives.)

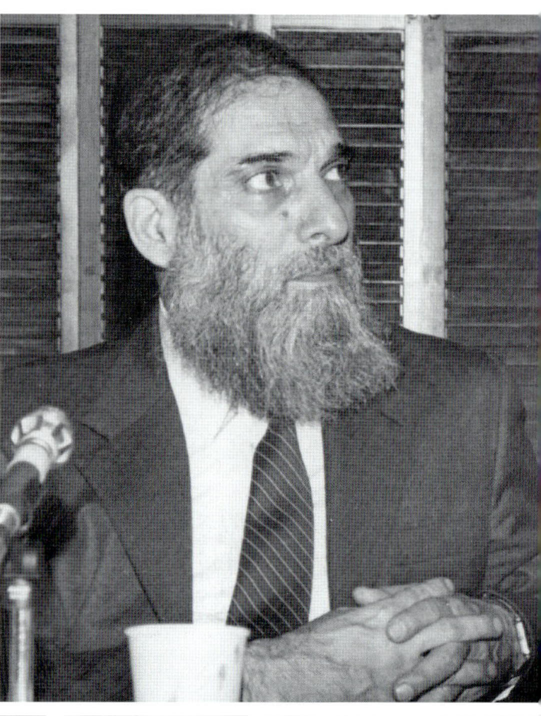

Rabbi Isadore Twersky

Rabbi Isadore Twersky was the descendent of a long line of Hasidic masters. He held religious services in his home in Brighton. He taught Jewish studies at Harvard and advised doctoral students. He was renowned as a scholar and interpreter of Jewish tradition and for his work on Maimonides and other central Jewish thinkers. He was a significant force in the growth of Jewish learning nationwide and a builder of institutions and programs. He died in 1997. (Center for Jewish Studies, Harvard University.)

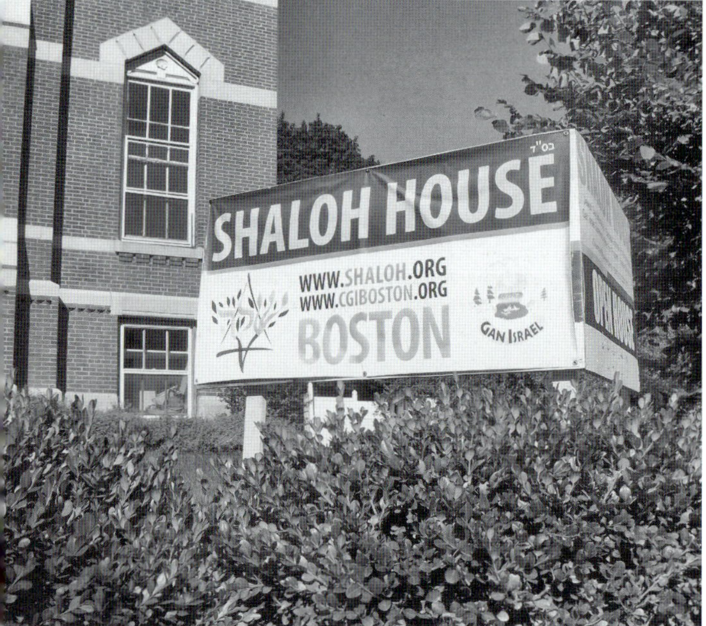

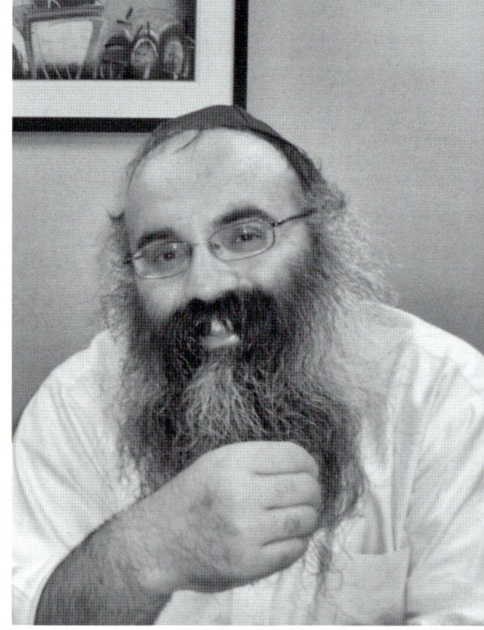

Rabbi Dan Rodkin

Rabbi Dan Rodkin is head master of Shaloh House School, where he has implemented a challenging and well-rounded curriculum that includes both Judaic and secular subjects. He was born in Russia, attended seminaries in Russia, Israel, and the United States, and earned a master of arts degree in theology from the Rabbinical College of America. Rabbi Rodkin and his wife live in Brighton, where they are raising their six children. (Photographs by Linda Mishkin.)

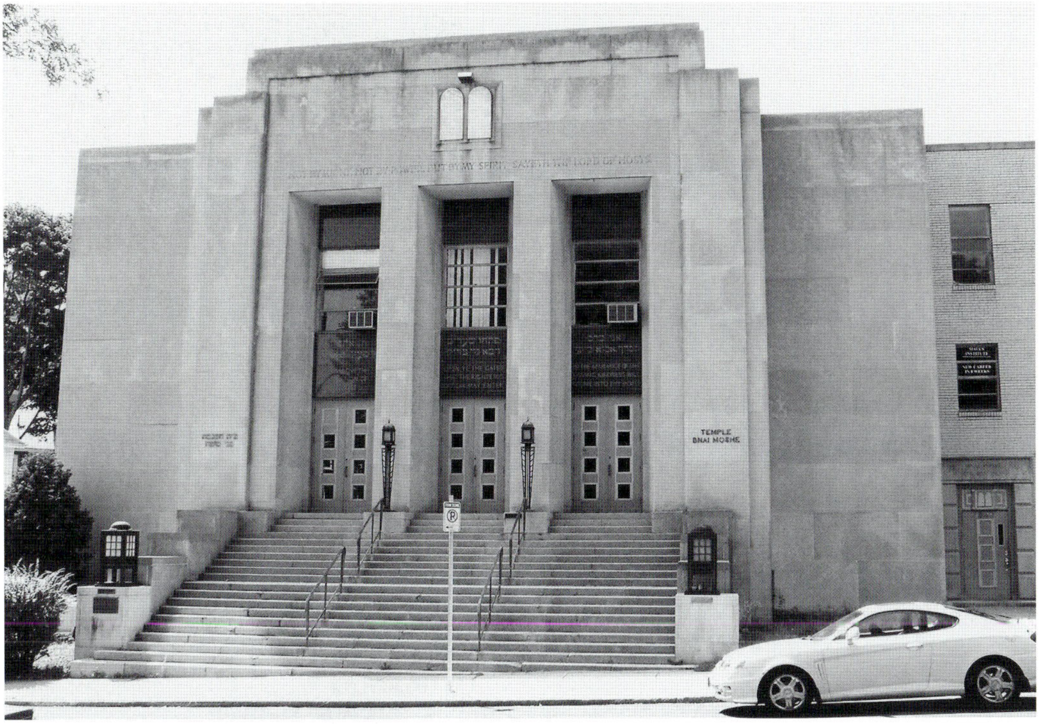

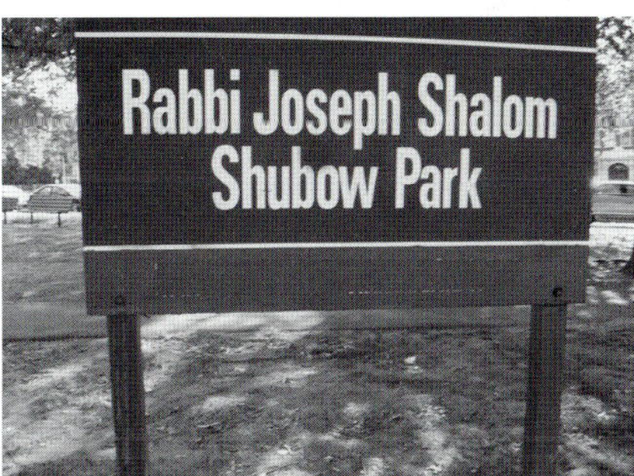

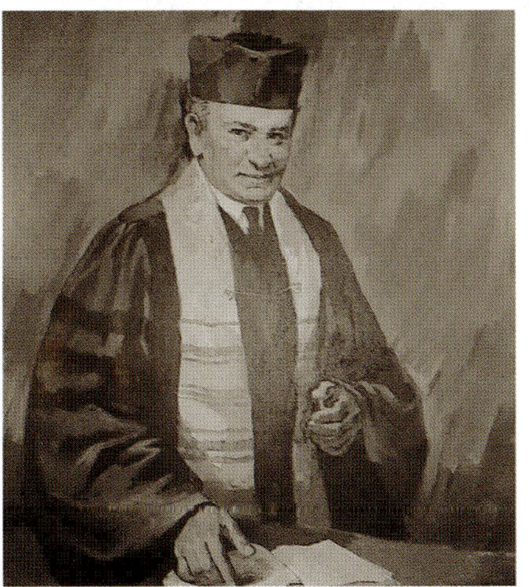

Rabbi Joseph Shubow (1899–1969)

Rabbi Joseph Shalom Shubow, who presided over Brighton's largest Synagogue, Temple B'nai Moshe, for many decades, was born in 1899 in Olita, Lithuania. He came to the United States with his family at a young age. At Harvard, he received a bachelor of arts in 1920, a master of arts in 1921, and doctorate of philosophy in 1959. Shubow was a leader of both the Boston Jewish community and the American Zionist movement. In 1943, then in his early 40s, he enlisted in the US Army, serving as a chaplain in Europe with the 9th Army through 1946. Shubow served as president of the New England Division of the American Jewish Congress (1941–1943), as president of the Greater Boston Rabbinical Association (1950–1953), and as vice president of the Zionist Organization of America (1961–1969). Shubow died in Brighton in 1969. (Photograph by Vlad.)

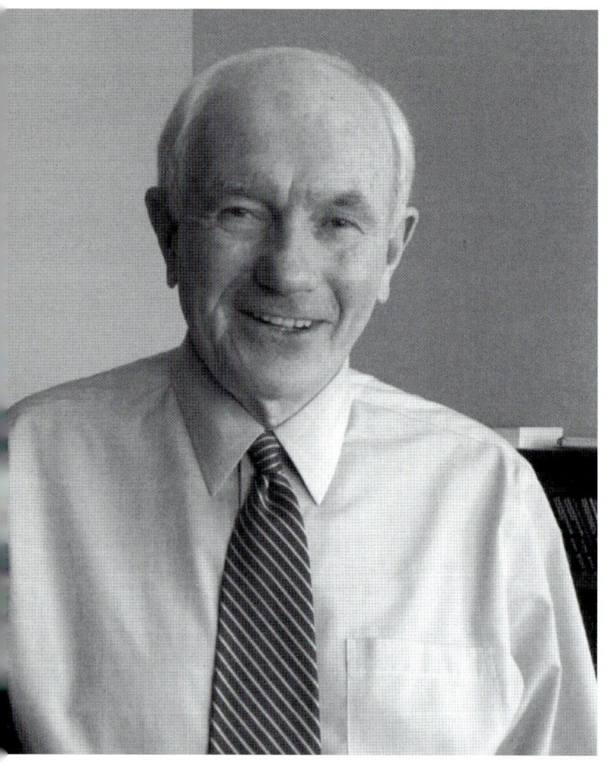

Judge Robert J. McKenna Jr.
Robert J. McKenna Jr. was born in Brighton and has lived there ever since. Growing up, he remembers winters when hundreds of ice skaters crowded onto Chandler Pond and summers when he worked as a caddy at what was then Commonwealth Golf Course, all within a short walk of his family home on Brayton Road. He worked for many years in the Suffolk County District Attorney's office and was appointed judge in 1997 when William Weld was governor of Massachusetts. For five years, McKenna served as first justice of the Concord District Court and then returned to Boston when the gun session was introduced in response to gang violence. Early in his career, McKenna worked on a new initiative called Elderly Hot Lunch Program. His natural writing ability was discovered years before. As an undergraduate, McKenna took a creative writing course taught by Harry Kemelman, well-known author of the successful Rabbi Small series of mystery books. Kemelman praised and encouraged McKenna's writing. The world of fiction was not to benefit from McKenna's writing skills, but the legal world certainly has. (Photograph by Linda Mishkin.)

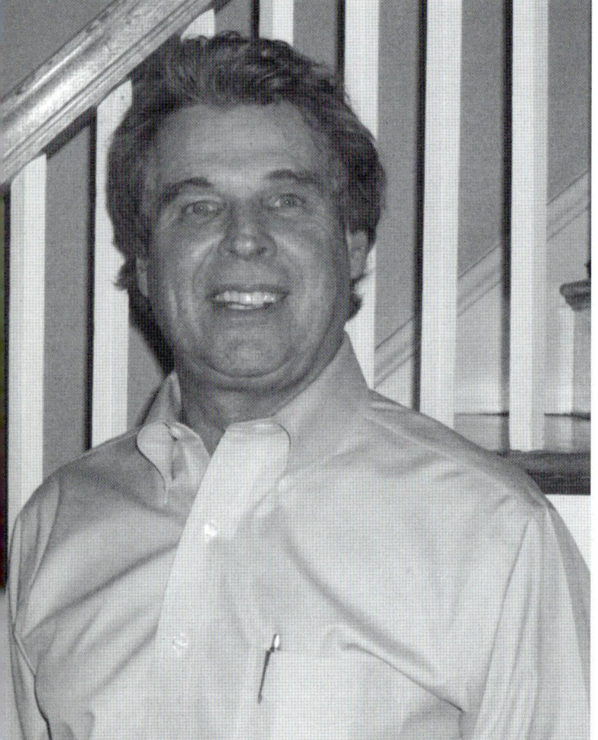

Attorney Richard Dyer
Richard Dyer grew up in L.A. (Lower Allston) and attended St. Anthony's school. He was an award-winning boy scout in the troop led by Joseph Smith (page 56), but as a teen, Dyer sought other adventures. Spending time with a new crowd in Harvard Square, he became involved with drugs. Eventually, he appeared In Brighton District Court before his former neighbor, Judge Charles Artesani (page 124). Dyer was sentenced to jail, halfway houses, and drug programs. Giving credit to Artesani, his parents, and others, Dyer was able to turn his life around. He got his GED degree while in jail, then he went to Boston State College. His volunteer work as counselor to young people in the court system was noticed by attorneys, who encouraged Dyer to study law. Only Northeastern University School of Law admitted him. After being pardoned by Governor Dukakis, Dyer successfully appealed for permission to sit for the bar exam; he passed, and practiced business law before switching to criminal defense. He now practices in the same Brighton court where he was convicted. Today, along with enjoying a successful career, Dyer is happily married and raising six great kids. (Photograph by Linda Mishkin.)

CHAPTER EIGHT

Artists, Athletes, and Entertainers

The artistic and athletic talent of Allston-Brighton is well documented in the narratives collected in this chapter. Only time and space placed limits on the number of people to include. Whether their art is displayed in a theater, gallery, street corner, side of a building, or playing field, here are examples of what members of our community have achieved. Natural ability, arduous training, and unique insight combine to give lucky audiences and onlookers the opportunity to experience the art of these legendary locals.

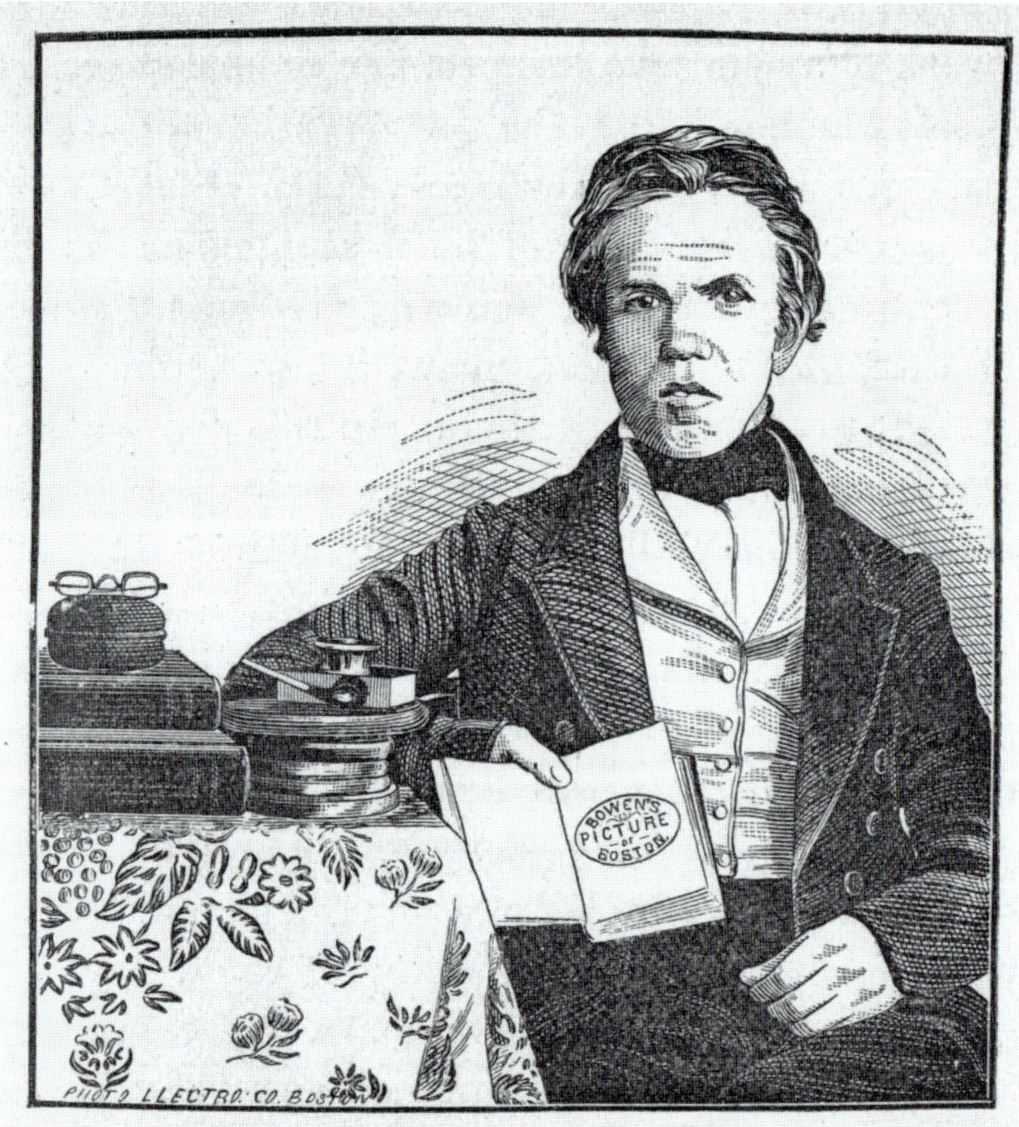

Abel Bowen (1790–1850)
Leading American illustrator and engraver Abel Bowen was not only a writer of American history but also an artist who preserved pictures of its past. He was the originator and publisher of Snow's *History of Boston*, a new form of history in which illustrations were to "predominate" (1825). Born in New York City in 1790, this self-trained engraver moved to Boston in 1812 to work as a printer in the Columbian Museum, Boston's oldest museum, which was owned and operated by his uncle Daniel Bowen. Abel Bowen's *Picture of Boston, or the Citizen's and Stranger's Guide to the Metropolis of Massachusetts* (1829) was an early pocket guide to the history and "present time" sites of Boston. It mentions Brighton, the Brighton Fair, and the fact that in 1837 the town had 1,500 inhabitants. Bowen resided with his uncle on an estate in Brighton called Lime Grove, west of Oak Square. He moved to Boston in 1814, following his marriage to Elizabeth Healey, where he continued as one of the city's leading illustrators and publishers. (Boston Public Library.)

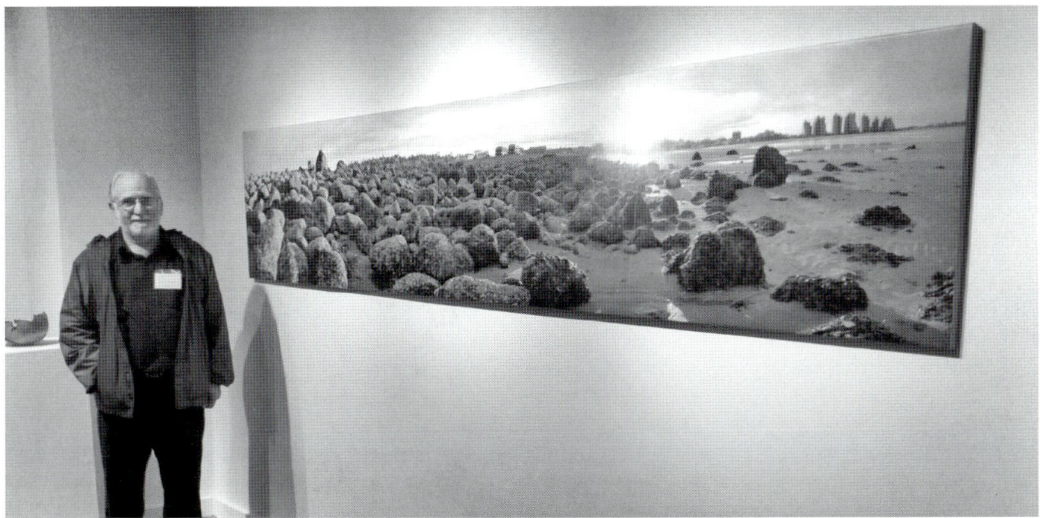

Fran Gardino

Fran Gardino is a painterly photographer. He majored in painting at Massachusetts College of Art but took many courses in photography. He works with digital cameras and is partial to printing on unconventional materials as well as traditional photograph paper. He likes to use canvas and rice paper. He enjoys using these materials because they not only add soft texture, but also because the finished product looks like calligraphy or watercolor paintings. The canvas also frees him to print massive images. When he mounts photographs for shows, he prefers not covering them with glass so that the observer experiences the photographs more directly. In addition to appearing in art shows and museums, Gardino is represented by a gallery in Vermont. His work is also available through Allston's Open Studios. (Both, Fran Gardino.)

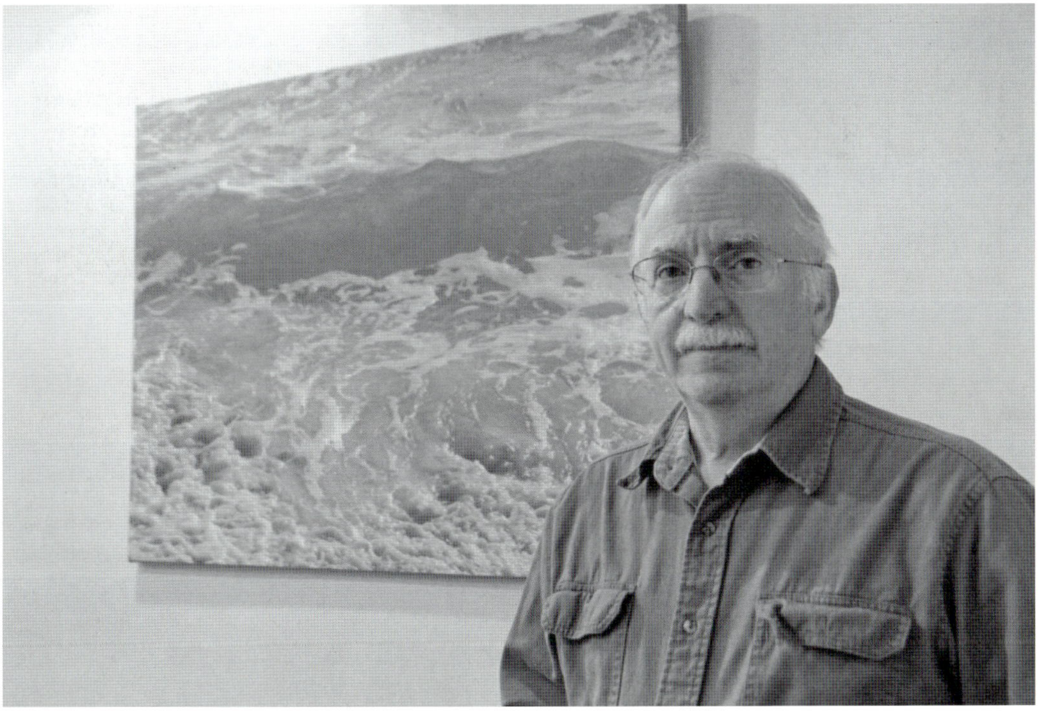

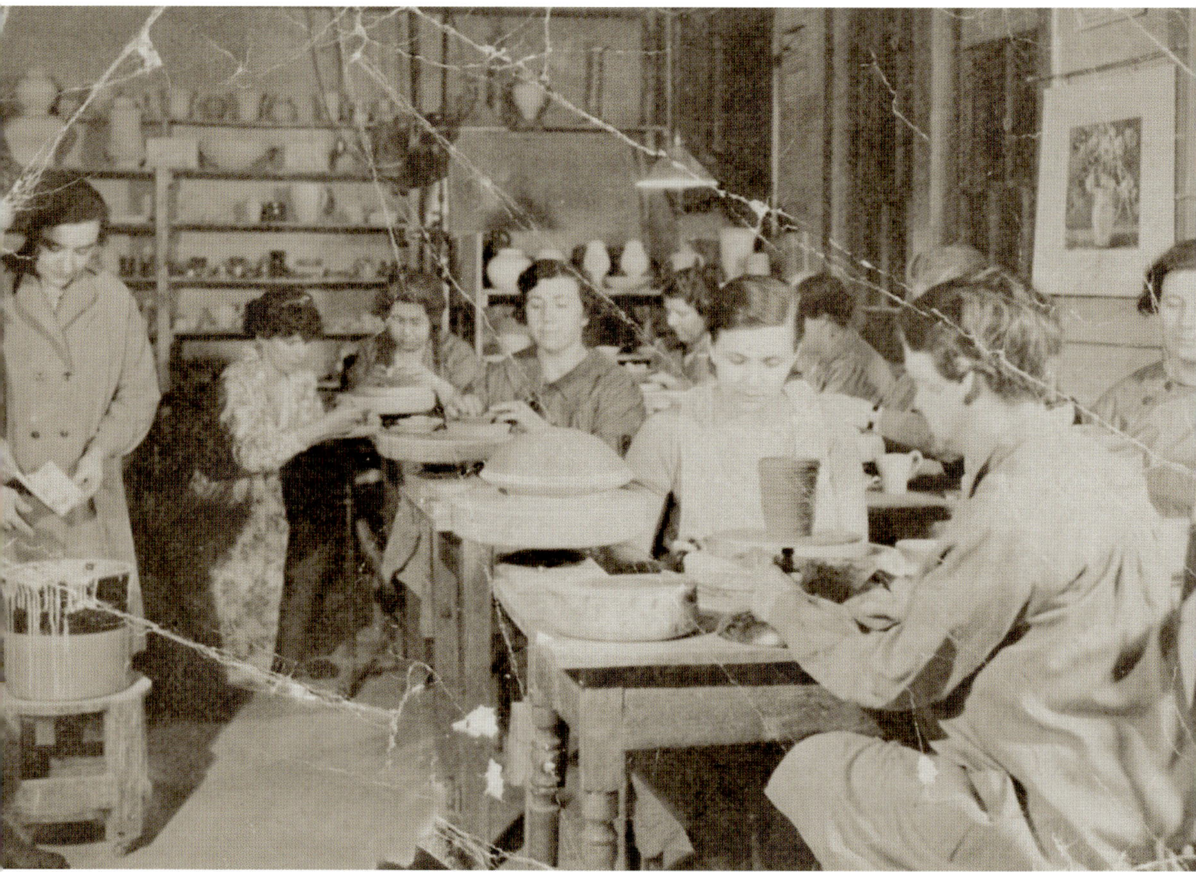

Edith Guerrier and Edith Brown

Edith Guerrier and Edith Brown moved their pottery workshop and training center, Paul Revere Pottery, to the Aberdeen section of Brighton in 1915. The move from the North End of Boston was instigated by a need for more space. Guerrier and Brown had established Paul Revere Pottery as a means to provide daughters of recent immigrants (mostly Jewish and Italian) with reliable, healthy, and financially rewarding employment. Compared with the prevailing conditions in factories, where such young women might otherwise have taken jobs at much lower wages, the Paul Revere Pottery workshop was well-lit, well-ventilated, and always decorated with flowers. Guerrier and Brown designed the English-style stucco Brighton building that included space for the two of them to live. The pottery opened with a workforce of 12 girls, a "jigger man" (pottery wheel operator), two potters, and an Evangelical minister, whose job it was to fire the kiln and to act as watchman. The workshop remained in Brighton until 1942, when it finally went out of business. (BAHS archives.)

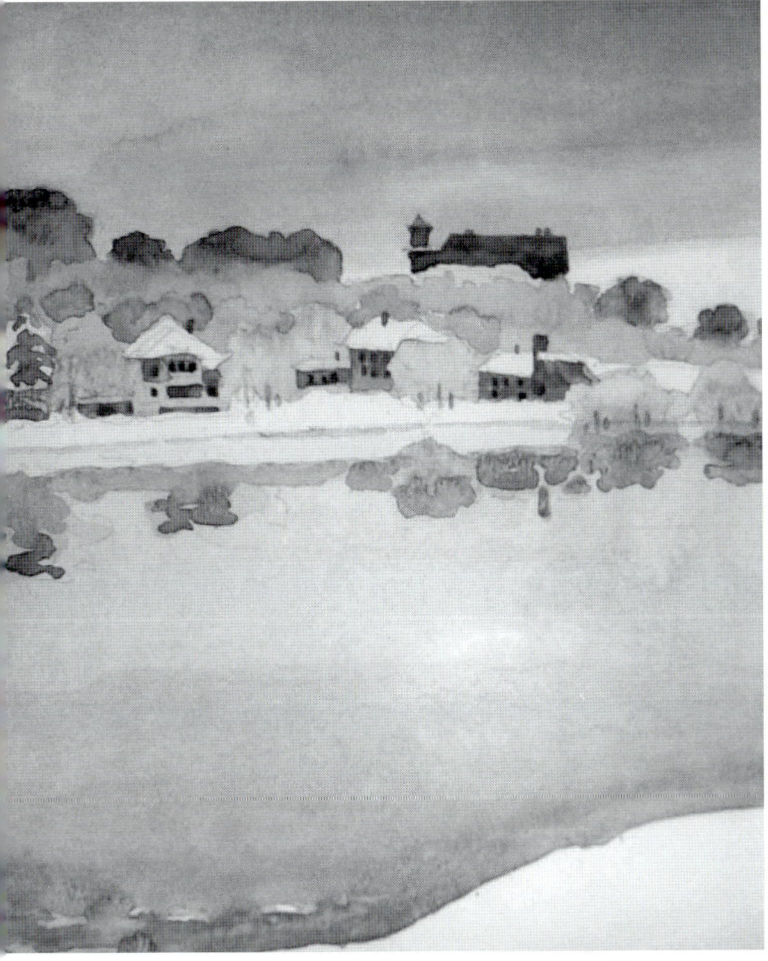

Sofya Suller

Sofya Suller was a successful architect and artist in St. Petersburg (then Leningrad), Russia. She, her husband, and their 21-year-old son decided to leave because of growing anti-Semitism. They arrived in Brighton in 1980 and stayed with friends before moving to the apartment where she and her husband still reside. She found work as an architect. Later, when she was laid off, she focused full-time on her artwork. She had been well known in St. Petersburg, but here, she was starting new. For a while, she worked with an art dealer who had several other clients. She enjoys working with watercolor, acrylic, and charcoal. She especially likes watercolor because of its unpredictability. It flows. She has a body of work that depicts scenes of Boston and Brighton in particular. (Photographs by Linda Mishkin.)

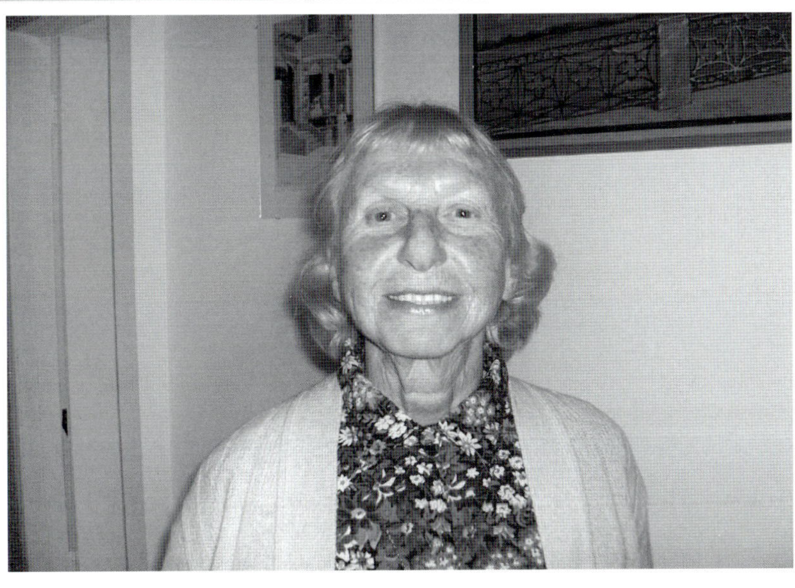

Edward Everett Rice (1847–1924)
A pioneer of American musical theatre, composer, and producer of full-length burlesques (musical comedies which parodied literary works or personalities of the time), Edward Everett Rice was born in Brighton. According to Brighton historian J.P.C. Winship, Rice was "well remembered by the old residents of Brighton as that 'Rice boy,' who at an early age turned his attention to drama." Weekly farces performed in his father's barn were smash hits, and Rice left home in his teenage years to become an itinerant actor. He returned to Boston to work as a printer and later as advertising agent of the Cunard steamship line. It was as a member of the dining clubs Papyrus and Orpheus that he gained a reputation for musical entertainment. No evening was considered complete without Rice performing at the piano. In 1869, Rice married Clara E. Rich, daughter of Isaac E. Rich, an important theatrical manager. (Library of Congress.)

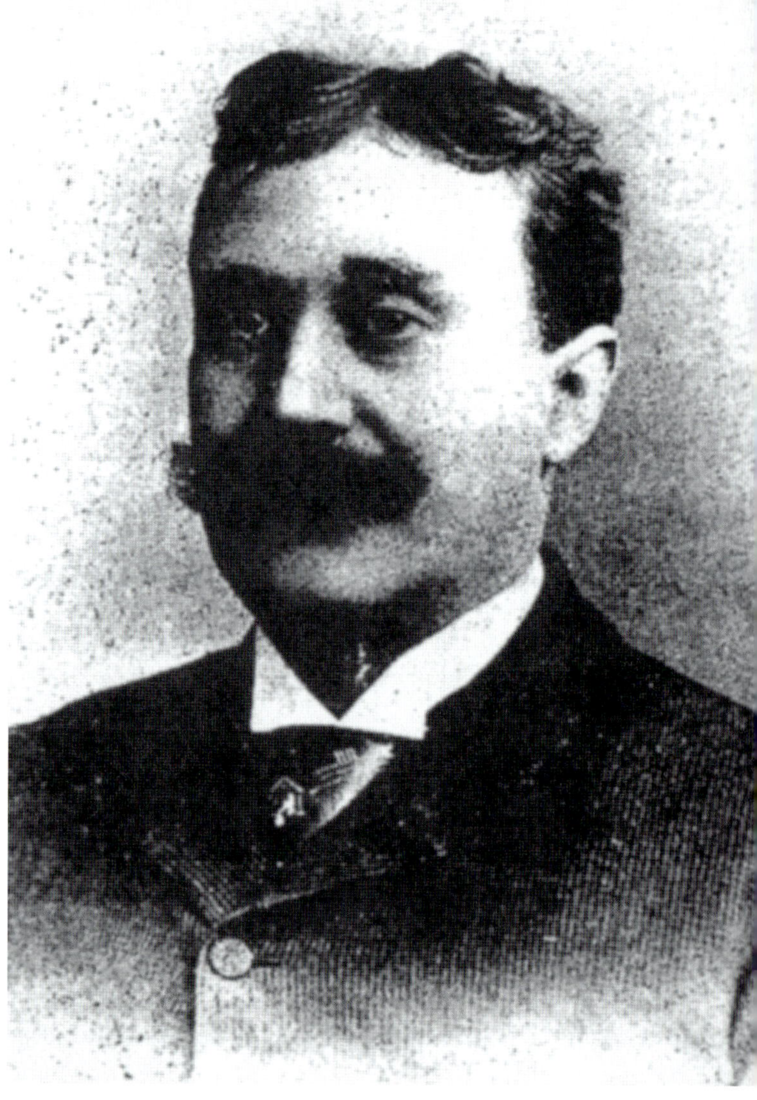

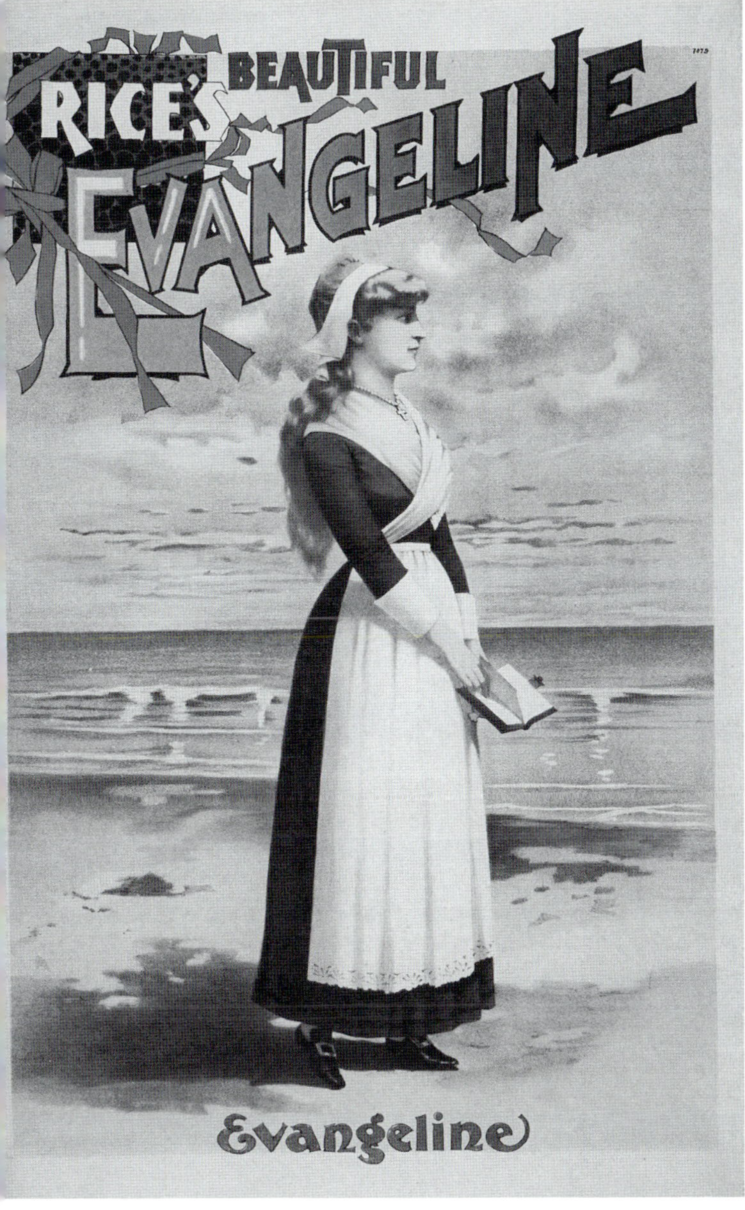

Evangeline Playbill
Rice joined forces in 1874 with John Cheever Goodwin to write *Evangeline*, a hugely popular burlesque musical based upon a poem by Henry Wadsworth Longfellow, the first American production billed as musical comedy. The opening number gives this accolade to the American poet (and helps to give a flavor of the production): "There's a man you all have heard about, / Who poetry has written, / That all of you have read, / And on it have been smitten." In 1884, Rice's smash hit *Adonis* was the first musical to run more than 500 performances in New York. In 1898, he produced *The Origin of the Cake Walk; or, Clorindy*; it was the first time a musical written and acted by African Americans was presented to white audiences. Rice introduced many major personalities to the theater world, including Lillian Russell, Jerome Kern, Fay Templeton, Julian Eltinge, and Henry E. Dicey. (Boston Public Library.)

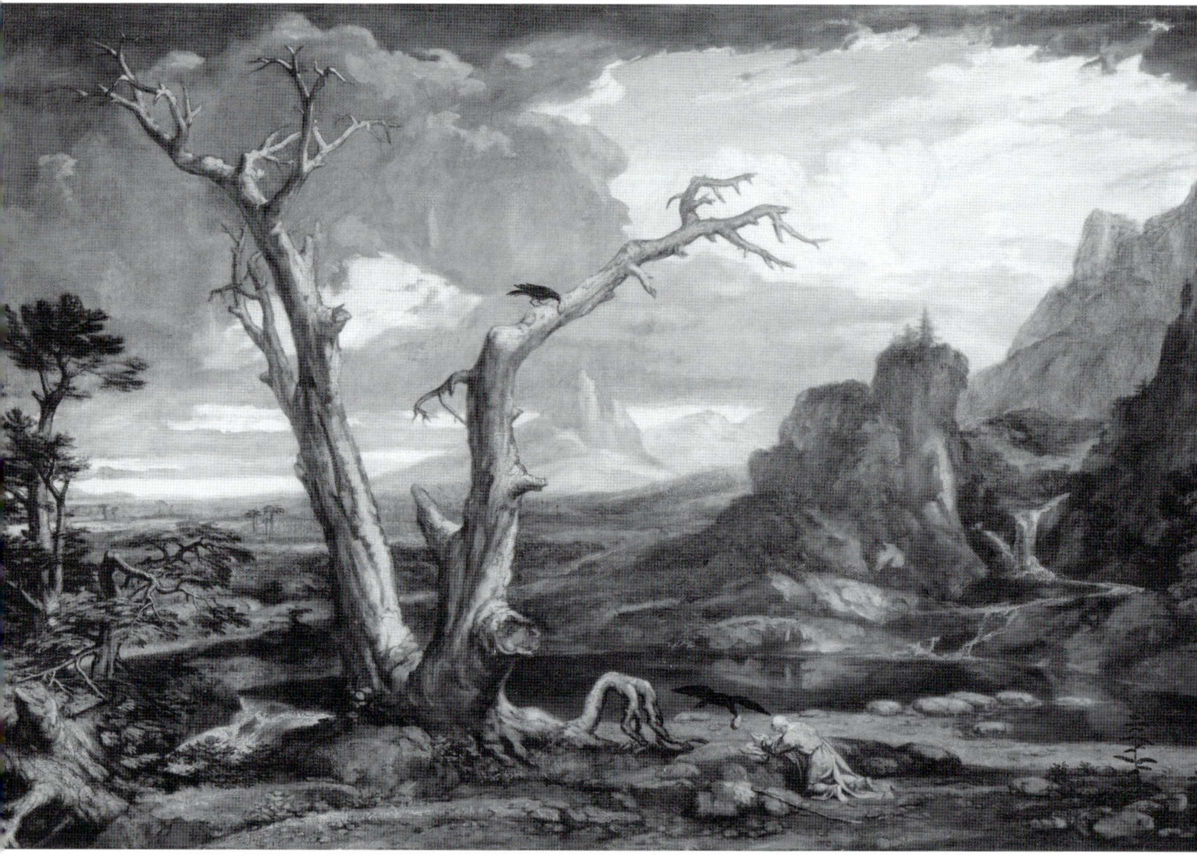

Washington Allston (1779–1843)
Washington Allston pioneered America's Romantic movement of landscape painting and influenced its development. His work is known for its vibrant color contrasts and dramatic subject matter. After graduating from Harvard in 1800, he traveled throughout Western Europe. He studied at the Royal Academy in London. For a few years, he lived in Rome. He became enamored of the great Venetian Renaissance painters for their use of technique and tone, which he emulated. He has been referred to as the "American Titian." In addition to painting, he was also a published writer of poetry and the book *Lectures on Art, and Poems*. Allston's work was admired by Samuel Taylor Coleridge, Ralph Waldo Emerson, and Henry Wadsworth Longfellow. After living in Europe for several years, in 1818 he returned to the United States and lived in Cambridge until his death. The community of Allston is named in his honor. (BAHS archives.)

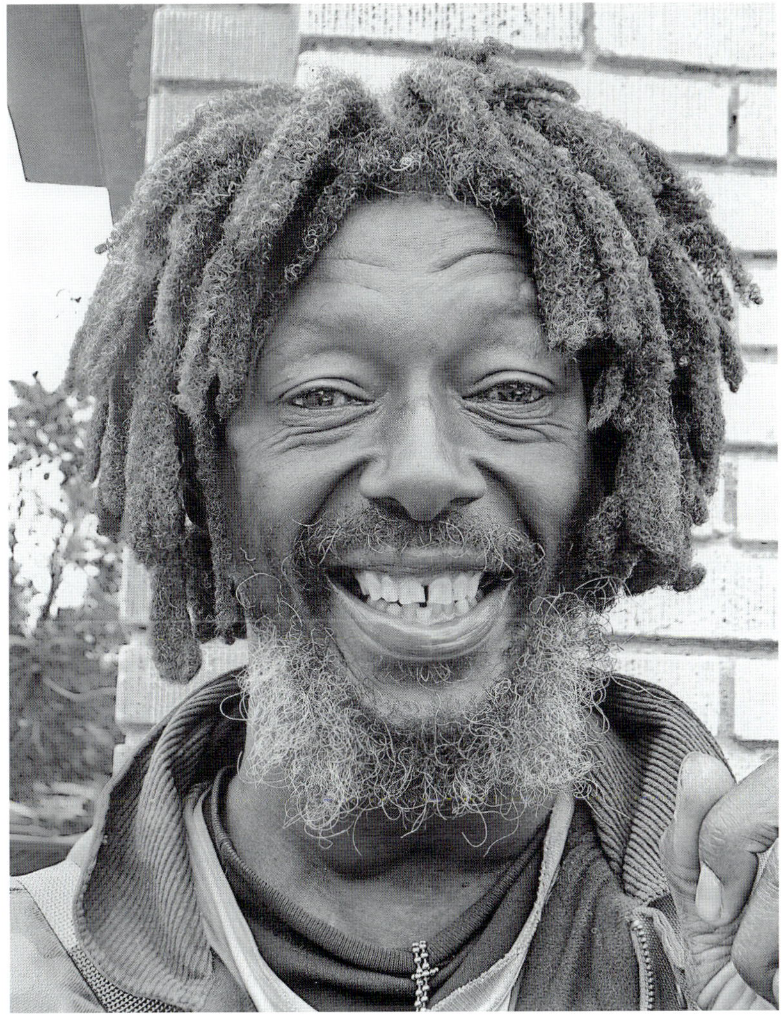

Harold Madison III "Mr. Butch" (1951–2007)

"I do art with all my heart," said "Mr. Butch," a musician and street philosopher. Called "The Mayor of Allston," Harold Madison III traveled the streets of Allston dispensing his brand of wisdom. He was one of seven children of Virginia Moore and Harold Madison Jr. from Worcester, Massachusetts, and started playing an acoustic guitar when he was 10. He settled in Boston sometime in 1976. From 1981, he lived on the streets. Generous merchants of Allston cared for his well being, banked his money, and provided him with places to sleep. Mr. Butch was an "exceedingly gentle soul" with a gift for connecting with people. He was a friend to students at the local colleges, especially Berklee School of Music, and played on their albums and appeared on project videos. During the 1980s, Mr. Butch's fame among the local musicians grew, and he performed gigs at various local venues. In 1984, Butch went on WMBR FM's *The Mystery Girls* to announce his platform for a gubernatorial run. Co-host Spencer Gates expected a wild ride, but remembered, "[Butch] made total sense. It was not crazy-drunk talk. He was clear, lucid. Who would've thought that? If only he had won. He was truly a better man than ANY politician." Mr. Butch is immortalized in an Allston mural by artist Elli Crocker. Mr. Butch died in 2007 at the age of 56 from a scooter accident. He was widely loved and remembered by the 1,000 people who attended his memorial parade and left messages on his remembrance pages. "He would have thought this was awesome," said Madison's sister, Janette. "This is Mr. Butch-style. Nothing fancy; just rejoicing." (Hercule Dubois.)

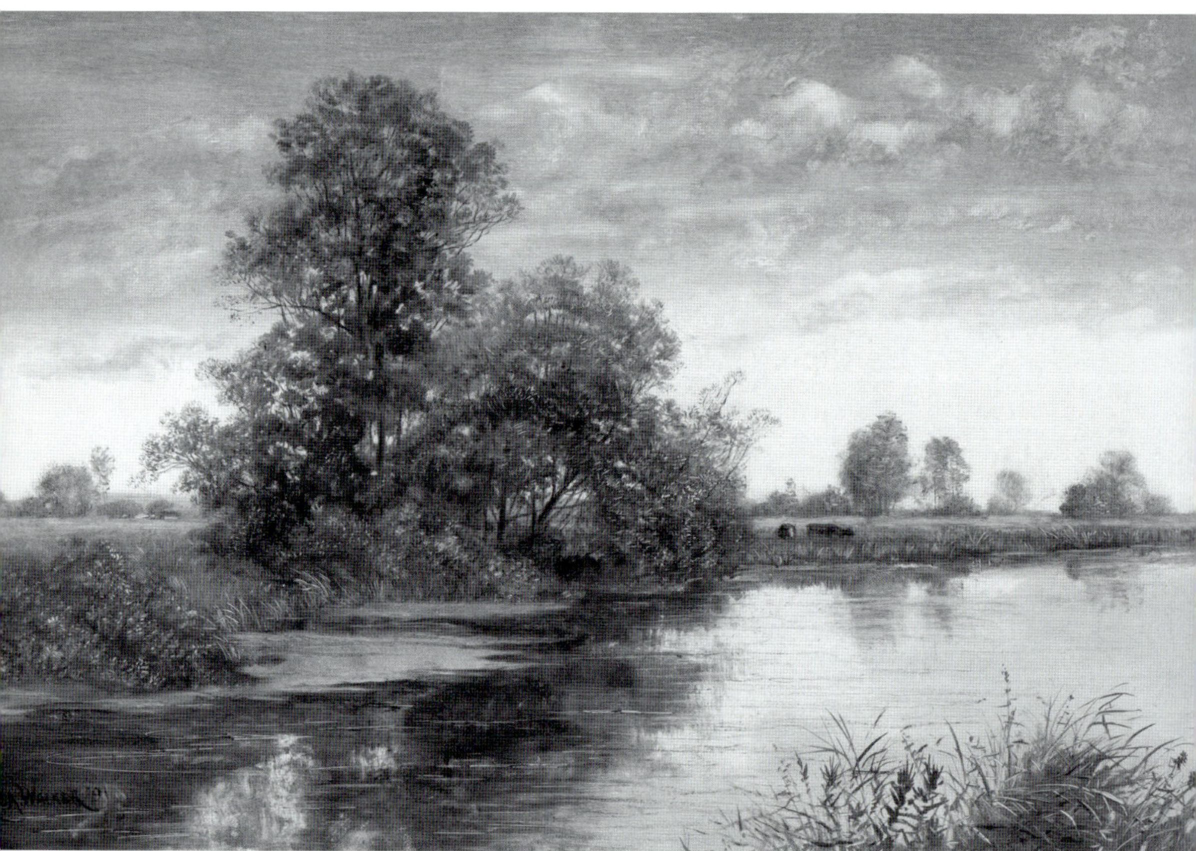

Charles Alvah Walker (1848–1925)
An interesting rivalry grew between artist Albion Bicknell and Charles Alvah Walker as to who first used the term "monotype" in print (November 1881). Odds went to Brighton citizen Charles Alvah Walker, a largely self-taught artist who lived in Brighton's Aberdeen section for many years. He exhibited chiefly at the National Academy of Design in New York using oils, etching, wood and steel engraving, and monotype as his media. He showed his work at many important Boston galleries. Walker's monotypes were concerned with nature, light, and atmosphere. A 1997 exhibit at the Smithsonian, "Singular Impressions: The Monotype in America," featured works by Walker alongside works by William Merritt Chase, Frank Duveneck, Maurice Prendergast, and Jasper Johns. This photograph shows Charles Alvah Walker's *Pastoral Landscape.* (Smithsonian American Art Museum through the Robert Tyler Davis Memorial Fund.)

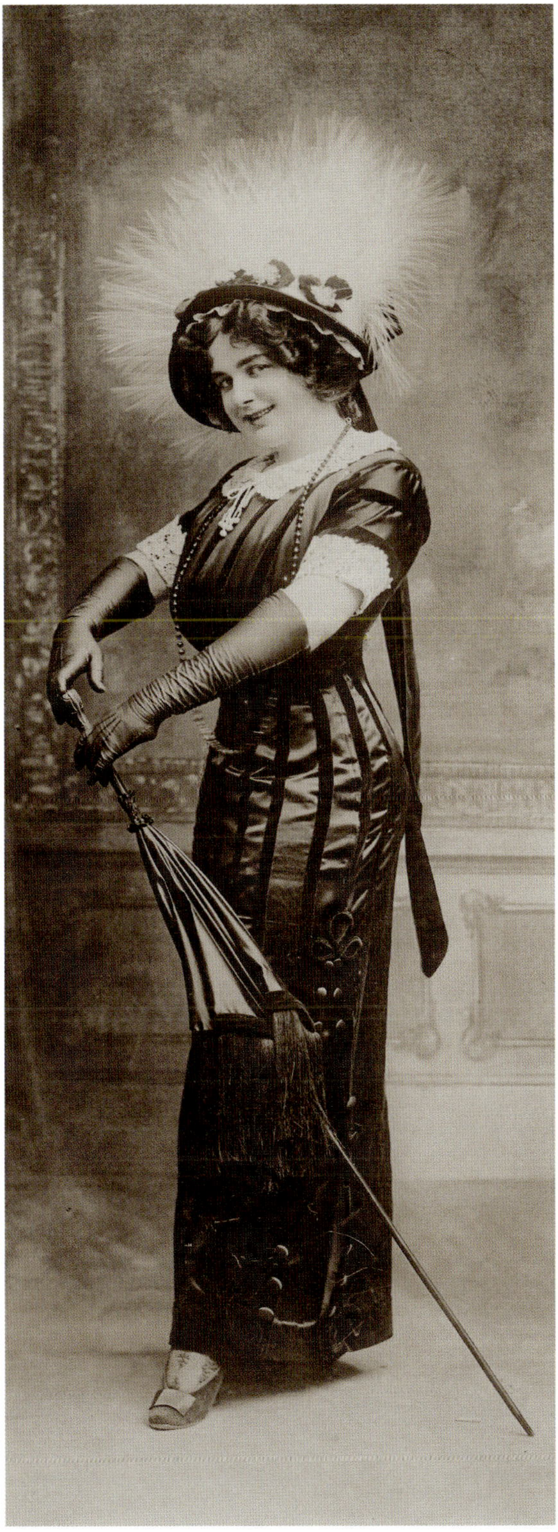

Julian Eltinge (né William Julian Dalton) (1881–1941)

American stage and silent screen actor Julian Eltinge was the greatest female impersonator of his day. Eltinge grew up in Allston on Mechanics Street and attended the Washington Allston Grammar School. His was introduced to the Boston stage (playing a little girl) at the age of 10. A rousing success, he continued to hone his art, making his New York debut in 1904. He crafted his female characters tastefully, imitating the stereotypical female images of the day rather than portraying women in the highly burlesque style of his time. Off stage, Eltinge strove to create a public impression of manliness that sharply contrasted with his stage persona. By the 1930s, audience tastes were changing. He suffered from alcoholism and financial problems, and his career began to go into decline. (Harvard Theatre Collection.)

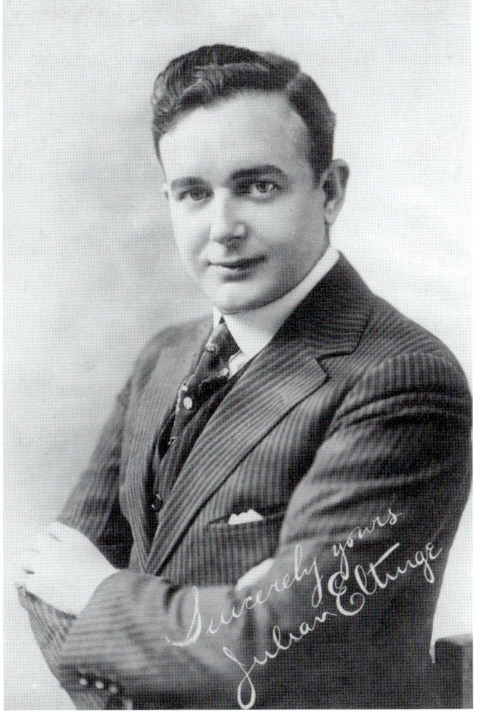

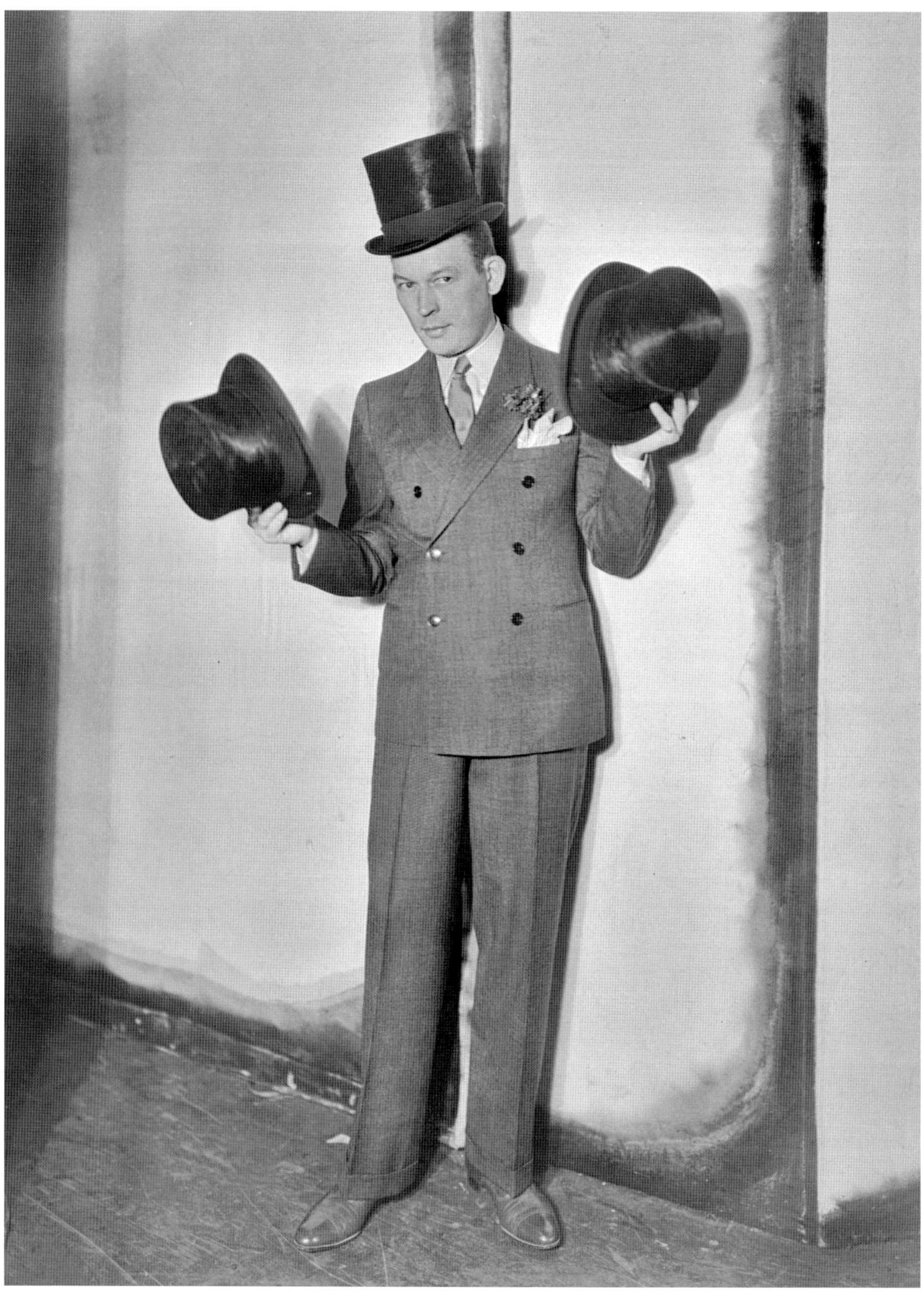

"You can count on the thumb of one hand the American who is at once a comedian, a humorist, a wit, and a satirist, and his name is Fred Allen."
—James Thurber

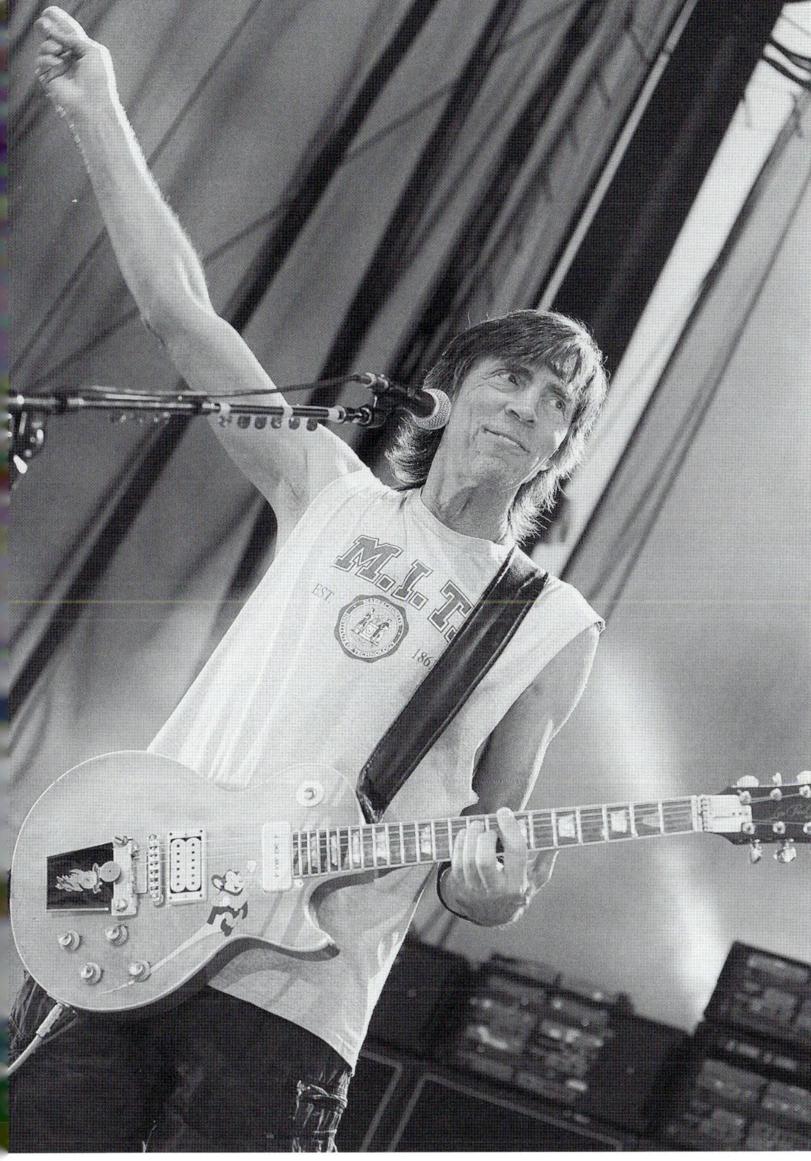

Tom Scholz
Songwriter, guitarist, inventor, and sound design engineer, Tom Scholz is the creative force behind the band Boston. As a high school student in Toledo, Ohio, he would tune into Boston's WBZ (then a music station) to listen to British rock and area bands that had the "Boston" sound. Scholz lived on Parkvale Avenue and Market Street (Brighton) in the late 1960s while attending MIT and playing in local bands. (Matthew Becker, Melodic Rock Concerts.)

Fred Allen (1894–1956) (OPPOSITE PAGE)
Born John Florence Sullivan, this famous radio personality of the 1930s and 1940s grew up on Bayard Street in the home of his aunt and attended the neighboring North Harvard Grammar School. Allen began performing on stage as an amateur teenage juggler, eventually adding patter and turning pro, with the billing "World's Worst Juggler." By about 1946, Allen's show was ranked number one on network radio. In spite of his ratings, Allen's impromptu political and social satire was often at odds with network censors. His later career included the television program, *What's My Line?* (Boston Public Library.)

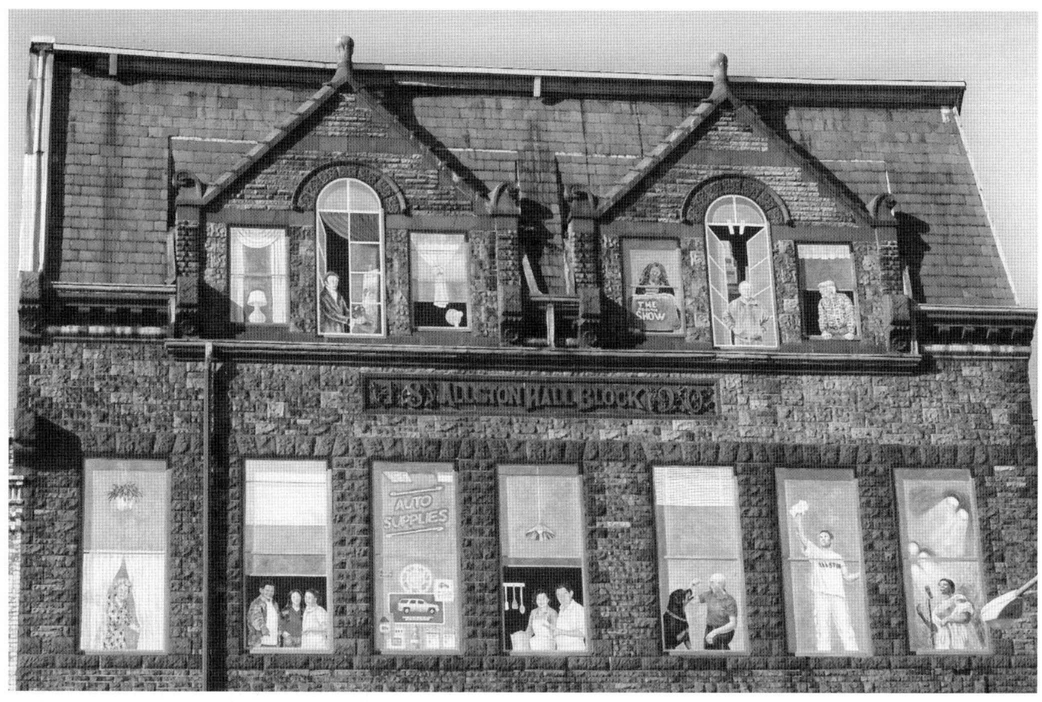
THE
SHOW
ALLSTON HALL BLOCK
AUTO
SUPPLIES

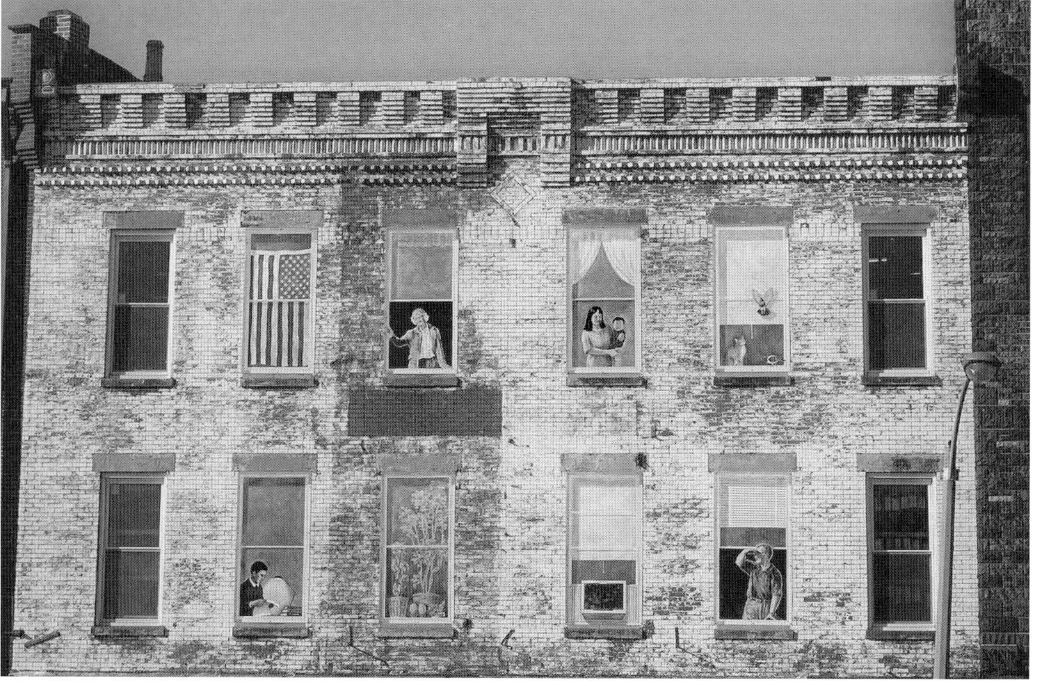

Elli Crocker

A former Brighton resident, artist Elli Crocker honors the people of Allston through her iconic mural, "Windows on Allston." This project, commissioned in 2001 by the Jack Young Company and Allston Village Main Streets Association, is designed to restore a sense of liveliness and stature to these Allston building sites (one of which is a prominent local landmark) as well as to depict and celebrate the diversity of the local population. The piece is painted in a loose trompe l'oeil manner in order to preserve the architectural integrity of the buildings. The panels on the opposite page are meant to imitate the windows that might actually be there while including portraits of citizens and a few historical figures, among them the namesake for this neighborhood, the American romantic painter Washington Allston (1779–1843). (Photograph by Liane Brandon.)

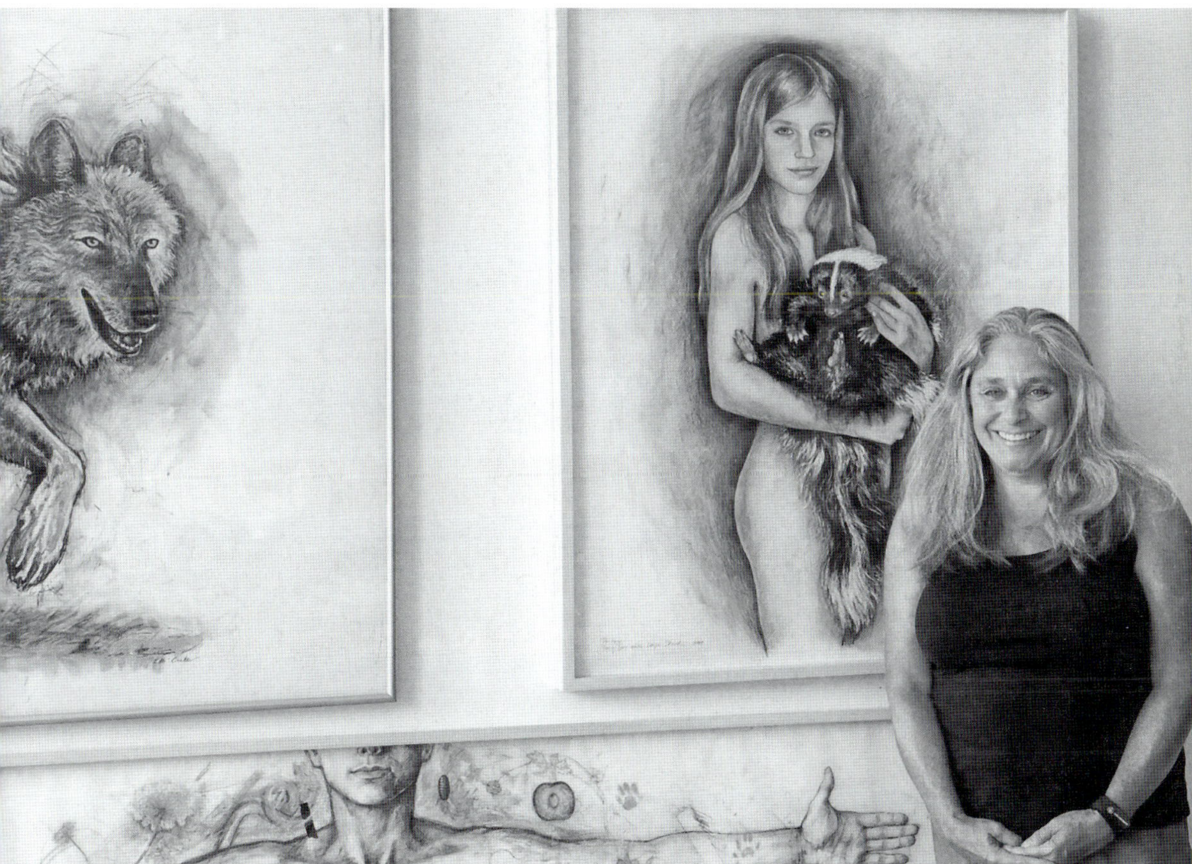

Crocker's Art

The commission fit in well with Crocker's focus on a realistic style of painting and particular interest in the human figure and portraiture. She enjoyed interviewing neighborhood personalities and working with the neighborhood association and the building owners to shape a vision of how the panels should appear. Crocker received her bachelor of arts from Smith College and master of fine arts from Tufts University in a collaborative program with the School of the Museum of Fine Arts. Her artwork is drawn from many sources and speaks to the contemporary imagination as well as ancient, undying myths. Onto these, she grafts her own stories and imagery. Crocker currently maintains a studio in Waltham, Massachusetts. In addition to her work as an artist, Crocker is associate professor of art at Clark University in Worcester, Massachusetts. She has served as director of the studio art program since 2002 and is currently gallery director at Clark. (Photograph by Liane Brandon.)

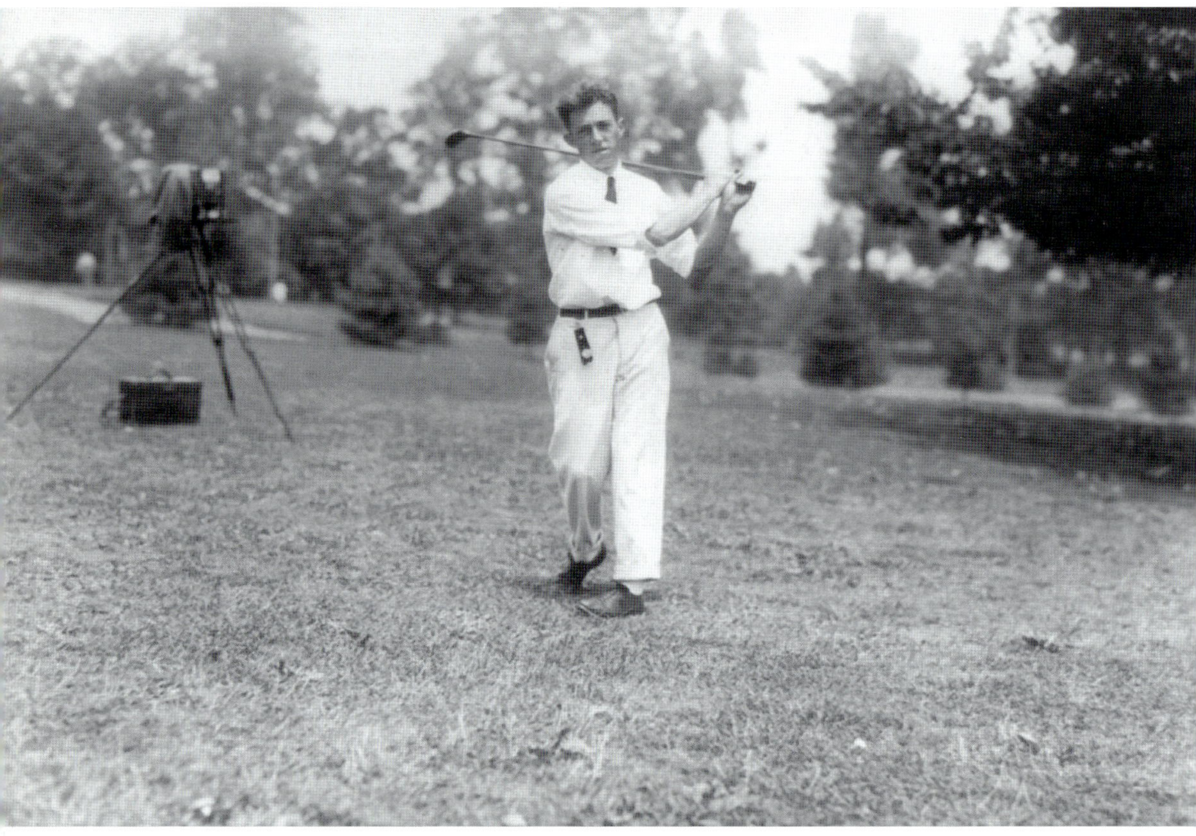

Francis Ouimet (1893–1967)
He really had not planned to convert the aristocratic game of golf to a sport for all. Yet, Francis Ouiment's unexpected victory at the 1913 American Open democratized and changed the perception of an entire sport. Born in 1893 in Brookline, Massachusetts, to immigrant parents, Ouimet lived in a working class neighborhood near The Country Club (Brookline). He learned the game of golf by caddying and observing the players at this fabled (and stuffy) country club. According to Ouimet, he and his brother built three makeshift holes in the family backyard using sunken tomato cans as cups. Often, he would sneak onto the course and play a few holes late in the day after the members of The Country Club had gone home. In 1918, Ouimet married Stella Sullivan, daughter of a well-to-do Brighton building contractor, and moved to Brighton's Lake Street to be close to his wife's family. While he later started a successful sporting supply business and became a stockbroker, golf remained his passion (and hobby). When friends wanted to present him with expensive gifts to celebrate the many honors he was receiving, Ouimet suggested, "Let's establish a scholarship fund to help boys and girls attend college." Started in 1949, the Francis Ouimet [Golf] Scholarship Fund is one of the largest independent scholarship organizations in New England. In 1974, he was elected to the World Golf Hall of Fame. His career inspired a book (2002) and film (2005), both called "The Greatest Game Ever Played." (Library of Congress.)

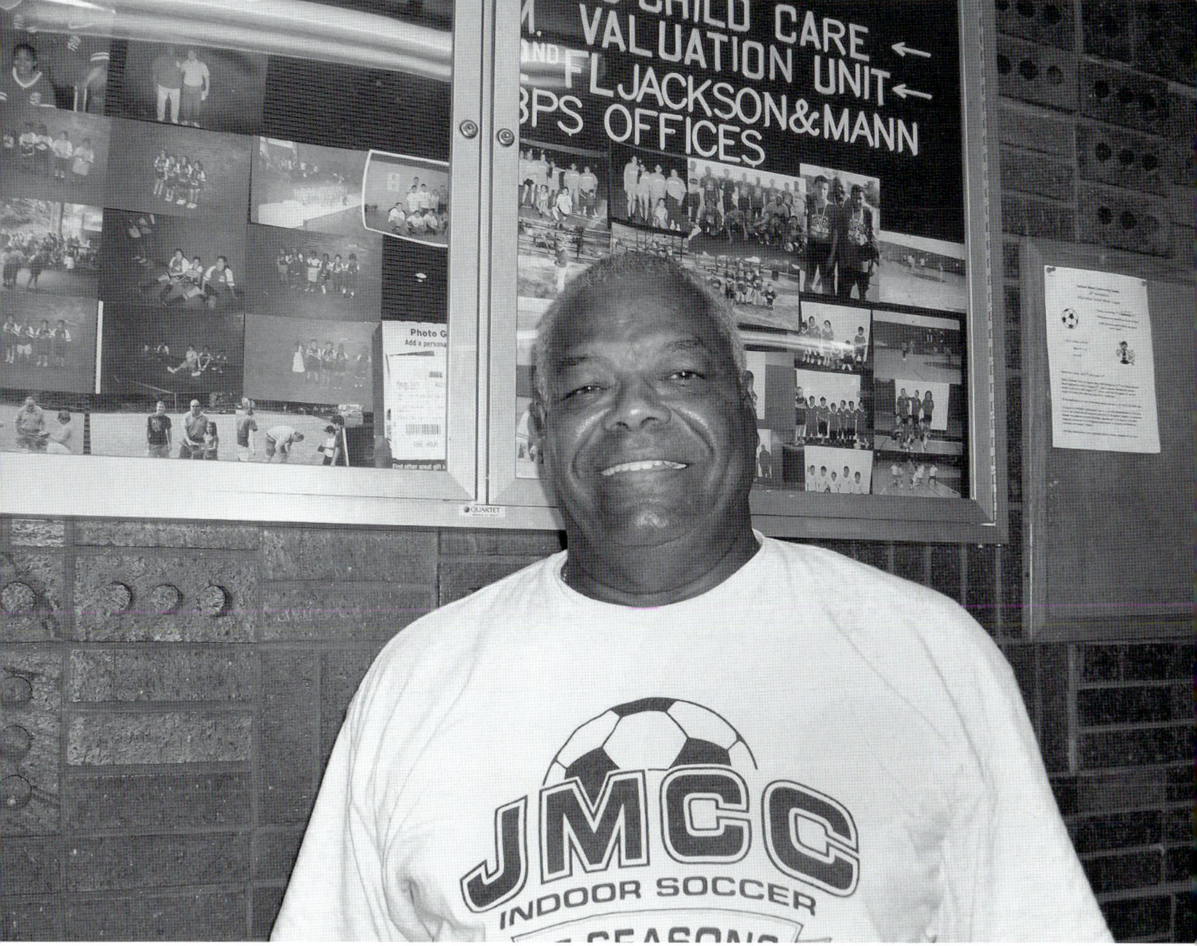

Lazaro Ponce
Lazaro Ponce is director of sports at the Jackson Mann Community Center, where he has worked for 18 years. He has been involved in sports his whole life. He was born in Cuba and played on the Cuban team in the Pan American baseball games in 1955 at age 16. Starting in 1956, he played for eight years on and off in the Philadelphia and Minnesota minor league baseball systems. He came to the United States when he was 20 years old. Traveling alone in a small boat, he became stranded. He was picked up by an American cargo ship and landed in Miami but wanted to move to the north, having heard good things about Boston. He eventually settled in Brighton, where he and his wife raised two girls, whose college education he financed. In 1969, he opened his own mechanic business called Ponce Chevron. In 1993, after a fire destroyed his business, he learned about the job at Jackson Mann through a prior customer at Ponce Chevron. He applied, was hired, and has been there ever since. He coaches teams of girls and boys of different age groups in basketball, soccer, and baseball and is proud of the many trophies his kids have won. (Photograph by Linda Mishkin.)

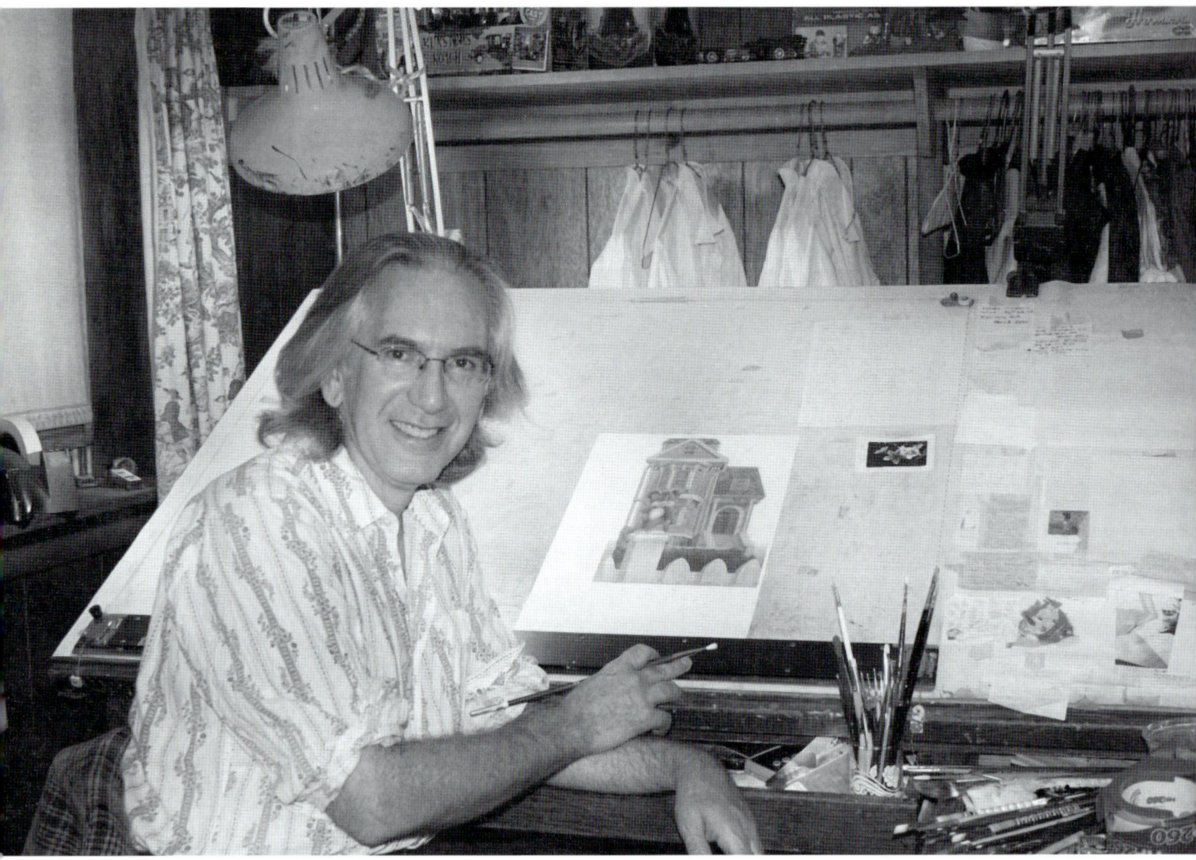

Richard Salvucci

When his grandmother bought him an *Incredible Hulk* comic book, illustrator Richard Salvucci was hooked. Says this lifelong resident of Brighton: "That moment was the beginning of my love for 'larger than life' stories, especially the illustrations telling those stories." After graduating from the Massachusetts College of Art, Salvucci became a freelance illustrator, producing magazine illustrations with a specialty in covers for science fiction and fantasy books. For many years, he has painted scenes of nature, animals, and birds. His exhibitions feature nature-inspired paintings that tell very personal stories. One of Salvucci's most cherished awards is his commission to produce a drawing presented to Dr. Jane Goodall as an award for her achievements in the conservation of chimpanzees. "It was exciting for me at the time," says the artist. "I was 31." (Photograph by Marjorie Hilton.)

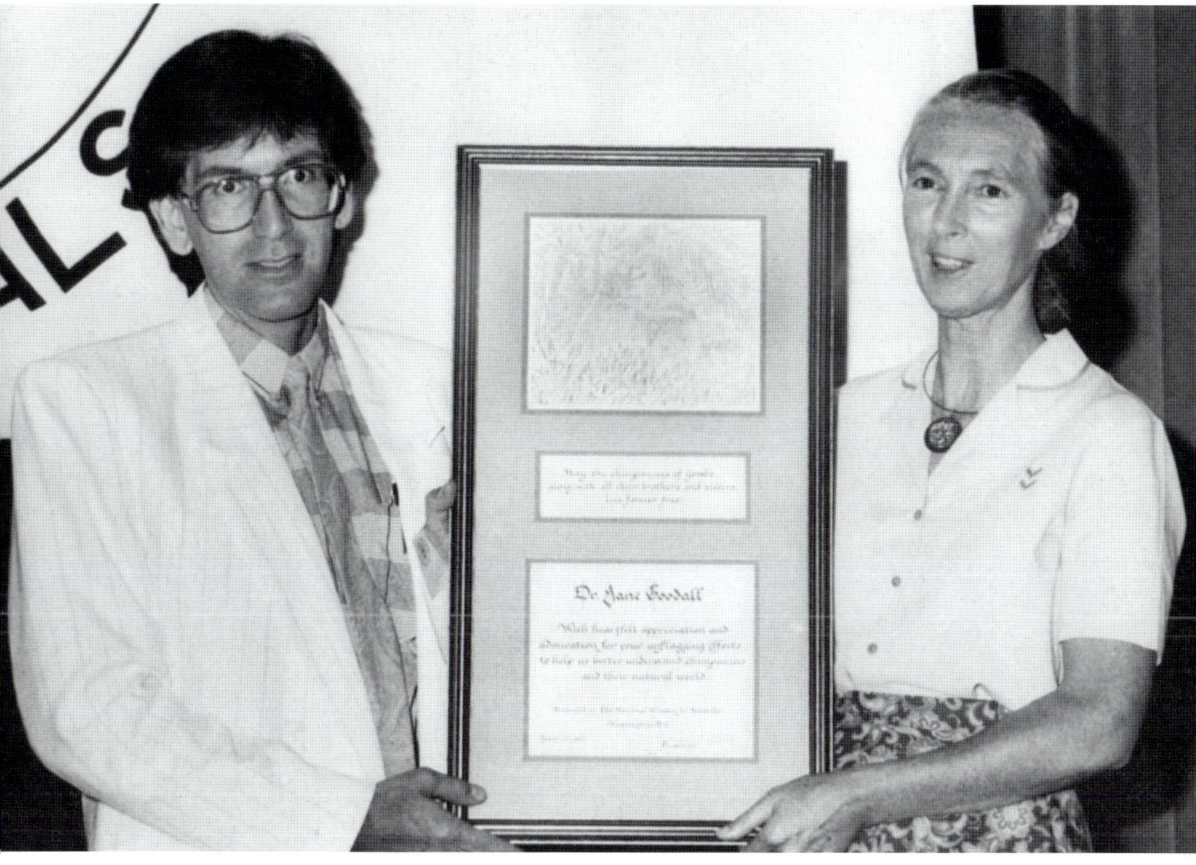

Richard Salvucci and Jane Goodall
In 1999, the first juried exhibition at the Norman Rockwell Museum, Made in Massachusetts, selected Salvucci's piece *The Snow Owl*. The exhibit honored original works by 47 of the Bay State's top contemporary illustrators. Primarily a painter of realism, Salvucci also enjoys experimenting in different styles and formulating new ways of "seeing." To produce his artwork, he uses a broad spectrum of media including oil, pencil, and ink. (Tanya Tuell.)

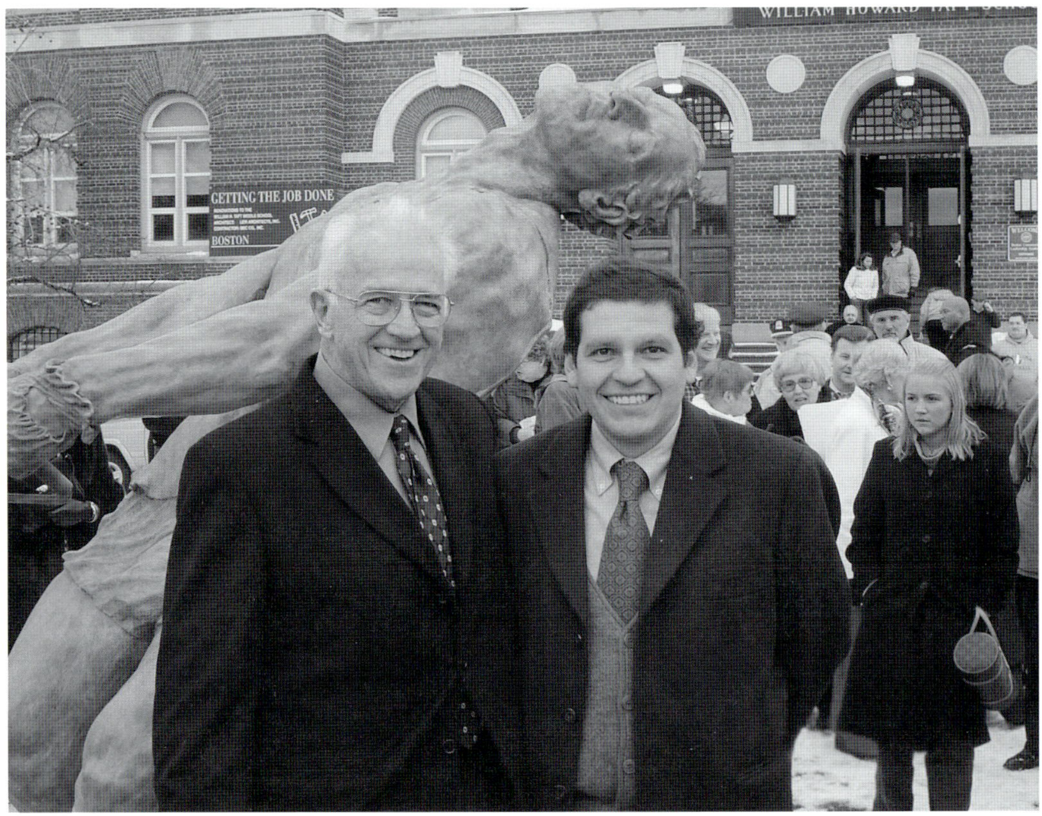

Harold Connolly (1931–2010)

As a young boy, Harold Connolly did not think that he would become one of the world's most influential athletes and a legend in the annals of the Olympic games. Yet, this winner of an Olympic gold medal for hammer throwing at the 1956 Olympics in Melbourne, Australia, was born with one arm four inches shorter than the other. Through patience and perseverance (his personal ethic), this extraordinary athlete was an inspiration to others who are physically challenged. Harold Connolly grew up and trained in Brighton. Connolly recalled, "I was a neighborhood kid who came up in the local schools right from kindergarten through Brighton High School. I was really a part of that neighborhood. In fact, I lived with my family in the same place for 26 years." He also remembered struggling to keep from being assigned to classes for the handicapped. As he wrote of his childhood, "I wanted to push myself into the 'normal' society. I was a handicapped person who knows the agony of all-out trying and not accomplishing. They didn't treat the disabled with dignity then. I couldn't stand to be treated differently." While attending Boston College, Connolly took up hammer throwing. He developed his own style of throwing to compensate for his left arm utilizing his great leg strength. His Aunt Mary, a ballet instructor, helped him with his footwork, and he transformed a pair of ballet slippers into a new kind of track shoe that is commonly worn today. After retiring from competition, Connolly spent 30 years as a high school teacher and administrator in Santa Monica, California, and 10 years as director of US programs for Special Olympics (1988–1999). "The thought of being patronized made me sick," said Connolly. "I wanted to play by the rules, not rules adapted for me because I was disabled. My coming to the Special Olympics was strictly a quirk of fate, but now I think it was my calling all the time." He was elected to the National Track and Field Hall of Fame in 1984. In 2005, a statue of Connolly was erected outside the Taft School in Brighton. "I am eternally grateful to all of you," he said to the assembled crowd. "I am here today, filled with intense pride for being a member of this community that made me into the man I became." He is pictured with the statue's sculptor, Pablo Eduardo. (James Connolly.)

Liane Brandon

Liane Brandon has had success as a public school teacher, stuntwoman, certified ski instructor, college professor, documentary filmmaker, and photographer. Underlying it all is her passion for social justice. Involved in the civil rights and women's movements, Liane used film as a vehicle for change. This started back when she was a public school teacher of a "discipline" class. Frustrated by her students' apparent lack of motivation, Liane asked them what they wanted to learn. They quickly replied that they wanted to learn how to make a movie. With limited exposure to filmmaking from her work with the antiwar collective Newsreel, Liane combined her teaching with her filmmaking. Together, she and her students worked, learned, and made a film. Always drawn to challenging the status quo but growing up in a time that offered few opportunities for women, Liane joined the legendary feminist collective Bread and Roses at the start of the Women's Movement in 1969. Here she combined her politics with her filmmaking, making some of the very first films of the Women's Movement and becoming one of the first independent women filmmakers in Massachusetts. She became an award-winning documentary filmmaker, receiving a Blue Ribbon at the American Film Festival for an early film, *Anything You Want To Be,* and international acclaim for another film, *Betty Tells Her Story*. During this time, Liane also became a professor at the University of Massachusetts in Amherst. Liane is a founding member of New Day Films, the pioneering film distribution cooperative. New Day, which now has over 100 members, played a major role in advancing the ideas and awareness of the Women's Movement and was recently celebrated at the Museum of Modern Art in New York. Liane has lived in Brighton for many years, drawn by the close-knit community. Her recent artistic focus is photography. Her work in film influences the vivid photographs she has done for PBS's *American Masters* and *NOVA*. She is also known for her photographs of historically significant sites around Allston-Brighton. (Photograph by Boyd Estus.)

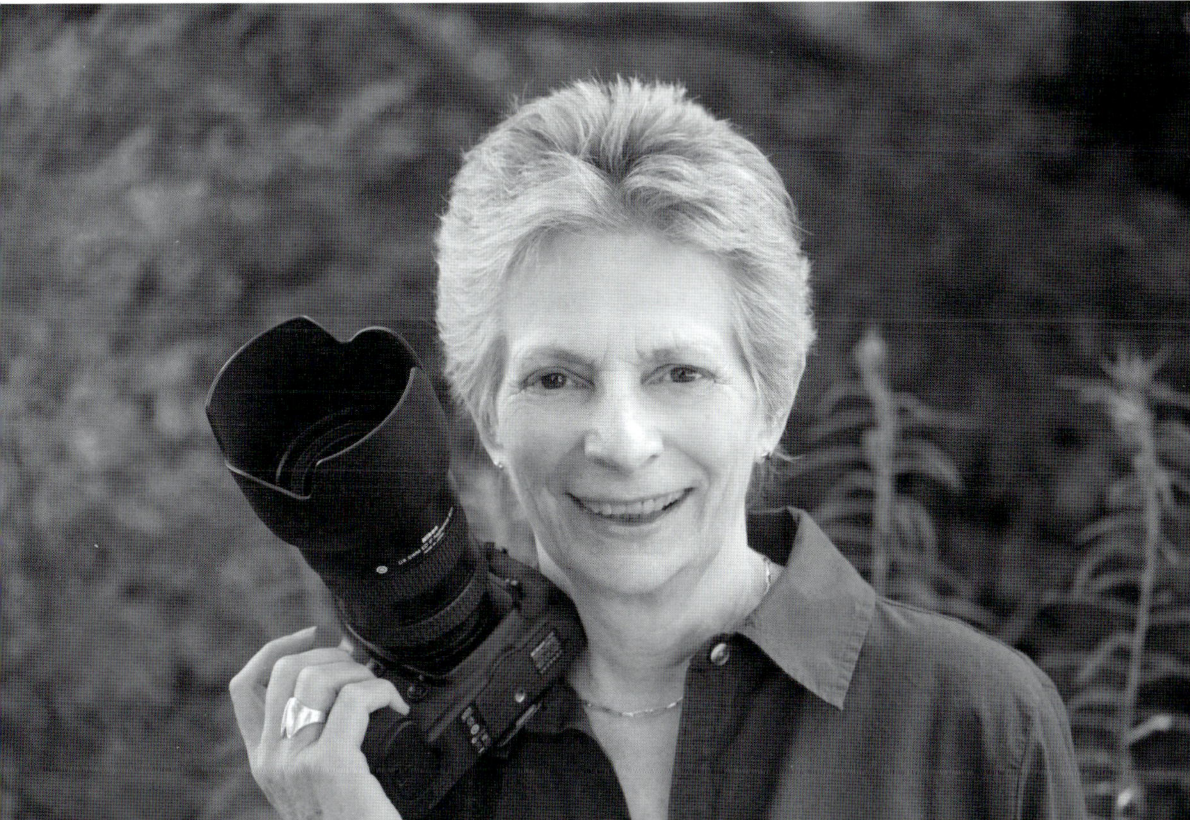

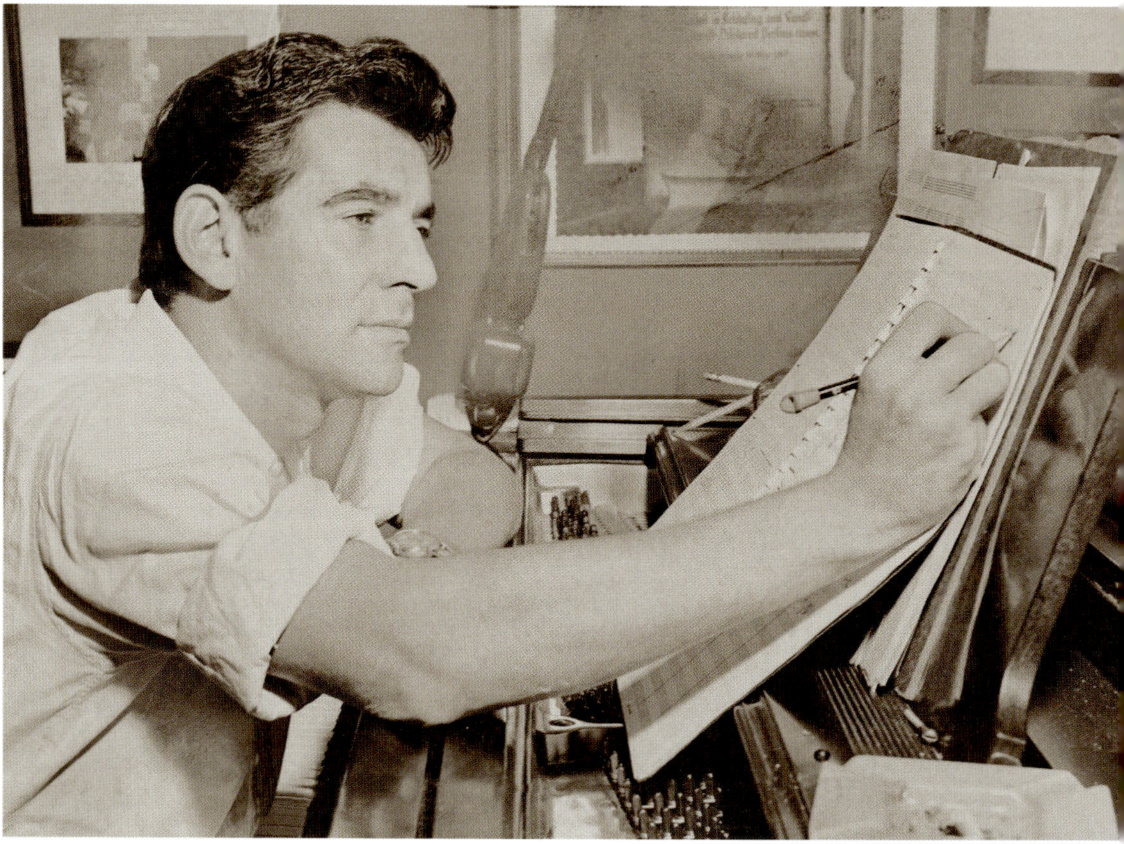

Leonard Bernstein (1918–1990)

Multifaceted and multitalented Leonard Bernstein brought the joy of music to the world with a fusion of many genres and styles. Bernstein and the New York Philharmonic enlightened understanding of music with his educational series the *Young People's Concerts* (1958–1973) on CBS. Bernstein also was a social and political activist, which ultimately led J. Edgar Hoover and the FBI to monitor his activities. Twenty-seven-year-old Bernstein became an overnight sensation on November 14, 1943, when he unexpectedly filled in for Bruno Walter at Carnegie Hall for a live national radio broadcast. Bernstein's father was once criticized for having failed to provide his talented son with more encouragement as a youngster. "How was I to know," his father replied, "that he would grow up to be Leonard Bernstein?" Bernstein lived in Allston from 1920 to 1923. (Library of Congress.)

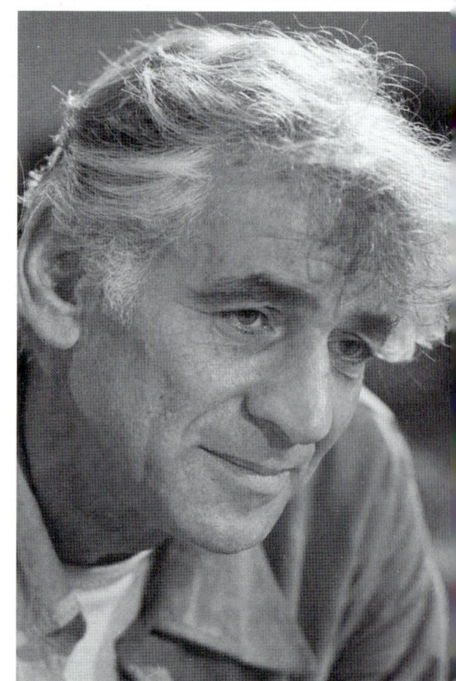

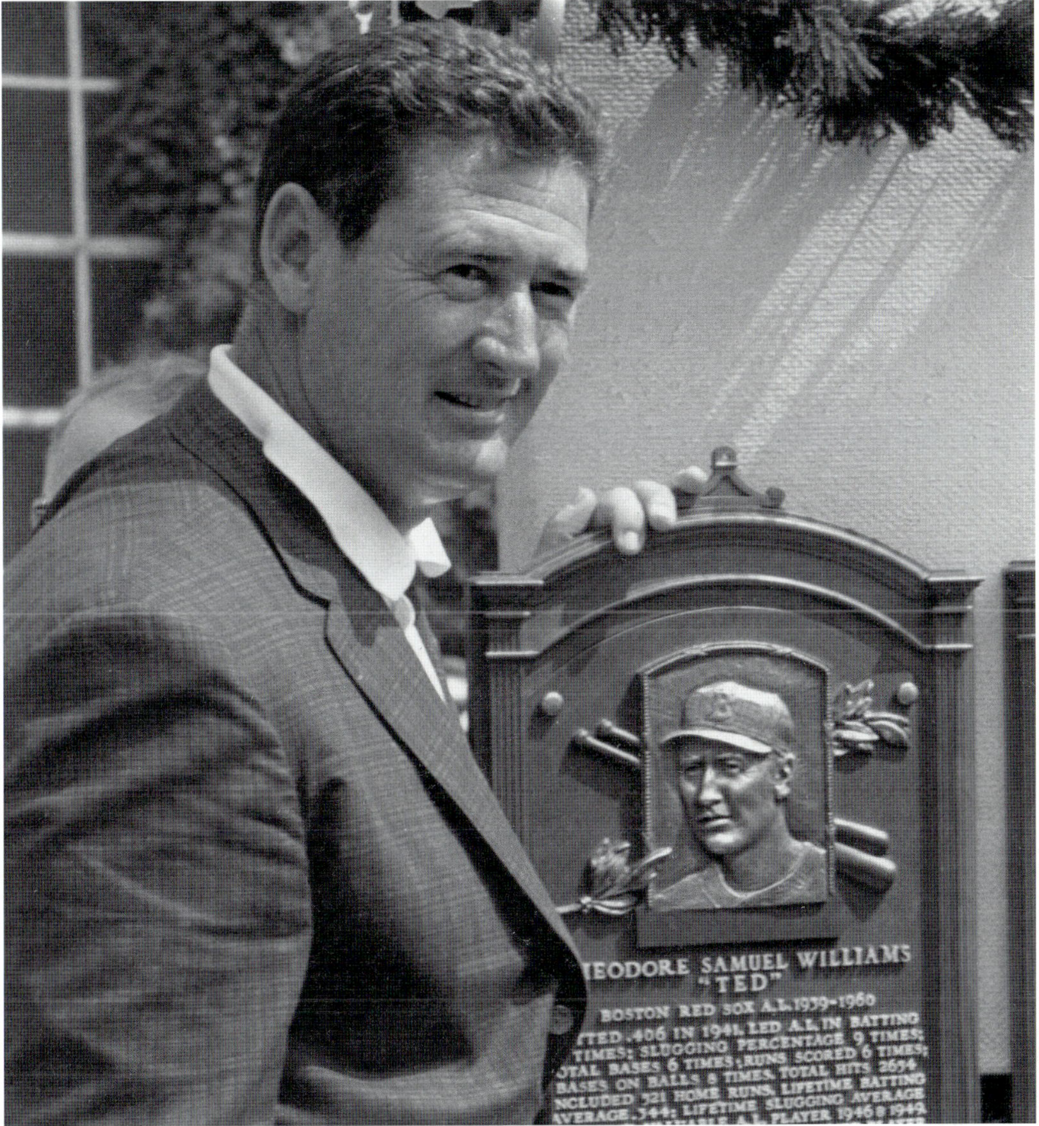

Theodore Samuel "Ted" Williams (1918–2002)
Arguably baseball's greatest hitter, Ted Williams resided on Foster Street near Brighton Center for a number of years during his two decades as a Red Sox player. Williams played for the Boston Red Sox from 1939 to 1960. His baseball career was interrupted by tours of duty in two wars. He was a decorated Marine pilot who believed in service to country. Though his reputation was often as a crusty personality, Williams had a compassionate side. He used his induction speech at the Baseball Hall of Fame (1966) to call for the recognition and enshrinement of the great Negro League stars. Williams gave generously to those in need. He is often thought of as the patron saint of the Jimmy Fund of the Dana-Farber Cancer Institute, which provides support for children's cancer research and treatment. At the age of eight, he was taught how to throw a baseball by Saul Venzor (one his mother's four brothers), a former semipro baseball player who pitched against Babe Ruth in an exhibition game. Williams ended his career dramatically, hitting a home run in his very last time at bat on September 28, 1960. (Ted Williams Enterprises Ltd.)

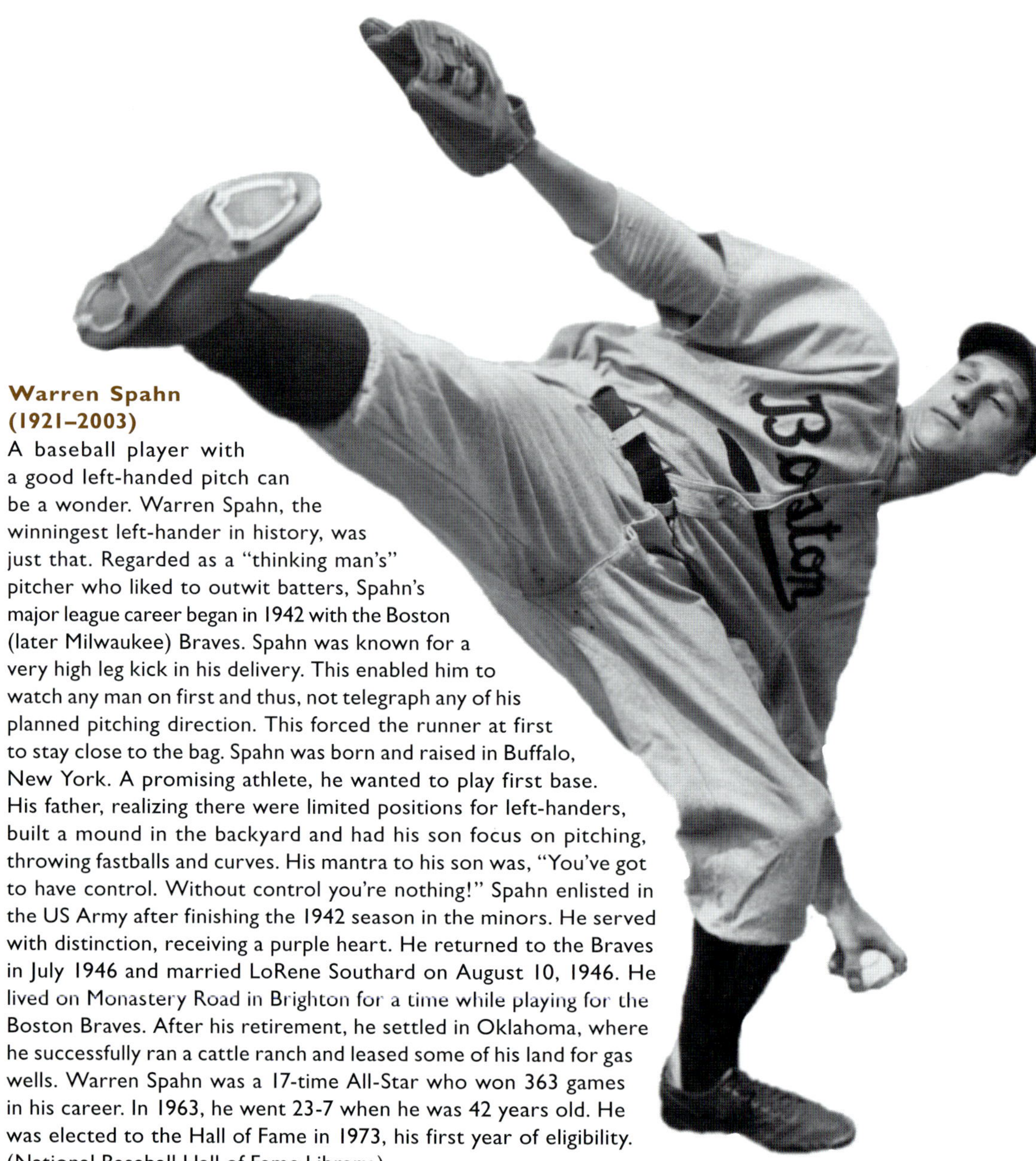

Warren Spahn (1921–2003)

A baseball player with a good left-handed pitch can be a wonder. Warren Spahn, the winningest left-hander in history, was just that. Regarded as a "thinking man's" pitcher who liked to outwit batters, Spahn's major league career began in 1942 with the Boston (later Milwaukee) Braves. Spahn was known for a very high leg kick in his delivery. This enabled him to watch any man on first and thus, not telegraph any of his planned pitching direction. This forced the runner at first to stay close to the bag. Spahn was born and raised in Buffalo, New York. A promising athlete, he wanted to play first base. His father, realizing there were limited positions for left-handers, built a mound in the backyard and had his son focus on pitching, throwing fastballs and curves. His mantra to his son was, "You've got to have control. Without control you're nothing!" Spahn enlisted in the US Army after finishing the 1942 season in the minors. He served with distinction, receiving a purple heart. He returned to the Braves in July 1946 and married LoRene Southard on August 10, 1946. He lived on Monastery Road in Brighton for a time while playing for the Boston Braves. After his retirement, he settled in Oklahoma, where he successfully ran a cattle ranch and leased some of his land for gas wells. Warren Spahn was a 17-time All-Star who won 363 games in his career. In 1963, he went 23-7 when he was 42 years old. He was elected to the Hall of Fame in 1973, his first year of eligibility. (National Baseball Hall of Fame Library.)

CHAPTER NINE

Public Officials and Politicos

Here are stories of dedicated public officials who work to ensure fairness and opportunity for all. They improve and protect the structure of the community so that it remains a place where people representing a wide variety of interests and backgrounds choose to live and work. Included here are officials who work with organizations that support communities both local and abroad. Several people mentioned in this chapter grew up in Allston-Brighton, attended local schools and nearby colleges, and still reside here. Several narratives show career paths in the public sector that include success in more than one position.

The 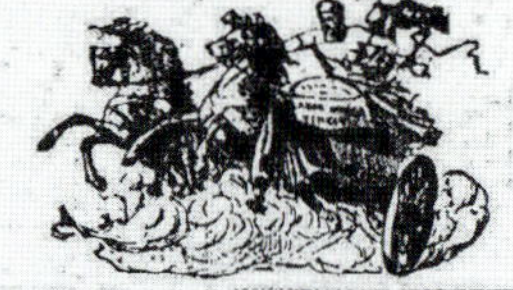 People

VOL. VI. NO. 16. NEW YORK, JULY 19, 1896.

LABOR CHAMPIONS

Presidential Candidates of the Socialist Labor Party.

Lines Drawn Sharply.

The American Division of the International Army of Emancipation Hangs its Banners to the Outer Wall.

On the 9th inst., the National Convention of the Socialist Labor party nominated, amidst thundering applause, two wage slaves of its own ranks for their Presidential candidates: Charles H. Matchett of New York for President, and Matthew Maguire of New Jersey for Vice-President.

CHAS. H. MATCHETT.

Charles H. Matchett, the nominee for President, is a resident of Brooklyn, N. Y. He is a genuine New England American. His ancestors emigrated from England in 1630 and 1788. He was born in 1843 at Needham, Middlesex County, Mass., and attended the public schools of Boston until he was sixteen years of age, when he went to sea. At the outbreak of the Civil War, in 1861, he enlisted on the warship Isaac Smith, stationed in the South Atlantic blockading fleet, and was present at the storming of Fort Royal, South Carolina, and of Fort Pulaski at Savannah. During the next three years he made several voyages to Africa and South America, and then settled down to the grocery business. That not being to his taste, he became a carpenter and finally a builder and was wrecked in the commercial crisis of 1873; he then again took to the carpentering trade, in which he remained until 1886, when he became an employee of the New York and New Jersey Telephone Cable Company.

From early childhood he was endowed with a strong love of freedom and equality, his radical ideas being inculcated by his father, who was acquainted with the Brook Farm Socialist Colony experiment, and a spectator of

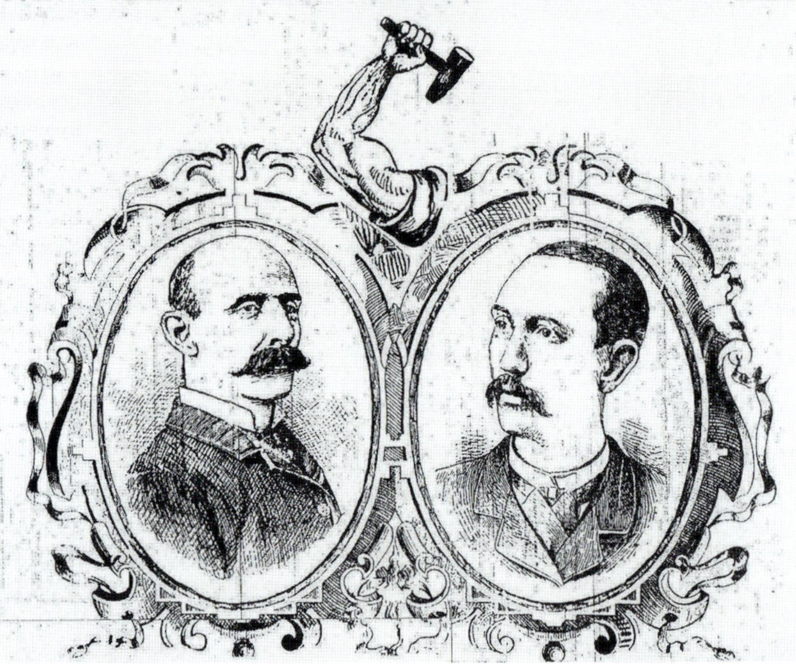

Charles Horatio Matchett (1843–1919)

Charles Horatio Matchett, Allston-Brighton's only presidential candidate, was born in Brighton at the family homestead just west of Oak Square. After a career of several years in the US Navy, Matchett helped found the Socialist Labor Party. He became that party's candidate for vice president in 1892, for governor of New York in 1894, and finally, in 1896, for president of the United States, receiving only 36,000 votes in that contest. The Socialist Party's platform in 1896 called for government ownership of all means of production and distribution. In the summer of 1901, Matchett left the Socialist Labor Party and helped found the more successful Socialist Party of America under the leadership of legendary labor leader Eugene Debs. Matchett died in Allston, Massachusetts, after a long illness in 1919. (BAHS archives.)

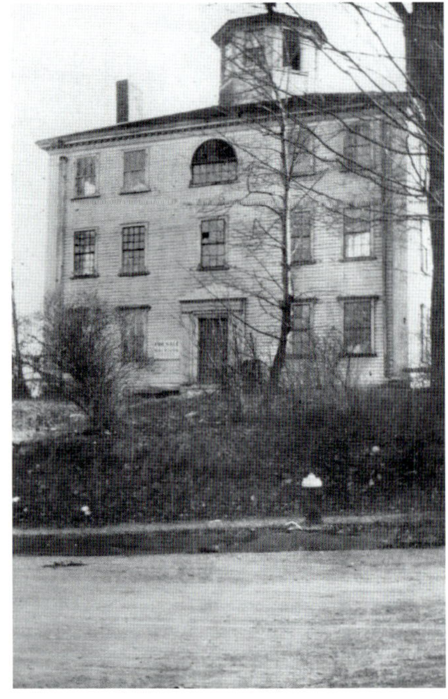

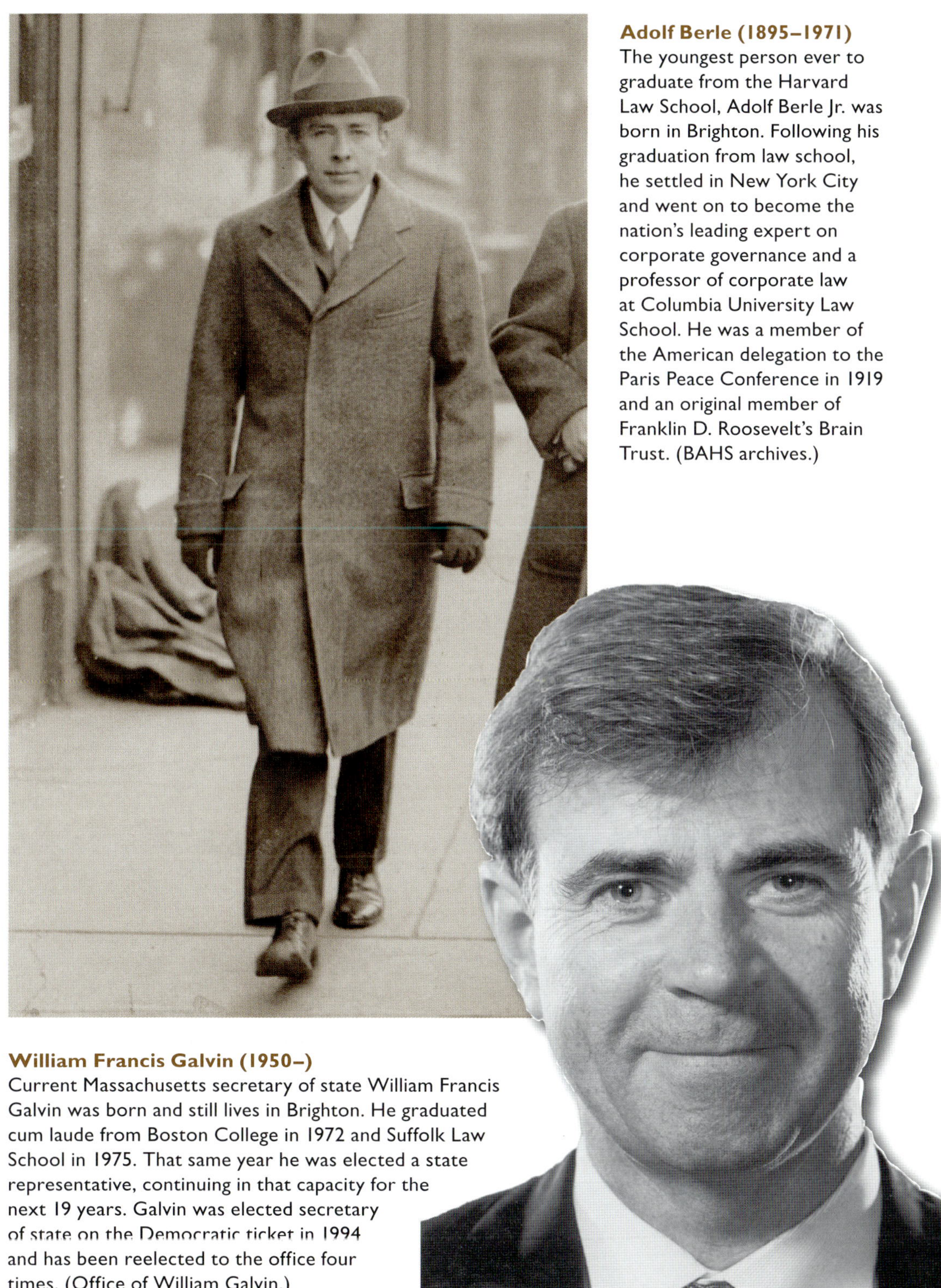

Adolf Berle (1895–1971)
The youngest person ever to graduate from the Harvard Law School, Adolf Berle Jr. was born in Brighton. Following his graduation from law school, he settled in New York City and went on to become the nation's leading expert on corporate governance and a professor of corporate law at Columbia University Law School. He was a member of the American delegation to the Paris Peace Conference in 1919 and an original member of Franklin D. Roosevelt's Brain Trust. (BAHS archives.)

William Francis Galvin (1950–)
Current Massachusetts secretary of state William Francis Galvin was born and still lives in Brighton. He graduated cum laude from Boston College in 1972 and Suffolk Law School in 1975. That same year he was elected a state representative, continuing in that capacity for the next 19 years. Galvin was elected secretary of state on the Democratic ticket in 1994 and has been reelected to the office four times. (Office of William Galvin.)

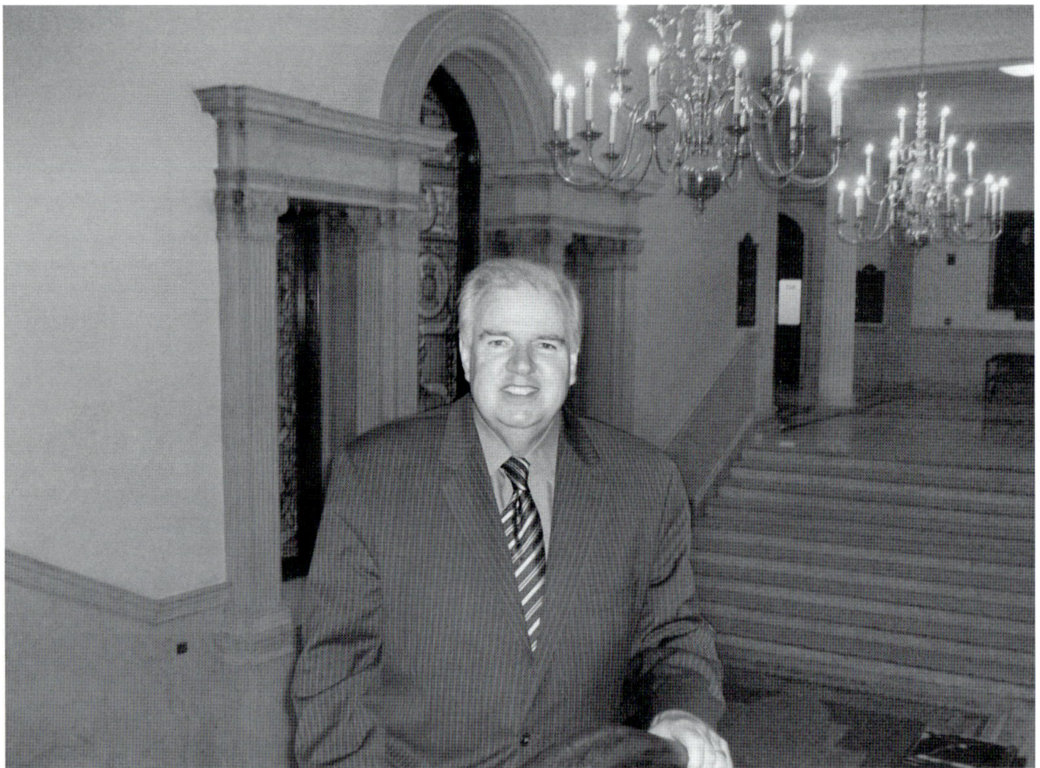

Kevin Honan

Kevin Honan comes from a family of community activists and political leaders. He grew up in Allston, where his parents still reside. Kevin now lives in Brighton. His mother, Mary Honan, did volunteer work for the Boston Public Schools and the Allston Civic Association. She was a member of the Democratic Ward Committee until the early 1980s. His father, Patrick, was active in labor unions. He was in the Local 550, the Sprinkler Fitters Union. His uncle Charlie Doyle was chairman of the Democratic Ward Committee for many years. Charlie's annual cookout, held at the Honan family home, drew hundreds of people, including anyone running in statewide primaries. Kevin earned his undergraduate degree from Boston College, a master's degree from Lesley University, and a master of public administration from Harvard's Kennedy School of Government. Kevin's career in public service began soon after he graduated from college. He worked for Action for Boston Community Development and then the Boston Parks and Recreation Commission. He stayed in the job until 1986, when he ran for the office of state representative. His campaign was successful and he has held the position ever since. As state representative, he is chairman of the Housing Committee, which works with the Department of Housing and Community Development and Allston-Brighton Community Development to make sure that funding is available for affordable housing, which he strongly supports. He was the chief sponsor of a bond bill of $1.25 billion, the largest in the state's history. He works hard to ensure that future generations are not priced out of the Allston-Brighton housing market. (Photograph by Linda Mishkin.)

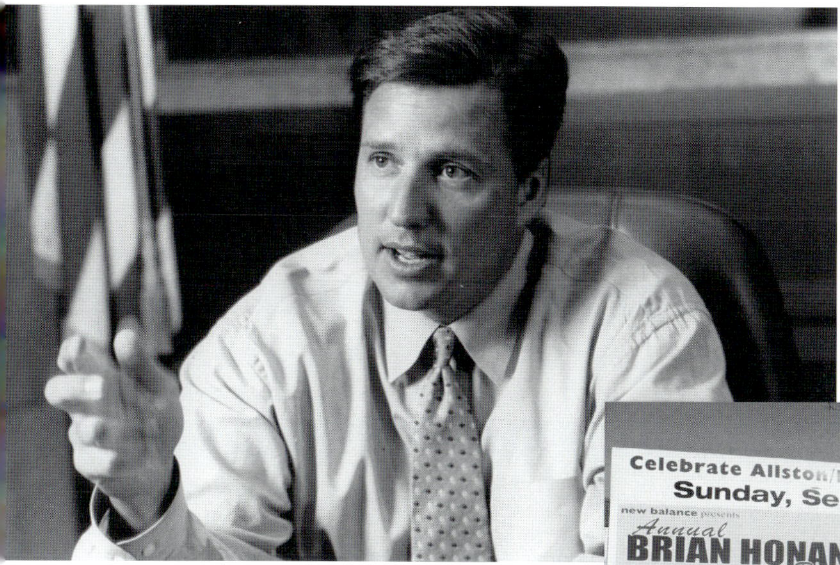

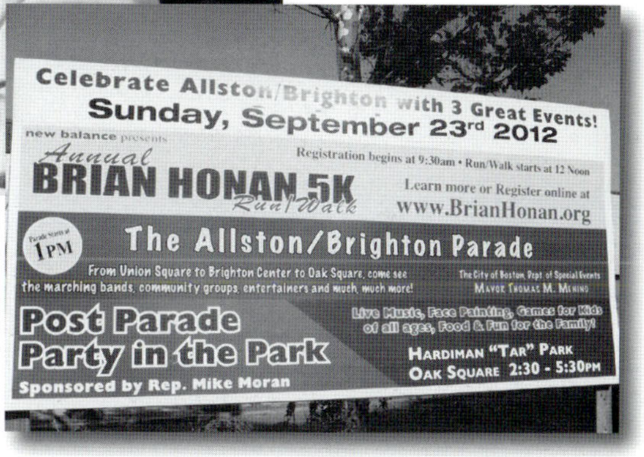

Brian Honan

Throughout his all-too-short life, Brian Honan was dedicated to the Allston-Brighton community. After earning his law degree, he took a job as assistant district attorney general in Suffolk County. In 1995, Brian was elected to the Boston City Council, representing Allston-Brighton, where he championed the cause of affordable housing. Brian passed away in 2002 from complications linked to cancer surgery. He will be remembered for his generous spirit, loyalty to family, friends, and constituents, and his commitment to public service. (Kevin Honan's office.)

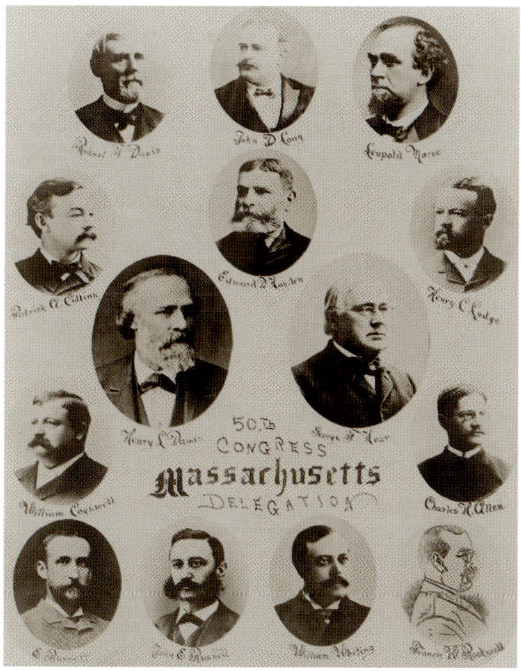

Patrick Collins (1844–1905)

Boston mayor from 1902 to 1905, Patrick Collins was one of the leading Democratic politicians of late-19th-century Massachusetts. During the last years of his life, he resided in Brighton. After earning a law degree from Harvard, he became one of the city's leading attorneys. He served in both houses of the Massachusetts legislature from 1868 to 1871, judge advocate of Massachusetts in 1875, the US Congress from 1883 to 1889, chairman of the Democratic State Committee from 1884 to 1890, and US consul general in London under Pres. Grover Cleveland from 1893 to 1897. (BAHS archives.)

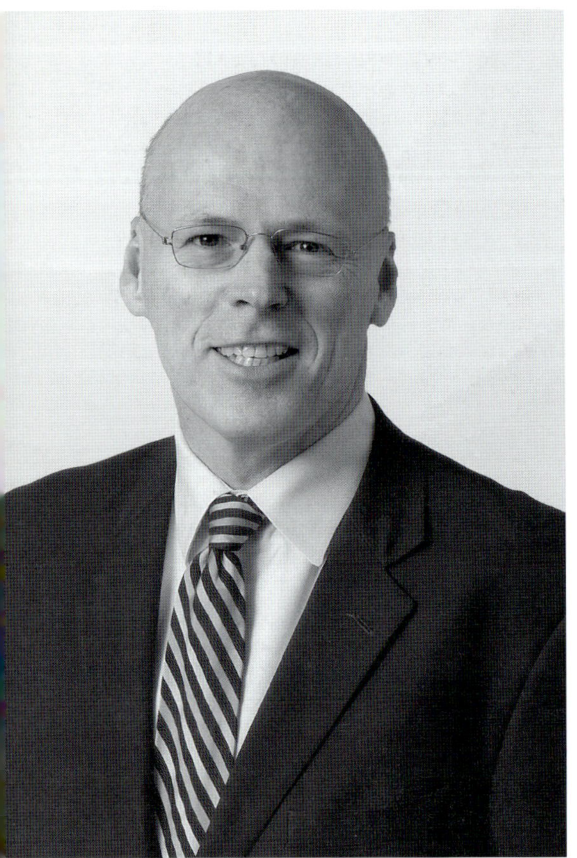

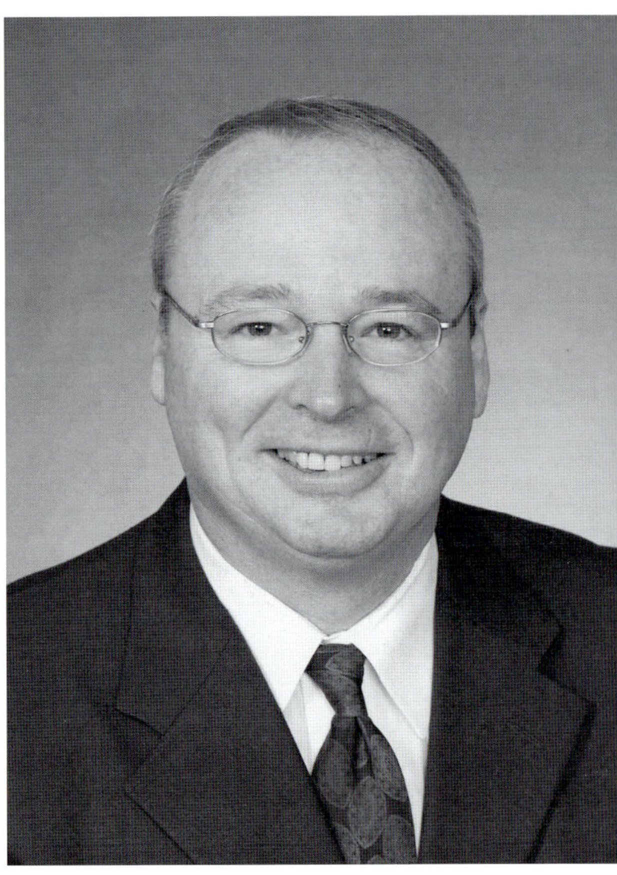

The Brothers Tolman

Brothers Steven and Warren Tolman were born in Brighton in 1954 and 1959 respectively. Warren attended Amherst College and Boston College Law School, was elected to the Massachusetts House of Representatives in 1990 and then to the Massachusetts State Senate in 1994. He ran unsuccessfully as both the Democratic nominee for lieutenant governor in 1998 and the Democratic gubernatorial nomination in 2002. He practices law with the firm of Holland and Knight. Steven Tolman entered the labor force straight out of high school and quickly became a Massachusetts labor leader. A resident of Brighton, he was elected state representative in 1994, serving two terms. In 1998, he ran for the Massachusetts State Senate seat that his brother held previously. Steven Tolman held that seat until October 13, 2011. He stepped down to become president of the American Federation of Labor and Congress of Industrial Organizations (AFL-CIO) of Massachusetts. (Tolman Offices.)

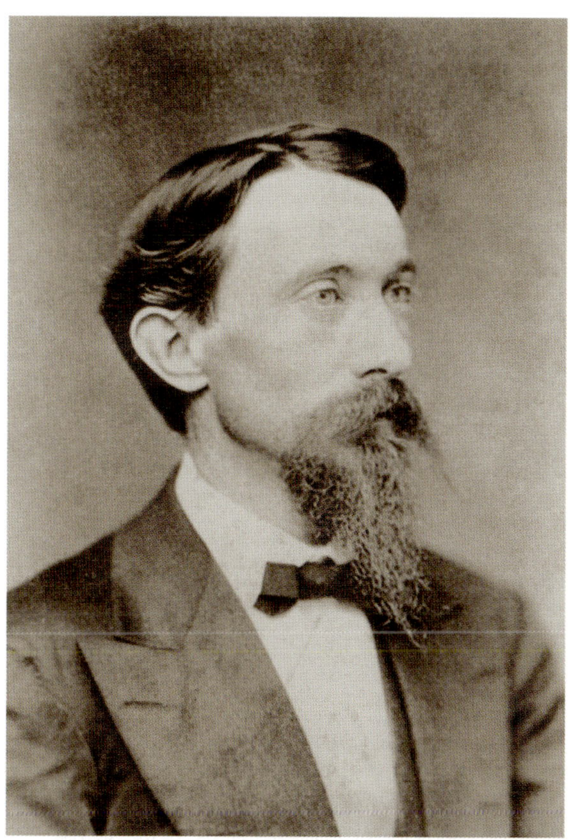

William Wirt Warren (1834–1880)
William Wirt Warren was the US congressman and Massachusetts state senator who helped mastermind the 1874 annexation of the town of Brighton to the city of Boston. He graduated from Harvard University in 1856 and was admitted to the practice of law in 1857. He was elected state senator in 1870 and congressman in 1874, serving from 1875 to 1877, but failed to win reelection. Warren practiced law in Boston until his early death at the age of 47. (BAHS archives.)

Norman Weinberg
Norman Weinberg has lived in Allston-Brighton since his birth in 1919. He was elected state representative in 1952 and held that office for 26 years. In 1981, Governor King appointed Weinberg as judge. For many years, Judge Weinberg has been involved with the West End House Boys and Girls Club and is on the board of directors. West End House moved to Allston-Brighton in the 1950s, following the destruction of the West End neighborhood. (Weinberg family.)

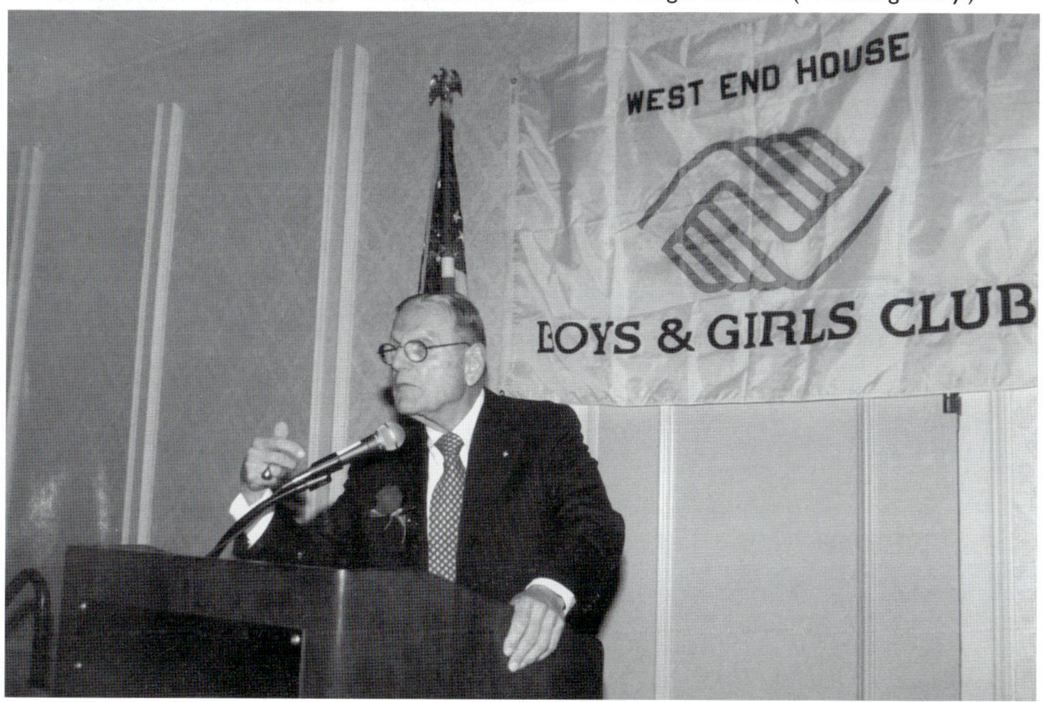

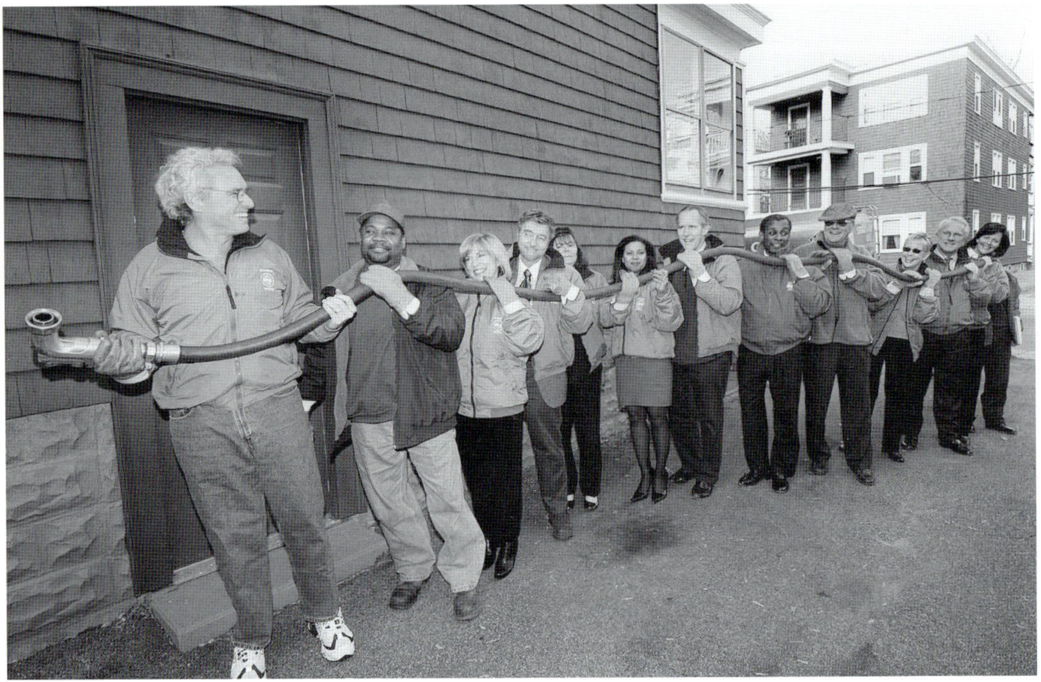

Joseph P. Kennedy II (1952–)
Joseph Patrick Kennedy II is the eldest son of Senator Robert F. Kennedy. In 1979, Kennedy II founded Citizen's Energy, a nonprofit organization that provides discounted heating fuel to low-income families. Upon the death of House Speaker Thomas P. "Tip" O'Neil in 1986, Kennedy was elected to the House of Representatives from the Massachusetts Eighth Congressional District, a seat previously held by his uncle, Pres. John F. Kennedy. After six terms, during which time he lived in Brighton, Kennedy announced his retirement from Congress. (Don West for Citizen's Energy Corporation.)

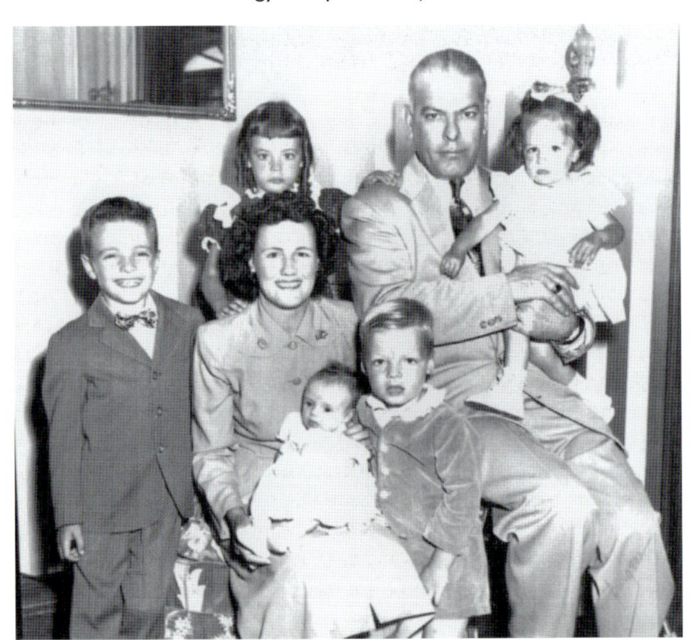

Charles J. Artesani (1911–1992)
Charles J. Artesani served as state representative for Allston-Brighton's Ward 22 from 1939 to 1958 and judge of the Brighton District Court from 1958 to 1981. Reaching the mandatory retirement age of 70 in 1981, he stepped down from the Brighton Court. Artesani organized and managed the Artesani Team in the Boston Park Baseball League. He also served as grand knight of the Knights of Columbus, Allston Council 555. (Artesani family.)

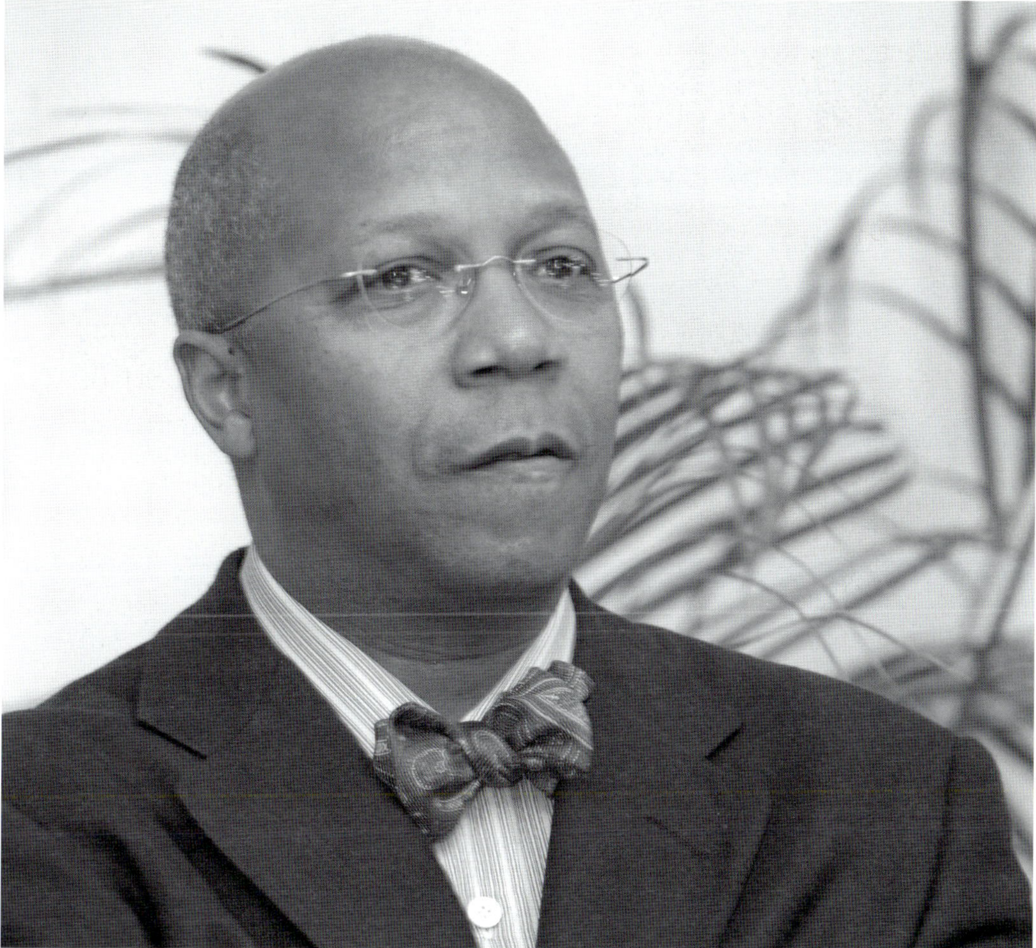

Charles Richard Stith (1949–)
Ambassador Charles Richard Stith is currently the director of the African Presidential Center at Boston University and resides in Brighton with his wife, Deborah Prothrow Stith, a consultant with Spencer Stuart and adjunct professor at the Harvard School of Public Health. Stith earned a master of divinity from Harvard, among other graduate degrees. By the time he was 30, he was the senior minister at the Union United Methodist Church in Boston. Pres. Bill Clinton appointed Stith US ambassador to Tanzania, where he served with distinction during a period of great turmoil in the traumatic period after the August 1998 bombing of the US embassy in Dar es Salaam. Under his leadership, the embassy was restored to stability and set a new standard for US embassies promoting American trade and investment in Africa. His achievements as ambassador included the signing of the first-ever Open Skies Agreement between an African country and the United States, and the successful negotiation of code-share agreements for Delta and Northwest Airlines. In September 1999, Ambassador Stith organized Tanzanian president Mkapa's historic visit to the United States, involving the largest delegation of African business leaders ever to accompany an African head of state on a visit to a Western nation. Stith worked with the Tanzanian government to enable it to become the first sub-Saharan African country to reach the decision point for debt relief under the enhanced Heavily-Indebted Poor Countries Initiative (HIPC). He has written a variety of newspaper articles and two books, *Political Religion* and *For Such a Time as This: African Leadership Challenges*. He founded the Organization for a New Equality and has served on a number of advisory boards. (BAHS archives.)

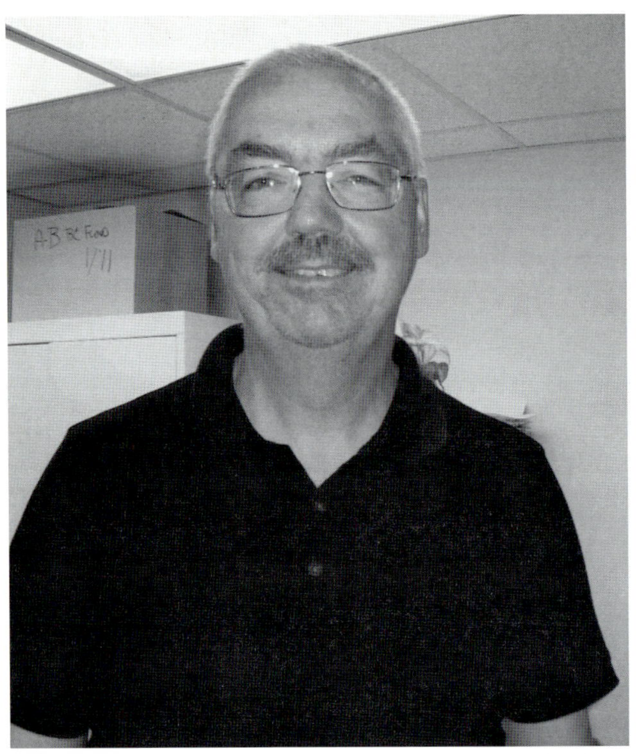

Brian McLaughlin

After six successful terms as Allston-Brighton city councilor, Brian McLaughlin was ready for a change. He became executive secretary of the Boston Parks and Recreation Commission, which he considered the best job in the city. As a recent college graduate in the early 1980s, he served as president of the Brighton-Allston Historical Society. In 1981, he responded to a *Boston Herald* invitation for the public to write editorials about neighborhood and city issues. His editorial, which argued for district representation on the city council, was published. Allston-Brighton had not had a councilor in decades. The issue had previously been on a ballot but had lost. In 1981, it was again on the ballot and won, which inspired his run for office. (Photograph by Linda Mishkin.)

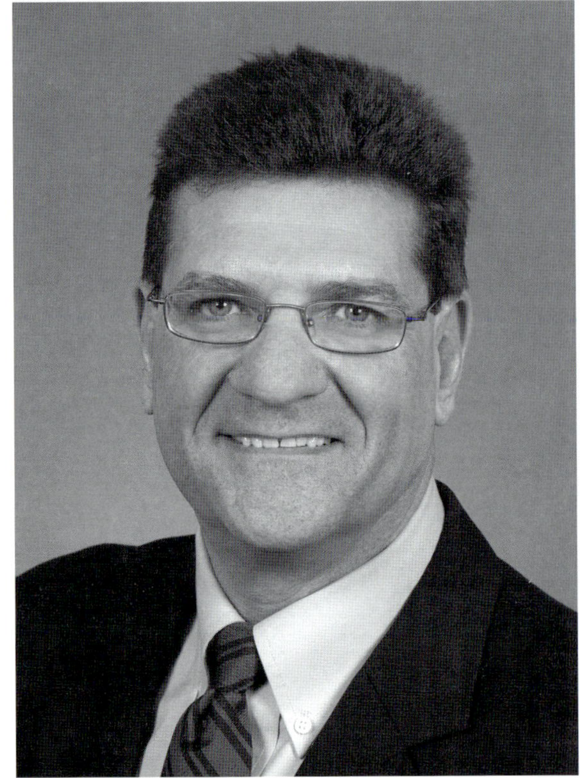

Mark Ciommo

Mark Ciommo was born and raised in Allston-Brighton, where he and his wife are raising their two sons. Since winning election in 2007, Ciommo has represented Allston-Brighton on the Boston City Council, where he chairs the Committee of Ways and Means. Much of his earlier career also focused on Allston-Brighton. He held positions such as youth outreach worker and then assistant director of the Jackson Mann Community Center and executive director of the Veronica Smith Multi-Service Senior Center. Growing up in a working class family with a single mom, Ciommo appreciates the additional guidance and encouragement he received from teachers, coaches, and community leaders. He is dedicated to his family and to the community that gave him so much along the way. (Ciommo office.)

INDEX

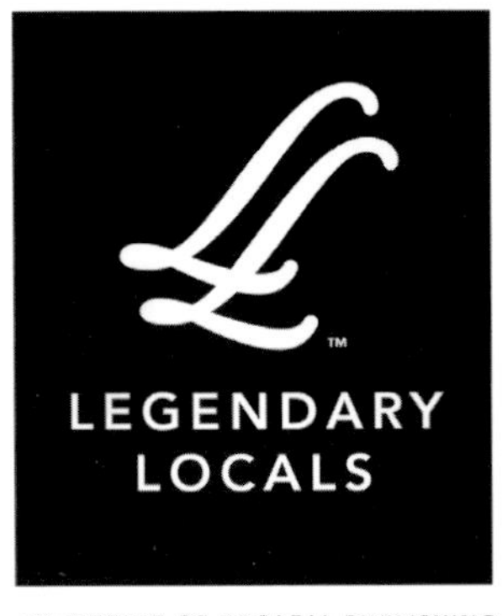

AN IMPRINT OF ARCADIA PUBLISHING

Find more books like this at
www.legendarylocals.com

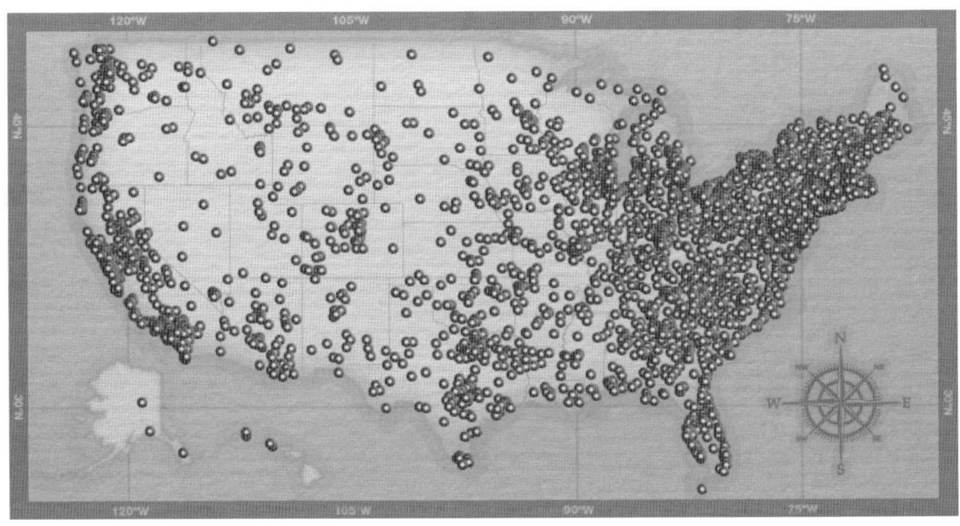

Discover more local and regional history books at
www.arcadiapublishing.com

Consistent with our mission to preserve history on a local level, this book was printed in South Carolina on American-made paper and manufactured entirely in the United States. Products carrying the accredited Forest Stewardship Council (FSC) label are printed on 100 percent FSC-certified paper.

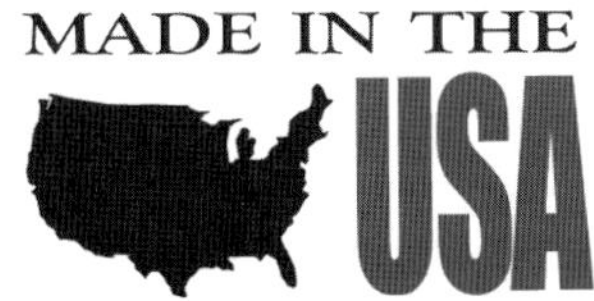